Building Temples in China

Much has been written on how temples are constructed or reconstructed for reviving local religious and communal life or for recycling tradition after the market reforms in China. The dynamics between the state and society that lie behind the revival of temples and religious practices initiated by the locals have been well analyzed. However, there is a gap in the literature when it comes to understanding religious revivals that were instead led by local governments.

This book examines the revival of worship of the Chinese deity Huang Daxian and the building of many new temples to the god in mainland China over the last 20 years. It analyzes the role of local governments in initiating temple construction projects in China and how development-oriented, temple-building activities in Mainland China reveal the forces of transnational ties, capital, markets, and identities, as temples were built with the hope of developing tourism, boosting the local economy, and enhancing Chinese identities for Hong Kong and Taiwanese worshippers.

The book includes chapters on making religious places, heritage and authenticity, women temple managers, and the role of entrepreneurs in managing some successful temples. Based on extensive fieldwork, Chan and Lang have produced a truly interdisciplinary follow up to *The Rise of a Refugee God* which will appeal to students and scholars of Chinese religion, Chinese culture, Asian anthropology, cultural heritage, and Daoism alike.

Selina Ching Chan is Professor of Sociology and Associate Director of the Contemporary China Research Centre at Hong Kong Yue Shan University.

Graeme Lang was a Professor of Sociology in the Department of Asian and International Studies at City University of Hong Kong until his retirement in 2014.

Anthropology of Asia Series
Series Editor: Shaun Malarney,
International Christian University, Japan

Asia today is one of the most dynamic regions of the world. The previously predominant image of 'timeless peasants' has given way to the image of fast-paced business people, mass consumerism and high-rise urban conglomerations. Yet much discourse remains entrenched in the polarities of East versus West', 'Tradition versus Change'. This series hopes to provide a forum for anthropological studies which break with such polarities. It will publish titles dealing with cosmopolitanism, cultural identity, representations, arts and performance. The complexities of urban Asia, its elites, its political rituals, and its families will also be explored.

Hong Kong
The anthropology of a Chinese metropolis
Edited by Grant Evans and Maria Tam

Folk Art Potters of Japan
Brian Moeran

Anthropology and Colonialism in Asia and Oceania
Jan van Bremen and Akitoshi Shimizu

Japanese Bosses, Chinese Workers
Power and control in a Hong Kong megastore
Wong Heung Wah

The Legend of the Golden Boat
Regulation, trade and traders in the borderlands of Laos, Thailand, China and Burma
Andrew Walker

Cultural Crisis and Social Memory
Modernity and identity in Thailand and Laos
Edited by Shigeharu Tanabe and Charles F. Keyes

The Globalization of Chinese Food
Edited by David Y. H. Wu and Sidney C. H. Cheung

Culture, Ritual and Revolution in Vietnam
Shaun Kingsley Malarney

The Ethnography of Vietnam's Central Highlanders
A historical contextualization, 1850–1990
Oscar Salemink

Night-time and Sleep in Asia and the West
Exploring the dark side of life
Edited by Brigitte Steger and Lodewijk Brunt

Chinese Death Rituals in Singapore
Tong Chee Kiong

Calligraphy and Power in Contemporary Chinese Society
Yuehping Yen

Buddhism Observed
Travellers, exiles and Tibetan Dharma in Kathmandu
Peter Moran

The Tea Ceremony and Women's Empowerment in Modern Japan
Bodies re-presenting the past
Etsuko Kato

Asian Anthropology
Edited by Jan van Bremen, Eyal Ben-Ari, Syed Farid Alatas

Love in Modern Japan
Its estrangement from self, sex and society
Sonia Ryang

Food and Foodways in Asia
Resource, tradition and cookery
Sidney CH Cheung and Tan Chee-Beng

Varieties of Secularism in Asia
Anthropological explorations of religion, politics and the spiritual
Edited by Nils Bubandt and Martijn van Beek

Building Temples in China
Memories, tourism and identities
Selina Ching Chan and Graeme Lang

Building Temples in China

Memories, tourism, and identities

**Selina Ching Chan and
Graeme Lang**

Routledge
Taylor & Francis Group

LONDON AND NEW YORK

First published 2015
by Routledge
2 Park Square, Milton Park, Abingdon, Oxon OX14 4RN

and by Routledge
711 Third Avenue, New York, NY 10017

Routledge is an imprint of the Taylor & Francis Group, an informa business

British Library Cataloguing in Publication Data
A catalogue record for this book is available from the British Library

Library of Congress Cataloging in Publication Data
Chan, Selina Ching.
Building temples in China: memories, tourism, and identities/Selina Ching
Chan and Graeme Lang.
pages cm. — (Anthropology of Asia series)
Includes bibliographical references and index.
1. Wong Tai Sin (Taoist deity) 2. Taoism—China—
History—20th century. 3. Taoism—China—History—21st century.
4. China—Religion. 5. Temples—China.
I. Title.
BL1942.85.W65C43 2014
299.5'14350951—dc23
2014022490

ISBN: 978-0-415-64224-8 (hbk)
ISBN: 978-0-203-08100-6 (ebk)

Typeset in Times New Roman
by Swales and Willis Ltd, Exeter, Devon, UK

MIX
Paper from
responsible sources
FSC
www.fsc.org   FSC® C013604   Printed and bound by CPI Group (UK) Ltd, Croydon, CR0 4YY

Contents

Illustrations   viii
Abbreviations and transliteration   x
Acknowledgments   xi

1   Building temples in China: memories, tourists, and identities   1

2   History of the worship of Huang Daxian   10

3   Making religious places: memories and transnational ties   30

4   Heritage and temples: authenticity, tourists, and pilgrims   49

5   Two grand temples in Jinhua   71

6   A female temple manager and the popularization of a temple   94

7   A popular temple in Guangzhou built and managed by
    a secular entrepreneur   121

8   Conclusion   145

Appendix: The lives of a saint—compiling stories about
Huang Chuping in Jinhua, Zhejiang   156
References   167
Glossary   173
Index   176

Illustrations

Figures

2.1 Statue of Huang Daxian at the foot of Xiqiaoshan in Guangdong
  (built in 1996, demolished by 2012)   27
4.1 Notice board displaying charitable scholarships for
  underprivileged girls   63
4.2 A primary school girl drew the picture. In the picture, the black
  cat detective committed corruption by accepting illegal gifts in the
  form of cash and luxurious banquets. He was jailed later   65
5.1 Empty Courtyard in front of YYY   75
5.2 Worshippers lighting candles, with used candle wax collected
  underneath the candles (Zugong temple, Jinhuashan)   76
5.3 At the installation of a new Huang Daxian statue at Gunglu temple,
  the statue-maker sprayed sacred water on the crowds   79
5.4 Spirit medium delivering a message from the deity, with a group
  of devoted female villagers   81
6.1 Foundation of CSDY, 1996, laid by Ms Luo and local cadres   98
6.2 Ms Luo with calligraphers and painters. The wall was painted by
  one of the priests at CSDY   103
6.3 On behalf of the Jinhua municipal government, the management
  team from CSDY presented a statue of HDX to former KMT leader,
  Lien Chan   105
6.4 A priest stationed at the courtyard in front of the main altar, CSDY   108
6.5 Daoist priests performing music while worshippers are praying,
  CSDY   110
6.6 Statues of the brothers Huang Chuping (known as Huang Daxian)
  and Huang Chuqi, at Chisonggong, Jinhuashan, Zhejiang   112
7.1 The Guangzhou HDX temple (main building), 2001   124
7.2 Guangzhou HDX temple staff, with goggles (to protect against
  incense smoke)   128
7.3 Crowds in Guangzhou HDX temple courtyard   130
7.4 Relics from the original temple built in 1899, which was destroyed
  in the 1930s, reinstalled in a commemorative wall in the garden,
  Guangzhou HDX temple   134

Map

1.1 China, showing locations of the Jinhua and
     Guangdong temples   8

Tables

3.1 Jinhua temples: location, construction, and financing   30
7.1 Revenue at Guangzhou Huang Daxian temple   137

Abbreviations and transliteration

Abbreviations

CSDY: Chisong Daoyuan (temple above the reservoir in Jinhuashan, Zhejiang
HDX: Huang Daxian (the deity)
SSY: Seseyuan (the organization which manages the public HDX temple in Hong Kong)
YQG: Yuan Qing Ge (the organization which manages the private HDX temple in Hong Kong)
YYY: Yuan Yuan Yuan (temple next to Huang Peng village near Lanxi, Zhejiang)

Transliteration

Chinese terms are transliterated using the *pinyin* system, except for place names for which an alternative transliteration is commonly used (e.g., Hong Kong, Kowloon, and Taiwan) or personal names for which a different transliteration has been adopted by that person (e.g., Leung rather than Liang).

Acknowledgments

This book is the product of fieldwork and interviews during the past 15 years in Hangzhou, Jinhua, Guangdong, and Hong Kong. We are grateful for financial support for these fieldwork trips by City University of Hong Kong, Hong Kong Shue Yan University, and the National University of Singapore.

While the authors mostly wrote the chapters separately—with the first author concentrating on temples and developments in Jinhua and the second author on temples and developments in Guangdong and some comparisons with the Jinhua developments (e.g., in the Appendix)—we shared ideas, commented and made suggestions on each other's chapters, and had discussions on the various topics. Our "voices" and perspectives reflect our differing backgrounds in anthropology and in sociology, but we have benefitted greatly from the collaboration. Both of us presented earlier drafts at different conferences and received constructive feedback from conference participants.

We have especially benefitted from discussing this research with academic colleagues, including Kim-kwong Chan, Adam Yuet Chau, Stephan Feuchtwang, Patrick Hase, Maria Jaschok, David Jordan, Yunfeng Lu, David Owyong, David Palmer, Lars Ragvald, Joseph Tamney, James L. Watson, Rubie S. Watson, Der-ruey Yang, Fenggang Yang, and Xudong Zhao. We are also grateful for the comments by two anonymous reviewers and for the advice and guidance (and much appreciated patience) of the editor, Hannah Mack.

This book is in a sense a sequel to the earlier book, *The Rise of a Refugee God: Hong Kong's Wong Tai Sin* (Lang and Ragvald 1993), which tried to describe and explain the development of worship of this deity and his eventual great success in Hong Kong. As we finished that book in 1993, we were already aware of the rebuilding of temples to the saint in China, described some of these developments, and concluded the book with these lines:

> The one hundredth anniversary of the founding of the cult of Wong Tai Sin in southern China will be in 1997, and it will be interesting to observe whether that year marks the beginning of hard times, or a new phase of growth, for the cult of this refugee god. As folk religion experiences a cautious revival inside China, it will also be interesting to watch his progress and travels in the land of his birth. (p. 160)

This book is the result of those further observations and investigations, and the story is as fascinating to us as we expected.

The research could not have been accomplished without the generous help and assistance of the many people we interviewed and with whom we discussed the research in Hong Kong, Guangdong, and Zhejiang, including temple managers, local officials, retired cadres, male and female clergy, local villagers, worshippers, and members of various religious associations in Hong Kong and mainland China. We regret that we cannot thank all of these people by name, but we would especially like to express our appreciation to Dr William S.L. Yip, Mr Alfred F.C. Leung, Mr Siuchi Chow, Ms Meiyu Luo, Ms Hongmei Hu, Mr Wenxing Zhao, Mr Yannan Shao, Mr Fumin Ren, and Mr Gengzhi Mao. Of course, any errors of fact or interpretation in the book are ours alone.

1 Building temples in China

Memories, tourists, and identities

Introduction

This book is about the revival of the Daoist immortal Huang Daxian (hereafter usually abbreviated as "HDX"), as seen from the construction and management of a series of temples dedicated to him in China over the past three decades. Several research questions are asked in this book. Why were so many temples dedicated to HDX constructed? How did different temple-builders obtain legitimacy for building the temples? How are the temples managed and promoted to attract tourists and locals? How do temple-construction and temple-management strategies reveal market forces, as well as local and transnational factors, and create an impact on the local people's religious life and identities?

Diversity in the trajectories of temple-building projects

Much has been written on how temples are constructed or reconstructed for reviving local religious and communal life or for recycling tradition after the market reforms in China. A bottom-up approach has been used in the existing research to investigate how and why the locals have taken the lead in temple-building activities in village communities (e.g., Jing 1996; Chau 2006). The locals who take the leadership in temple construction or revival of religious practices are peasants in village communities or charismatic leaders (e.g., Jing 1996; Feuchtwang and Wang 2001; Chau 2006). Constructing or reconstructing temples were ways of "reasserting their identity and dignity and regaining social status" for some of these locals (Jing 1996; Chau 2006; Goossaert and Palmer 2011: 250) and also reflect the rise of local power and communal authority (Eng and Lin 2002). Additional research on how locals have revived their religious beliefs and practices examines the financial and cultural support of overseas kinsmen and the support given by local governments to temple revivals (Dean 1993; Kuah-Pearce 2000; Dean and Zheng 2010). The dynamics between the state and society that lie behind the revival of temples and religious practices initiated by the locals have been well-analyzed. However, there is a gap in the literature when it comes to understanding religious revivals that were instead led by local governments. Although a few researchers noted that the local governments or businessmen got involved in temple renovation or revival, they did not provide a detailed account of the process and the state–society dynamics behind it (e.g., Dott 2010; Sutton and Kang 2010; Svensson 2010).

Unlike the majority of existing studies which argue that religious revival took a bottom-up approach, our book suggests that a top-down approach in religious revival is instead the case in Jinhua. The book examines why the local governments were the ones who took the lead in initiating a series of temple-construction projects in China. Who was involved in these projects and how were they involved? Another feature of our research which distinguishes it from the existing literature on temples in China is that we studied the similarities and differences in the process of construction, development, and management of a number of temples, all dedicated to the same deity, in two provinces (Zhejiang and Guangdong) in China since the 1980s. These temples are of different sizes and each of the temples was unique in its coalition of sponsors, supporters, resources, and management. The complexity and diversity in the trajectories of construction and development among this particular sample of temples dedicated to one deity shows that there are a variety of ways to build and operate a temple despite what appears to be a relatively standard set of regulations for the construction and supervision of temples. As other researchers have noted, there are many ways to accomplish projects in China, given the resourcefulness and political sophistication of some of the initiators of these projects and the dynamic interactions that occur between the various parties in the government and the local community (Ashiwa and Wank 2006; 2009; Goossaert and Fang 2009; Sutton and Kang 2010; Svensson 2010).

Among all temples dedicated to the same deity, some were built or renovated by locals, some were sponsored by local governments, some were funded by overseas pilgrims, some were constructed by local investors, and others were built by foreign investors. Why is such a diverse pattern found for these temples dedicated to the same deity? Funding of these temples projects can come from local banks or local companies operating in the area, which have been instructed to support a project or see commercial advantages in doing so. It could also be supported from local village fund-raising, as well as from overseas Chinese investors who have business interests or personal networks in the area. Some of these new temple projects have required 10 or 20 million RMB for construction and land acquisition alone, and when most of these projects were initiated in the 1990s, this was a major investment. How local coalitions put together this kind of funding, typically but not always with local government support, is one of the most striking features in the construction of new temples in the two provinces.

Our book delineates the multiple motivations of temple-building projects. It also examines the particular sociopolitical context and the developmental discourse behind these motivations. The way in which different local governments assumed leadership in initiating a series of temple-building activities due to visits by overseas pilgrims will be investigated. It analyzes how the transnational flow of knowledge on the popularity of the HDX in Hong Kong has led to the awakening of memories and later to temple-building activities in China.

Regarding religious memories, Jing (1996) has demonstrated how temple memories were related to the collective trauma of forced resettlement and Cultural Revolution and symbolized the local protest against the state in the past. Narratives of suffering and the politics of revenge were remembered through the process of temple construction (Jing 1996; Aijmer and Ho 2000; Mueggler 2001). Instead of focusing on the confrontational relationship between the state and locals, we examine how memories were evoked for economic purposes by the locals and local governments. How did local villagers revive legends and invent memories for their own advantage? How did remembering and forgetting take place at many levels, each possibly with different agents and each with its own agenda? What was the impact on the local identities?

Our research reveals that selected materials from the distant past, in the forms of legends and stories from Daoist literature and oral tradition, were recovered or invented by the locals with the help of local governments and intellectuals. We also investigate the morality evoked through these awakened legends and oral narratives and argue that they are reflections of concerns in the wider society and responses to the "moral vacuum" in China after market reforms began. Such a process of reawakening and inventing memories has reinterpreted and trans-formed the meaning of the homecoming religious symbol and made places. Our book will demonstrate how local identities were constructed with new meanings and place-making, while memories were reawakened and invented by the govern-ment, intellectuals, and locals as a result of the transnational flow of knowledge, people, and money.

Legitimacy of temples

With religion being known to be closely monitored by the state in China, how could so many temples for the same deity be allowed to be constructed in Jinhua city alone? Goossaert and Palmer (2011: 347) have provided an account of the regulations on places of religious worship that were enacted by the State council in 1994. In practice, all new temple projects need to put up a strong case in order to gain approval and support from the local government. There are different ways of interpreting the regulations to claim legitimacy.

First, it is usually necessary to establish the legitimacy of the temple in the con-text of local religious and cultural history. Second, legitimacy is obtained through downplaying religion as folk culture—thus providing the assurance to the govern-ment that it is kept under control—while exploiting its market value (see, e.g., Sutton and Kang 2010: 122). For instance, temple construction by overseas Chinese in their hometowns could only be conducted after economic contribution in public works had been made (Dean 2010: 247). Third, legitimacy is obtained through utilizing the symbol of religion to serve the goal of nationalism, such as to enhance Chinese cultural nationalism among the Chinese living both inside and outside China and to promote national harmony. For instance, legitimacy of religious activities could be obtained through putting them within the framework of cultural nationalism and the PRC government's goal of reunifying Taiwan to China (e.g., Dean 1998). The maintenance of social stability, the acceptance of the state's established political authority, and Chinese cultural nationalism are also legitimate grounds for promoting the Confucius cult ceremony in Qufu (Yan and Bramwell 2008: 985). At Wutaishan in Shanxi province, the national ideology of building a harmonious society is also put forward as a justification to host the cultural (religious) festival (Ryan and Gu 2010: 171). The aims of promoting harmony among different ethnic groups as well as loyalty to the state are legitimate grounds for renovating religious sites of ethnic minorities (e.g., Sutton and Kang 2010: 115). Indeed, economic development, tourism, historical heritage, nationalism, and social stability are the common grounds for the state to compromise with local groups seeking to rebuild temples or revive local religious rituals (Goossaert and Palmer 2011: 399).

While most of the earlier studies have mentioned the grounds of legitimacy for temple-building, they do not provide a detailed account on the process of justification and do not account for the importance of continuous endorsement from the different branches of the governments in the development of a temple. An exception was found at Longwanggou, where popular enthusiasm as well as environmental and educational achievements are all utilized by the temple manager to obtain legitimate status for the temple (Chau 2005: 260, 2009). In this study, we note that Chinese cultural nationalism serves as a general framework for the state to regulate the transnational flow of capital and information and to legitimize temple-building activities. The historical heritage of HDX in Jinhua and economic development are also important grounds for legitimacy. More importantly, we interrogate the process of obtaining legitimacy and demonstrate why some temples obtained approval more easily than others, although the same justifications had been put forward. Elsewhere in Sichuan, there was a case where a new temple was not officially approved or was even refused permission (Sutton and Kang 2010). Eventually, government officials gave in and later considered it as a tourism site and promoted it as a tourist stop on the old "Silk and Horse Trade Route" (Sutton and Kang 2010: 111–113). Instead of merely documenting the outcomes in obtaining approval, we will probe into the complexity in the process of seeking legitimacy and delineate how one particular temple manager in Jinhua overcame this challenge through utilizing various social and cultural capital from the local community, official networks, and transnational ties. In addition, this book also examines how the local governments, temple managers, and locals exploit the notions of historical heritage and the ideology of Chinese cultural nationalism for their own interests. It analyzes the different strategies in soliciting support from different local government offices for the development of temples. We address the politics behind making a case for historical authenticity, nationalism, or economic development, as well as the relationship between temple management teams and their respective local governments.

Temple management strategies

Instead of merely discussing religious practices conducted at temples, this book focuses on the strategies to manage temples and attract worshippers or visitors, as well as the complex dynamics of the transnational, national, and local forces behind them. This perspective has taken into account the fact that marketization and commercialization are found in temples.[1] Today, there are plenty of temples in China, which is different from two decades ago when there were fewer temples available for people to tour around and to satisfy their religious needs. It is therefore important to note that the popularization of religious beliefs and temples is not a necessary outcome of temple construction or revival. This is in contrast to the existing research in which temples or public religious rituals and festivals have always obtained support and worshippers from the start (e.g., Siu 1990; Jing 1996: 173). None of the past research seems to encounter or examine cases of temples being without adequate visitors. Among the different temples examined, we discovered that although some temples were successful in attracting crowds, there are others that did experience difficulty in attracting visitors. Our book argues that the popularity of a temple has to be understood both from marketing strategies implemented by temple managers as well as how these managers interact with the local governments and locals. As far as we know, nobody has pursued the question of strategies and management through interviews with visitors to religious sites in China or through detailed observations about how visitors spend their time and to which scenes they direct the most attention during a temple visit.

Some temples related to HDX were built in Jinhua with the clear intention of attracting overseas pilgrims and international tourists and boosting the local economy, whereas other temples built or renovated by local villagers were primarily for reviving local religious life. Nevertheless, none of these temples have consistently managed to attract large numbers of visitors. Why are these cases in Jinhua different from temples in Fujian (see, e.g., Dean and Zheng 2010; Kuah-Pearce 2000), where temples reconstructed by Taiwanese and Singaporean kinsmen have successfully attracted regular and frequent visitors from abroad? A related question is why some of the temples we examined have proven to be extremely successful in attracting domestic tourists and pilgrims, while others less so. This book will examine how and why these temples have achieved popularity and have become leisure sites for the consumption of tourists and why other temples have not become as popular as envisaged by their builders.

The book also delineates how the authenticity of HDX's hometown is a negotiated discourse and how it has then become the government's key promotional agenda for temples dedicated to HDX. We argue that HDX religious heritage has been reworked and represented as authentic Jinhua cultural heritage under the leadership of the local governments through various cultural media strategies. Our book will also examine how the sense of authenticity of HDX is constructed by the local government through introducing the new HDX cultural festival, as well as the central government's official recognition of HDX legends as a national intangible cultural heritage.[2] Are these authenticating strategies conducted at the governmental level effective in bringing many pilgrims, visitors, and tourists to these temples that are constructed and managed by them?

This book examines how impressive religious services have turned temples into popular religious sites because they resonate with people's spiritual needs and are "authentic" religious places. Our studies will investigate the factors that determine whether temple managers fail or succeed in soliciting help from religious specialists to enhance the religious aura of the temples. The development and subsequent popularization of temples also relies on how temples continue to satisfy the locals and visitors in secular aspect. Strategies used by temple managers to promote the temple's attractions, benefits, and virtues to visitors are hence important in determining the popularity of temples. We analyze how different features are added to the temples to satisfy the needs of the local community as well as those of domestic tourists and visitors from different backgrounds.

Complexity of state–society dynamics

Tensions as well as negotiation and mutual cooperation between the local government and locals over religious sites were often observed throughout temple-construction and management processes (e.g., James 1985; Dean 1998, 2003; Flower and Leonard 1998; Aijmer and Ho 2000; Tsai 2002).[3] It is therefore important that the supporters of a new temple project must work continuously to ensure good relations with relevant bureaus within the local government. Our ethnography will show how different management strategies cope with the constantly changing and complex state–society dynamics. The state–society dynamics are investigated through addressing the different and overlapping interests of multiple agents at various layers and sectors in the state bureaucracy and local society.

On the complexity of state power, we delineate it through examining the dynamics between governments at different levels as well as between different local county governments. State power appears in various forms—central government power, local government power, discretionary power of individual officials, and persuasion power of the official ideology—and do not often stay in coherence (Eng and Lin 2002: 1261). This book will demonstrate how various stances were taken up by a wide range of agents of state power at different levels and in changing times. Each of the layers of these governments has different perceptions of religion and how it should be tapped for development and tourism purposes. We argue that the different and fluctuating positions are largely due to changing socioeconomic and political environments in different counties as well as leadership changes that affect the development direction adopted by different government offices.

At the vertical level, we will address how temple-management strategies are affected by the power dynamics between local governments and provincial governments, as well as between locals and governmental authorities. In particular, temple managers often have to deal with different directions and stances taken by the various local governments. The stances of the respective local government are often a result of complex dynamics between local governments at the same level and between the local and provincial governments.

At the horizontal level, we delineate how development strategies in temples have been affected by the power dynamics of various agents of mobile and immobile groups. We have observed cooperation and/or competition among different actors, such as temple managers, local governments, local villagers, overseas pilgrims, tourists from overseas, as well as domestic tourists. The book examines how temple managers and locals use different strategies, including use of social capital and local networks, to negotiate with various government agencies in order to ensure the temples' legitimacy and reputation. It also analyzes how different strategies have been used to seek support or cooperation from local communities.

Methodology and chapter description

This book is mainly based on material collected from multisited fieldwork conducted over the last 15 years. We conducted fieldwork at various temples dedicated to HDX in Jinhua, of Zhejiang province, in 1999, 2000, 2003, and 2007. While most of the data were collected in Jinhua, in 2003 we also conducted a fieldtrip to Guangzhou and interviewed the temple management team at a temple there that was dedicated to the same deity in 2003. Throughout the past 15 years, we have developed long-term relationships with some of the informants. Some interviews were also conducted in Hong Kong in 2006, 2012, 2013, and 2014, either with informants who lived here or were visiting Hong Kong on a regular basis. We carried out in-depth interviews with a wide range of people in our fieldwork, including pilgrims, tourists, villagers, temple managers, businessmen, and officials from different government offices, including those from the United Front as well as at both the local and provincial levels. This wide range of informants has allowed us to analyze the multiple meanings of temple-building activities for various parties.

Our research at various temples dedicated to the same deity across a wide range of geographical areas uncovers the process of religious revival in various counties, as well as the unity and diversity of religious practices in postreform China.[4] The fieldwork also allows us not only to understand religious revival as a reflection of state–society dynamics but also to examine temple-building activities as cooperation and competition among different counties at various times in response to state policy. Our longitudinal fieldwork at various sites allows us to analyze the revival and boom in religious practices as a process which is closely related to economic, touristic, and political developments over the past few decades.

Our book mainly investigates temple construction and development in Jinhua and illuminates different roles and motivations played by the different actors— including individuals, local governments, and businessmen—over this time period (Chapters 3–6). Besides, we update some of the findings and analysis from earlier work by Lang and Ragvald (1993), providing a brief account on revival of a few temples dedicated to HDX in Guangdong (Chapter 2). This also includes a more in-depth analysis of one of the temples dedicated to the deity in Guangdong for making comparisons between strategies and initiatives of temple-builders and supporters in Guangzhou and in Jinhua (Chapter 7).

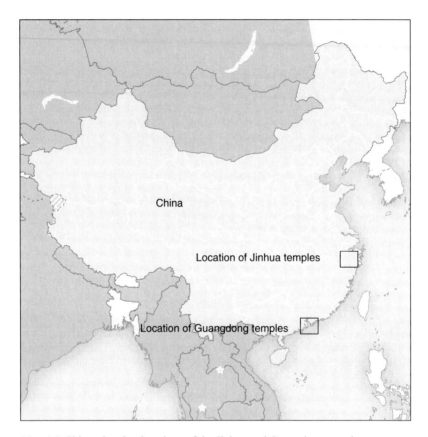

Map 1.1 China, showing locations of the Jinhua and Guangdong temples

In Chapter 2, we review the origins of the legends about the Daoist saint Huang Daxian and outline the history of worship of the saint in Zhejiang, and in Guangdong, up to the mid twentieth century. We note the eventual destruction or confiscation of almost all of the temples dedicated to the saint in China and the eventual great success of the one remaining major temple in Hong Kong to escape that fate since the 1950s. Then we describe the beginning of the revival of interest in this deity in Guangdong in the late 1980s, partly and sometimes entirely as a result of the deity's great popularity in Hong Kong, and the desire to attract Hong Kong's people back to sites associated with the deity in mainland China. In Chapter 3, we examine how narratives of memories of HDX in Jinhua have been evoked and reawakened in the forms of legends and stories by the local governments and used to justify various temple-building projects. In Chapter 4, we examine how the local government promotes HDX temples by highlighting HDX as authentic cultural heritage through various cultural media strategies. The way in which locals and tourists respond to these portrayals will also be analyzed. In Chapter 5, we describe the case of two large temples built in Jinhua in the 1990s which were launched and funded through the initiatives of the local government. One was next to a village, in the small town of Lanxi near Jinhua, where the saint had supposedly lived during his time on earth, in the fourth century CE. Intended as a project to attract Hong Kong tourists and investors, the temple initially attracted the interest of some Hong Kong believers but ultimately failed to sustain their interest or to attract many local visitors, tourists, or worshippers, despite some striking initiatives by the secular government-appointed temple manager. The other temple was built on Jinhua Mountain, also as a government-launched project, but failed to attract many visitors and was eventually "privatized" by allocating the management to a large secular firm in Zhejiang. We describe these two cases and explain the troubles and initiatives associated with each temple.

In Chapters 6 and 7, we describe one HDX temple which was built in a rural district near Jinhua by a Taiwanese business woman and the other which was built in a suburban district in Guangzhou by a Canadian-Chinese business man based in Hong Kong, respectively. Both of these managers arranged funding for temple construction and then devoted a great deal of their time and entrepreneurial energies in subsequent years to enhancing the temple's features, promoting it in the local community, and cultivating good relationships with the local government. They have been strikingly successful in these activities. We examine, review, and compare the somewhat different strategies and initiatives adopted by these managers in managing and promoting their temples. In the conclusions, we summarize the main findings and themes in the book.

Notes

1 The market provides freedom to conduct religious activities while "commercialization and commoditization are obvious characteristics of religious activity" (Goossaert and Palmer 2011: 12).
2 Indeed, the classification of national intangible cultural heritage is a new category for religious traditions, which is used for tourism development (see also Goossaert and Palmer 2011: 344).
3 Festivals and rituals reveal how state power operates and intervenes in cultural fields (Feuchtwang and Wang 2001: 41).
4 Some chapters draw from the material reported in earlier publications (Chan 2005; Chan and Lang 2005; Lang, Chan, and Ragvald 2005; Chan and Lang 2007; Chan and Lang 2011).

2 History of the worship of Huang Daxian

Introduction

This chapter provides a review of the history of worship of the Daoist immortal Huang Daxian, beginning with the legends and stories recorded in the fourth century CE in China and concluding with his great success in Hong Kong in the latter half of the twentieth century. This review includes key developments in the history of worship of Huang Daxian in the Jinhua area of Zhejiang and in Guangdong, including the use of spirit-writing in Guangdong in the 1890s, the building of new temples and shrines in Guangdong, and the eventual destruction of all of those temples between the 1920s and 1960s. The chapter describes the migration of the cult of HDX to Hong Kong in 1915 and the establishment of a large temple several years later, the great success of this temple in Hong Kong after 1949, and the reasons for the god's success in Hong Kong.[1]

The final section of the chapter describes the growing interest of the god's increasingly affluent Hong Kong worshippers in the sites of the original temples in Guangdong in mainland China, their attempts to learn more about and visit those sites, and the responses to those visits, as local governments and various other parties began to build new temples to the deity.

We begin with the origins of the legend and cult of HDX, in the Jinhua area of Zhejiang province, and the outlines of a history of worship in the area up to the 1950s, including the original versions of the cult focused on two brothers, Huang Chuping (who was eventually known as Huang Daxian in Guangdong and Hong Kong) and Huang Chuqi. Then, we relate the growing worship of one of the brothers, Huang Chuping, in Guangzhou in the 1890s, the temples that were built in Guangdong from the 1890s to 1930s, and the eventual migration of the cult to Hong Kong early in the twentieth century. While all of the temples to Huang Chuping and Huang Chuqi were eventually destroyed in China between the 1920s and 1960s, a temple to this deity in Hong Kong eventually became very popular and wealthy, especially from the 1950s. It was the great success of this temple among the Hong Kong people that eventually stimulated the construction or rebuilding of a number of new temples to the saint in Guangdong and Zhejiang from the late 1980s, and the appearance of some smaller shrines and temples among the Hong Kong emigrants in various cities in the United States, Canada, and Australia in the 1980s and 1990s.

Origins and transmission of the legend of Huang Daxian

The earliest clear reference to the figure eventually known as "Huang Daxian" is in the fourth century CE book *Biographies of Immortals* (*Shenxian Zhuan*) by the famous Daoist writer Ge Hong (284–364 CE). The book outlines the biographies of 84 Daoist "immortals" or saints, including Huang Chuping, who lived in the third or fourth Century CE, during the Jin dynasty (266–316 CE) in west-central Zhejiang, according to this account. Huang Chuping is the person who supposedly achieved immortality and Daoist perfection and was eventually worshipped as "Huang Daxian." Ge Hong's account of Huang's life states that when he was tending the family's herd of sheep at age 15, he met a Daoist who noted his qualities and invited him to go into the hills on Jinhua Mountain (*Jinhuashan*) to practice Daoist cultivation and seek the extraordinary powers which were supposed to result from success in this quest.

Forty years later, Huang Chuping's brother, Huang Chuqi, went to look for him, and was told by a Daoist to look for him on the mountain. The brothers finally met on the mountain and updated each other on what they had been doing. Huang Chuqi wanted to know what had happened to the sheep, which had been Chuping's responsibility when he disappeared 40 years earlier. Chuping pointed to a nearby hillside, but Chuqi told his brother that he could not see any sheep, only white boulders, whereupon Chuping called out to the white boulders, and they turned into sheep. A translation of Ge Hong's account of these events reads:

> Huang Chuping came from Danxi. When he was 15, his family had him tend sheep. A Daoist, seeing that he was good-natured and conscientious, took him to a stone cave in Jinhua Mountain. For 40 odd years Chuping stayed there without thinking of his family. His elder brother Chuqi searched for him for many years in the mountains but without success. Once in a market-place he saw a Daoist. Chuqi beckoned him and asked, "My brother Chuping who was sent out to tend sheep has not been seen for more than 40 years. I don't know where he is or whether he is dead or alive. Would you please find out by divination?" The Daoist said, "On the Jinhua Mountain there is a young shepherd by the name of Huang Chuping. Doubtless he is your brother." When he heard this, Chuqi followed the Daoist in search of his younger brother, and found him. The brothers told each other what had happened during the years they had been apart. Chuqi then asked his brother where the sheep were. "Not far from here on the eastern side of the mountain" Chuping answered. Chuqi went over and looked for them, but he saw only white stones. He went back and said to Chuping, "There are no sheep on the eastern side of the mountain." Chuping said, "The sheep are there, but you, my brother, could not see them." Chuping and Chuqi went over to have another look. Chuping shouted to the sheep to rise and all the stones turned into tens of thousands of sheep. Chuqi said to his brother, "You have now attained perfection in the secrets of the Dao [the 'way',]. Can I also learn to do that?" Chuping said, "Only if you are eager to learn the Dao will you attain perfection." Chuqi then abandoned his wife and children and stayed with his brother to learn the Dao.
>
> (adapted from the translation in Lang and Ragvald 1993: 4–5)

The passage continues with references to some medicines perfected by Chuping and states that a person who takes these medicines can even become immortal. It concludes with the two brothers changing their names: Chuping to Chisong Zi (Red Pine Master) and Chuqi to Lu Ban. This story has been transmitted through all of the later accounts of Chuping's life and work, and the miracle of transforming rocks into sheep is enshrined in a large relief-carving behind the altar in the main Hong Kong temple and in life-size statues of white boulders turning into sheep on a hillside near a temple in rural Guangdong. The typical ways for a Daoist to demonstrate the achievement of extraordinary powers are through healing others, and extraordinary longevity or immortality for himself. So, this unusual story about turning boulders into sheep, which is the only instance of such a story in the Daoist literature as far as we know, prompts the curious scholar to wonder whether there might be some secular event which prompted this miracle-story.

A secular explanation for the story is possible.[2] But Chuqi, believing he had indeed witnessed a miracle, was highly impressed, and asked if he could learn to exercise this kind of magical power. Chuping replied that if he was truly sincere and devoted, he could also acquire such abilities. Chuqi then left his wife and children and joined Chuping on the mountain, seeking Daoist perfection and the powers of the Daoist saint. The brothers subsequently developed medicines for healing and for attaining immortality (a preoccupation of many "Daoists" during that period) and allegedly became renowned in the area for these achievements. Ge Hong's account claims that Chuping succeeded in refining cinnabar (mercuric sulphide) into a drug which could be used to achieve immortality. This experimentation with cinnabar in the quest for longevity and immortality had been a preoccupation of some Daoists from as early as the first century CE (Williams 1960: 169; Welch 1965: 97). Chuping's reported success in this quest was included by Ge Hong in his biography of the saint.

Ge Hong was a high government official and military staff officer but was also interested in Daoist alchemy and eventually retired to Mt. Luofu in Guangdong province to experiment with cinnabar, herbal medicines, and Daoist cultivation (Lang and Ragvald 1993: 161–162) and became famous among later generations of Daoists and intellectuals for his writings on these themes.

All later versions of the life of Huang Chuping depend directly or indirectly on Ge Hong's account. One of those later versions of the story was published in the tenth century CE in a short encyclopedia titled the *Shilei fu* (*Rhapsodies on [one hundred] Subjects*) (Lang and Ragvald 1993: 37). A compilation of earlier writings on a wide range of topics, it was apparently consulted by many of the candidates for the imperial examinations. It included a summary of Ge Hong's account of Huang Chuping and Huang Chuqi, and it was probably through this book that many writers and poets in later centuries became aware of the two brothers.

Huang Chuping and Huang Chuqi were evidently worshipped in the Mt. Jinhua area in at least one and probably several local temples (Wong 1985). In the twelfth and thirteenth centuries CE, two Southern Song emperors reportedly bestowed titles on the two saints (in 1189 and 1262 CE), probably as part of their efforts to cultivate goodwill among the local population after political turmoil and invasions had forced a relocation of the royal capital to Hangzhou, not far from Jinhua (Lang and Ragvald 1993: 38). This attention to the two saints by several emperors was noted in some later writings such as the *Huitu Liexian Quanzhuan* (*Illustrated Complete Biographies of Ranked Immortals*) compiled in the sixteenth century CE, which contained short biographical sketches of about 500 Daoist saints from the supposed beginnings of Daoism up to the early sixteenth century, including the brothers Chuping and Chuqi (Lang and Ragvald 1993: 162). It seems likely that worship was more or less continuous in Jinhua from the fourth century CE, sustained by local pride, later accounts of their careers in the Jinhua gazetteer (Wong 1985), and no doubt also by occasional "healings" attributed to them, as has occurred in so many other Daoist saint-cults.

The shrines to these saints were renovated or rebuilt in the eleventh, fifteenth, and sixteenth centuries. The main temple on Mt. Jinhua had been called the Chisong (Red Pine) Gong and was renamed as the Baoji Guan (Temple of Assembled Treasures) in 1008 CE (Wong 1985). This was apparently part of a government-sponsored enhancement of Daoist temples in China, which was accompanied by increased central control over the temples by priests sent out for that purpose from the capital. The reconstructed temple to the two brothers was reported to have been the most impressive of the Daoist temples south of the Yangzte River during that time (Lang and Ragvald 1993: 183–184).

The cult of worship of the two Daoist saints was apparently confined to the districts around Jinhua, where it had a physical presence in the iconography of the temple to the brothers and a literary presence in the Jinhua gazetteer. We have not seen clear historical evidence that it had spread much beyond Jinhua into other provinces until the nineteenth century CE. However, the legends of the two brothers were also preserved in Daoist writings and collections from the fourth century CE (*Biographies of Immortals*), the tenth century CE (*Rhapsodies on [one hundred] Subjects*), and the sixteenth century CE (*Illustrated Complete Biographies of Ranked Immortals*), all of which apparently served as handbooks of saints and their achievements for Daoists throughout the country. Eventually, some Daoists in Guangdong adopted Huang Chuping as a deity worthy of special devotion who was prepared, in company with his fellow immortals, to deliver lessons (through these Daoists) to the world.

Veneration of Huang Daxian in Guangdong, 1890s to 1930s

All or nearly all of the current temples to Huang Chuping in mainland China are in Guangdong and Zhejiang. The first temple in the Jinhua region of Zhejiang was apparently built in the fourth century CE, but the shrines and temples to Huang Chuping in Guangdong were built only in the 1890s. We do not have strong evidence of earlier temples or worship of Chuping and Chuqi in Guangdong.

The upsurge in veneration of Huang Chuping in the late 1890s was led by a man who founded a shrine to Huang Chuping in Guangzhou and eventually brought the cult of the deity to Hong Kong early in the twentieth century. The temple which he founded in Hong Kong in 1921 became enormously popular in Hong Kong from the 1950s, and it was the great success of that temple which eventually stimulated the revival of worship of this Daoist saint in Guangdong and Zhejiang in the 1980s and 1990s.

But in the 1890s, we were aware of worship of Huang Chuping only in a shrine in Panyu, near Guangzhou. At that site, a man named Liang Renan conducted spirit-writing sessions (known as *fuji*) to record the words of various gods and deified humans who spoke through these writings to small groups of interested persons. In spirit-writing sessions, one or two people hold a stick or some other apparatus to which a stylus or pointer is attached, and the stylus writes Chinese characters on a table or in a tray of sand, which are read out and recorded by a person standing beside the table. (If a tray of sand is used, the sand is smoothed with a scraper after each character has been written in the sand and recorded, to prepare for the arrival of the next character.) The writer is thought to be possessed by a deity or immortal, and the words are the deity's messages to the assembled persons.

These kinds of groups have been studied in Taiwan (e.g., Jordan and Overmyer 1986) and sometimes evolve into sectarian organizations in which the deity is a kind of patron of the group, who receives the deity's special favor as a reward for their devotion. The deity uses the spirit-writing to issue moral guidance and sometimes specific instructions to various people among the group of devotees and also to communicate general messages about morality to the wider society and to the world.

In the 1890s, one of the topics that apparently led some attendees to seek the god's help was the plague-epidemic which afflicted and killed large numbers of people in Hong Kong and Guangzhou in 1894 and swept through urban areas of the two cities every summer until the end of the 1890s. Liang Renan had been an official in the Chinese Customs service but left the service to pursue his own interests in Daoism and herbal medicines. Like some other literati of his time, he began to use "spirit-writing" to interact with Daoist saints and to expound on Daoist themes and evidently gathered a group of like-minded seekers who believed that they were getting special messages from gods and immortals through Mr Liang's spirit-writing sessions.

We have a record of these messages from Huang Chuping and other immortals in spirit-writings which were published by the group several years later in a two-volume collection titled *Jing Mimeng* (JM), or *Awake [from] Illusory Dreams* (Lang and Ragvald 1993: 13; 164, n. 7). Most of the messages are general moral pronouncements reflecting the Confucian conservatism of the literati, advocating filial piety, honesty, obedience and loyalty toward the emperor, adherence to traditional virtues, and for women, modesty and respectfulness toward the husband and his family.

The spirit-writer brought a number of different figures to the sessions, including not only Daoist saints such as Huang Chuping but also deceased generals, emperors, and culture-heroes from the past. This diversity of voices and messages allowed the spirit-writer to hold the attention of most of his audience of worshippers and seekers for several years. Some of the comments from these supernatural figures addressed the social conditions and alleged social injustices in the society at that time. For example, the spirit of a long-deceased emperor descended to the session and delivered the following critiques:

> Those people who are wealthy should not exploit the common people. Observe how nature changes, and see that all things change. Even though you are wealthy, you labor only for money and for your descendants [because you may die before you enjoy the benefits]. It is better to build up credit for yourself by publishing [i.e., paying for the publishing expenses of] books on good morals, and by donating clothes and food to the common people. . . .
>
> Those people who make money in the market always intend to cheat their customers. They are not honest with their scales, and give less than what you pay for. Their goods are fake. They deceive simple people. While they may make money now through such practices, eventually they will lose everything, and will not even have a piece of roof above their heads.
>
> (*Jing Mimeng*, quoted in Lang and Ragvald 1998: 317)

We quote these examples from the spirit-writings to show that this kind of operation was much more complicated than just a channeling of Daoist deities for the purpose of providing medical remedies or other kinds of assistance to devotees. It was a kind of intense convocation between humans and their cultural predecessors in which the humans mobilized the supposed or imagined views of those predecessors to engage in critiques of their own society and to promote change through a kind of moral revival. At least, this is how a secular sociologist or anthropologist might view these events. Some of this has similarities with shamanistic movements elsewhere in the nineteenth and twentieth centuries (Lewis 1989) and with the Yahwist "prophetic" writings in ancient Israel and Judah (Lang 1989: 318).

Some of the spirit-writings produced by Liang Renan during those years mentioned the epidemic and explained to the attendees that "heaven" was sending this epidemic to those cities because of the wrong-doing of the people in an attempt to "wake them up" or shock them awake (Lang and Ragvald 1998). Other messages mentioned some of the political and military turmoil of that period, conditions which seem especially likely to produce spirit-writing groups among people anxious for guidance and help from the gods (Jordan and Overmyer 1986: 288). The plague seems to have added considerable urgency to these sessions, and this is reflected in some of the messages. For example,

> The plague, which produces such a horrifying scene [of crowds of people desperately beseeching the god] is actually caused by the wrong-doing of the people. It is due to their misbehavior that Heaven sends this kind of epidemic disease to fill up this whole region.
>
> (*Jing Mimeng*, quoted in Lang and Ragvald 1993: 15)

It seems likely that this was one of the reasons why the spirit-writer, Liang Renan, chose this particular deity as the main celestial patron and visitor to the spirit-writing sessions: Huang Chuping was said to be capable of prescribing various Daoist herbal and quasimagical remedies to cure a variety of illnesses. Liang himself was keenly interested in herbal medicines, and his shrines to Huang Chuping in Guangdong and later in Hong Kong had links to herbal medicine business operations. But Huang Chuping was not the only Daoist saint who supposedly had the ability to cure illness.

There are interesting puzzles which remain unsolved in regard to this focus on Huang Chuping in the Panyu shrine in the last decade of the nineteenth century. We have some evidence that Liang Renan was familiar with the writings of Ge Hong, since he cited them in *Jing Mimeng*. He also produced a spirit-writing message from Huang Chuping which was essentially a brief autobiography of the saint and related his miracle of turning rocks into sheep.

> I was originally a goatherd on Jinhua Mountain, which lies to the north of Jinhua prefectural town in Zhejiang. . . . To the north of Jinhua Mountain there is a mountain called Red Pine Mountain. I lived on this mountain. It was a place where people rarely came. The mountain-side was thickly wooded, and the clouds hung heavy over it. In the green-clad towering slopes, deep in a secluded valley there is a cave called Jinhua Grotto; it is one of the Thirty-six Grotto Heavens and Places of Good Fortune. When I was young, my family were poor, and we often did not even have chaff to eat. When I was 8 years old I began to herd sheep and continued until I was 15, at which time I was fortunate to receive instruction from an immortal elder. He led me into the cavern, and there prepared the medicine of immortality by nine times transforming cinnabar. Thereafter I cast aside all worldly matters. My elder brother Chuqi searched for me for more than 40 years without success, and it was only after he met a Daoist who was skilled in divination that he could find me, and we were reunited. My elder brother asked where my sheep were, and I replied that they were [grazing] on the eastern slope of the mountain. When we went to find them, all we could see were white stones lying all over the place. I called to the stones, and they all turned back into sheep! From that time onwards my elder brother took up Daoist practices, and he is now also ranked among the host of immortals. My family name is Huang and my given name is Chuping. I was born in the Jin dynasty and am a native of Danxi [near Jinhua]. Since I lived in seclusion on Mount Red Pine, I am also known as "Immortal Master Red Pin," [Chisong Zi]. However, I am not the same person as the immortal with this name who accompanied Zhang Liang on his travels.[3] If I did not make this clear, then no one would know anything about it; thus I have set down this autobiography.
>
> (adapted from the translation in Lang and Ragvald 1993: 3–4)

This "autobiography" of the saint, delivered by the deity himself in a spirit-writing session and published later in *Jing Mimeng*, is based on the account of the saint's life by Ge Hong in his book *Biographies of Immortals*. It was brought to Hong Kong by Liang Renan and adopted by the Hong Kong worshippers of the deity as the official story of his life and achievements.

But we do not know why Liang selected Huang Chuping, among all of the immortals profiled in Ge Hong's work and in later compilations of biographies of Daoist saints. Liang could not explain the reasons why he had chosen the deity, because he presented himself as a man chosen by the deity to write down his messages to the world. It was the deity, not Liang, who made the choice, for a deity's reasons. But perhaps there was some prior shrine or tradition of worship of Huang Chuping in Guangdong, which Liang had encountered in his own Daoist explorations.

We have not found firm evidence of earlier worship of Huang Chuping in Guangdong. But it is notable that a seventeenth century Ming Dynasty official, Huang Gongfu, who was a native of Guangdong, held some high positions in the regime of the last Ming emperor, lived for a time not far from the Jinhua area before returning to Guangdong, and had devoted some literary attention to Huang Chuping. When the Ming dynasty fell, he retreated to the Xinhui mountain area of Guangdong and lived near a hill called Yangshikeng, or "sheep stone pit." A memorial hall for Huang Gongfu was eventually built on the mountain to commemorate his life and achievements as a local-born patriot and scholar-official. Huang Gongfu wrote a poem about Huang Chuping around this time and also reportedly renamed the nearby hill as Chishi Yan, or "crag of shouting [at the sheep?]," which may have been a reference to Huang Chuping's one major miracle of calling to the boulders and turning them into sheep. Huang Gongfu was renowned as a patriot of the Ming dynasty, among local literati in subsequent generations (Wong 1985), and his interest in Huang Chuping may have led to some veneration of the saint among Guangdong literati. However, we do not have evidence for worship of Huang Chuping in the area between the time of Huang Gongfu in the seventeenth century and Liang Renan in the late nineteenth century. We can guess that veneration of Huang Chuping continued, in some small niches in the cultural landscape, during those two centuries, but at present, this is only a guess.[4]

In any case, after doing spirit-writing sessions at the shrine in Panyu in the 1890s, Mr Liang eventually gained enough wealthy backers to launch a new temple in a rural district called Huadi, just across the river from Guangzhou, in 1899. This temple featured a large gold-colored statue of Huang Chuping. The new temple attracted many worshippers, most of whom came across the river from Guangzhou in boats, and took the short walk up to the temple from a dock below the temple.

Eventually, it seems that it became difficult for Mr Liang to continue to produce messages from the immortals for all of the attendees seeking the gods' advice or favors, and the temple also attracted some powerful and wealthy patrons who wanted to expand the operation and take a larger role in its direction and management.

After several years, Mr Liang withdrew from the Huadi temple and moved back to his home village (Lang and Ragvald 1993: 20), where he built a new temple to Chuping in 1901, providing herbal medicines to worshippers from the area who came seeking medicines and Daoist cures. There was a gold-colored statue to Huang Chuping in the main temple building and a large medicine shop near the entrance to the temple, with a statue of Chuping's brother Huang Chuqi inside the shop. Some free medicines were offered to poor worshippers (with the costs presumably paid by rich patrons who could cultivate virtue by donating for that purpose), but worshippers were expected to pay if they could do so (Lang and Ragvald 1993: 27).

Liang also produced an additional compilation of spirit-writings during this period, which he titled *Xing Shi Yaoyan*, or *Important Words to Awaken the World*. These spirit-writings included some sharp comments on contemporary events in China, which were possibly more pointed from the safer location in the village than he could deliver to his audiences in Guangzhou. For example, after the central government of the Qing dynasty had been humiliated by the capture of Beijing by Western military forces during the so-called Boxer rebellion in 1900, Liang produced this message, supposedly received from the spirit of a famous deceased general:

> These general-officials boast of their power when there is no danger. But as soon as a dangerous situation arises, they are frightened and flee . . . even worse are those generals who secretly reduce the number of their soldiers, and keep the funds meant to pay for the soldiers. When an emergency occurs, they quickly recruit men to fill up the ranks, but these troops are untrained and have no discipline. They are not even able to fight against thieves, let alone external enemies . . . generals exploit the soldiers and steal their salary.
> (*Xing Shi Yaoyan*, quoted in Lang and Ragvald 1998: 317)

But Liang was also developing the Daoist-medicines aspect of the temple's operations. During this period, he compiled a set of numbered medical prescriptions, in which the petitioner's prescription was selected using the "fortune-sticks" method (*qiu qian*): the worshipper asks the god a question or seeks a prescription for a particular type of medical problem and then shakes a bamboo container holding these numbered sticks until one falls out. The number on the stick points the worshipper to the same-number prescription, which is the god's answer to the question. Somebody among the devotees also compiled a set of 100 *qian* or fortune-poems through which worshippers could seek the god's answers to nonmedical questions about family, business, travel, and studies. As with the medical prescriptions, the numbered stick which falls out of the container refers to the number of one of the 100 poems, and the "answer" to the question is encoded in that poem (see Lang and Ragvald 1993: Ch. 6, "Divination and the fortune-tellers," for elaboration and examples).

Huang Daxian in Hong Kong

Several years after the founding of the new temples in his home village in Guangdong, Liang Renan became increasingly anxious about the political and economic turmoil in Guangdong following the revolution of 1911, especially after some local "bad elements" began to try to extort money from him (according to one of his grandsons: Lang and Ragvald 1993: 31). So, after consulting the deity and getting a positive reply, he moved to Hong Kong in 1915, setting up a shrine to Huang Chuping in his herbal medicine shop. He used a painting of the deity in the shrine (rather than a statue, as at the temples in Guangdong and Zhejiang), and conducted spirit-writings in the back of the shop, producing prescriptions from the god which could be filled by Mr Liang himself from the various medicines sold in the front of his shop.

During this period, the original large temple in Huadi, across the river from Guangzhou, began to attract the hostile attention of zealots in the new Republican government in Guangdong, many of whom were antagonistic toward traditional popular-religion temples, which they considered to be hindering economic, social, and cultural progress with their superstitious practices and ability to extract money from worshippers for what secular revolutionaries and Christian reformists considered to be useless or fraudulent cures. Like many other temples in that era, the temple was confiscated around 1919 and converted by the local government to an orphanage, using funds from overseas Chinese, in the early 1920s. The gold-colored statue to Huang Chuping was taken out of the building, broken in pieces, and thrown among bamboo trees nearby. Eventually, the temple-orphanage was closed due to lack of funds, and later it was partially demolished by the Japanese in the 1930s to increase their military security along the river. Some of the bricks were also taken away by local entrepreneurs eager to use or sell bricks and stonework from the temple.

In the 1930s, a second and much smaller temple to Huang Chuping was built nearby, with support from a Guangdong warlord, which continued the worship of the deity in the area. That temple also provided medical services (which were remembered many decades later when Ragvald interviewed local elderly in the area). But that smaller temple was confiscated by the new Communist government of Guangzhou in the early 1950s, and the building was converted into residences.

Meanwhile, in Hong Kong Liang had acquired a number of wealthy patrons prepared to fund a free-standing Daoist temple in Kowloon, which they eventually built in 1921 on a large patch of marginal land near the Kowloon hills. The organization that managed the temple, the *Seseyuan* (which can be translated as "leave behind your earthly desires [when you enter this] garden": Lang and Ragvald 1993: 169, n. 6), was originally conceived as a kind of Daoist retreat for those wishing to pursue Daoist arts and to cultivate personal health and longevity through such arts and use of herbal medicines. Mr Liang died soon after the founding of the temple during one of his returns to his home village, but his son Liang Junzhuan continued as the temple manager of the new Hong Kong temple, assisted by people who had become affiliated with the temple as patrons and devotees. As the population in Kowloon grew in the 1930s, more people from surrounding districts began to visit the temple.

The Japanese invaded Hong Kong in December of 1941 and eventually formed a plan to destroy the temple and informed the temple manager (Liang Renan's son Junzhuan) of that plan (Lang and Ragvald 1993: Ch. 3). The manager and his staff anxiously consulted the god and were informed through spirit-writing that there was no need to worry, and indeed, the Japanese never confiscated and destroyed the temple. (The temple's own historical account claims that the Japanese officers came to deliver the final message about confiscation of the temple, but they slipped and fell in the mud when alighting from their car, retreated in embarrassment, and did not return to carry out the eviction, an outcome which the manager and his staff attributed to the god's subtle intervention during the arrival of the Japanese officers.

After the war, a large number of people who had left Hong Kong during the Japanese occupation returned to the city, some of whom were forced to occupy squatter housing in the districts around the temple. In the late 1940s and early 1950s, another very large stream of migrants arrived in the area from mainland China, seeking better opportunities in Hong Kong or fleeing the armies and administration of the new Communist government in China. Farmers and villagers in the area around the temple rented out squatter huts on this land to thousands of these migrants, who began to try to make a living and seek upward mobility in the colony.

In *The Rise of a Refugee God: Hong Kong's Wong Tai Sin* [Huang Daxian], Lang and Ragvald (1993) sought to explain why this deity had become one of the two or three most popular gods in Hong Kong and why the main temple to HDX had become the richest and most frequently visited of the city's temples. For purposes of this historical introduction to the present book, we can distill the explanation into the following key factors:

1   The temple compound was very large, because Mr Liang found enough wealthy patrons to establish a large Daoist temple and retreat, and he and his patrons located it on largely barren land against the hills but within an hour or so of travel from the growing towns in Kowloon (the "business model" was similar to that of the large temple in Huadi across the river from Guangzhou, which was built in 1899).

2   The temple was not closely associated with any local village or village alliance or ethnic group, as some other local temples were, and thus visitors from surrounding districts, including new migrants from mainland China, were welcomed.

3   The god had a reputation for efficacy with medical prescriptions (possibly also broader powers because of the story circulating after the war that the god had protected the temple from the Japanese plan to confiscate it).

4   The temple offered some free herbal medicines, with prescriptions provided by the god through *fuji* or through fortune-poems using the *qiu qian* procedure to select the prescription using numbered sticks (Lang and Ragvald 1993), at a time when most local people believed in these herbal medicines (and in any case many of them could not afford to pay for medicine).

5   The location of the temple was excellent: although it was not close to any large population of potential worshippers when it was built, it was close enough to the villages and towns in Kowloon to attract devotees and interested visitors in the 1920s and 1930s. Fortuitously (because Liang Renan

could not have anticipated this when he and his colleagues selected the site), it was also ideally located to benefit from later rapid population growth in the area around the temple in later decades, and particularly after World War II.

6　Tens of thousands of anxious and insecure migrants from mainland China crowded into huts and other squatter housing in the areas around the temple in the late 1940s and early 1950s and became the temple's natural constituency as they sought supernatural help and advice in their quest for security and upward mobility.

7　Many of the worshippers who sought the god's help and advice throughout the 1950s, 1960s, and 1970s experienced collectively, and on average, dramatic increases in their incomes, housing conditions, and socioeconomic status. As Hong Kong industrialized, the colony's economy boomed during this period and housing conditions greatly improved as a large-scale program of public housing was implemented by the Hong Kong government. Although it was always a struggle for each family and they all experienced much anxiety and insecurity, working hard to survive and also seeking the help of their favorite deities, collectively, over several decades from the 1950s, many of them prospered and saw considerable increases in their incomes and family status. The god got a lot of the credit for their successes (or in other words, the god rode Hong Kong's economic success to greatly increased popularity and fame among Hong Kong people). Indeed, since this big temple was the *only* substantial public temple to Huang Daxian in Hong Kong, the credit was also given to the temple itself, as the home of the deity in Hong Kong and the place where his "presence" was apparently very powerful.

It was also important that the leader and directors of the Seseyuan who managed the main Hong Kong temple to the deity shrewdly cultivated good relations with the Hong Kong government and with the local population, especially by using funds from the increasingly wealthy temple to sponsor kindergartens, schools, and homes for the elderly. The chairman of the Seseyuan also arranged in the 1950s to channel gate receipts and rents from the fortune-tellers' stalls at the temple to one of the major Chinese charitable organizations in the city, the Tung Wah group of hospitals. As part of the chairman's attempt to move the Seseyuan into the role of a major charitable organization, with responsible management using secular principles, the chairman also refused to allow further spirit-writing sessions at the temple after the elderly spirit-writing master died in the early 1970s. He told Lang that this was to avoid the use of this procedure to make "political" statements, which had occurred in Guangdong in the early twentieth century, and perhaps also to avoid challenges from the spirit-writer, supposedly representing the views of the gods and immortals, to the chairman's own careful management of the temple's activities and expenditures and to his good relations with the Hong Kong government.

The board of directors of the temple were comprised mostly of local Chinese businesspeople, some of whom were wealthy and used their association with the temple to pursue various charitable projects and enhance their status in the local community and with the colonial government. From the 1980s, some of these directors began to develop business interests in mainland China and to travel to the mainland periodically. The chairman of the Seseyuan, Mr Huang Yuntian, was also affiliated with a local Buddhist organization (he was not dogmatically Daoist) and developed good relations with mainland China's Buddhist Association. The head of that organization in China eventually visited the temple and contributed an inscription which was prominently displayed at the temple. The board of directors of the temple was expanded in the 1980s to include some government-appointed representatives, whose role was to help to ensure that the temple's wealth was properly managed and used at least in part for worthwhile projects in the community.

These directors of the temple were also cautiously keen to develop good relations with the central government in Beijing to try to ensure that the temple would not be adversely affected by the transition in sovereignty over Hong Kong from Britain to China in 1997. Partly for that reason, they were also willing to consider requests for visits and support from new temples to HDX which were being proposed and built in mainland China during the 1990s (see Chapter 3).

We must note that there was another important temple to HDX in Hong Kong, but unlike the main HDX temple operated by the Seseyuan, this temple was not public and was unknown to most worshippers of the deity in the city. The reason is that it was set up originally by Chaozhou migrants, whose dialect is strikingly different from the Cantonese spoken by most of the Hong Kong population, and whose religious culture and ritual practices were also somewhat different. Consequently many of the Chaozhou migrants retained a strong sense of ethnic identity even after their migration to Hong Kong.

Some of these Chaozhou migrants set up their own apartment-shrine to HDX in Kowloon, during the Japanese occupation, and began to worship privately rather than going out to the main temple. They also engaged in spirit-writing or *fuji* at the shrine. Eventually, they received a message from the highest supernatural authority, the Jade Emperor, instructing them that they had earned the right to have their own free-standing private temple to HDX, for which they were given the exalted title of *Yuanqingge*, which could be translated as "pavilion of the original request/invitation." (On the origins and development of this organization, see Lang and Ragvald 1993: 131–134.) The leader of this group for a time was a wealthy Chaozhou rice merchant, and the temple was eventually built on a hillside west of the main Seseyuan temple, about a kilometer up the hill from his shop in Kowloon.

As in the main public temple to HDX, they also used a picture of the saint, rather than a statue as in the temples in Guangdong. However, they did not have a copy of the Seseyuan's painting of the saint, so, the spirit-writer produced a "self-portrait" of the deity, using a brush attached to the spirit-writing stylus to paint a picture of the saint. HDX had previously delivered his personal biography to the Guangdong Daoists by spirit-writing, but he also delivered his self-portrait in Hong Kong, by spirit-painting, to the Chaozhou devotees in the Yuanqingge. These wealthy Chaozhou worshippers continued to support spirit-writing at the temple long after the Seseyuan had abandoned the practice and considered themselves to be at least as fervent as the Seseyuan, if not more so, partly because of these intense sessions with the deity.

Some members of the Yuangqingge eventually left the group and formed a new association which continued to worship HDX, and continued to practice *fuji*, but planned to set up a new shrine for themselves and for their *fuji* operation in a rented unit in the nearby urban district of Sham Shui Po, with free medical services several times each week.

When the opportunities to patronize and possibly support new temples to HDX in mainland China began to multiply in the 1990s, both the Seseyuan and the Yuangqingge had some influence on these developments through their visits and their worship at these sites and were important potential supporters and investors. Despite the split with the Yuangqingge, the members of the new group also continued to maintain contacts with and support some of the HDX developments in Jinhua.

New temples in mainland China

Our first intimations of the revival of worship of HDX in mainland China were reports in the mid-1980s that a new shrine to the deity had been installed in a Daoist temple at Mt. Luofu in northeastern Guangdong (see Map 1.1). Luofu had been a center of Daoist cultivation and temples at least since the time of Ge Hong's stay on the mountain in the fourth century CE, and some Guangdong Daoists believed that the mountain was actually the native place of HDX. In 1987, Ragvald and Lang journeyed to the mountain to investigate reports of a new shrine to HDX at Mt. Luofu and made an interesting discovery.

There was indeed a new shrine in one of the rooms in a temple on the mountain to "Huang Daxian." But we discovered that the "Saint [xian] Huang" at Luofushan was actually another legendary Daoist hermit, also surnamed Huang, who had supposedly achieved immortality on the mountain after spending several centuries living in the forests and occasionally making an appearance to visitors. This figure was known as Huang Yeren, or (loosely) "Huang the Wild Man", a reportedly slovenly hermit who did not achieve anything in particular except immortality. The Daoists in Luofushan knew that this "Saint Huang" was not the same character as the HDX of Hong Kong and hence, that attempts to claim that they were the same figure were illegitimate.

However, we discovered that local cultural affairs cadres and Daoists had collaborated in a revisionist history of this figure, merging the story of "Huang Daxian" (Huang Chuping) with their legendary local Daoist hermit-immortal (Huang Yeren) in order to draw tourists from Hong Kong and to increase the flow of religious tourism to the district for the sake of local economic aggrandizement (Lang and Ragvald 1993: 142–145). Local Daoists and some of the cadres were aware of this deliberate merging of the two figures. When we pointed out that the two saints appeared to us, from the literature, to be separate figures, one cultural affairs cadre replied: "Well, the masses want them to be the same, so, we can consider them to be the same". By "the masses", he evidently referred to local worshippers, Hong Kong people lured to the mountain to worship "Huang Daxian" through advertising in Hong Kong (some of whom we observed arriving by bus and car during our visit) and no doubt also the Luofushan villagers who benefited financially from the arrival and the spending of these tourists.

This was probably the first attempt to provide a new site for worship of HDX since the destruction of the last remaining temple to the saint in mainland China in 1967 (the temple which Mr Liang Renan had built in his home village in Guangdong, which was destroyed during the so-called Cultural Revolution). Notably, this merging of the two saints to create a site for worship of "Huang Daxian" at Mt. Luofu was designed primarily to attract Hong Kong tourists to the mountain. This also represents an instance of the merging of distinct deities into one figure for various reasons, a process which has happened many times in the history of religions, but for reasons which can usually only be inferred centuries later. In this case, the merging was recent and we could elicit the reasons for the merger from those who had actually accomplished and supported it.

Several years later, in 1989, the first free-standing temple to HDX was built in mainland China, on a mountain in Xinhui county, Guangdong. This temple was built by one of the members of the Seseyuan, Mr Huang Guang, who was a native of Xinhui and had emigrated to Hong Kong decades earlier and eventually became wealthy. He was also a believer in the deity Che Gong (who is also popular in Hong Kong) and wished to build two temples on the mountain, one for each deity. The villagers, expecting many benefits from these two projects, supported the application, and the local government approved it on the condition that Mr Huang provided all of the funds for the construction of the temples. He committed to using the temple's revenues, after maintenance and operating expenses, to provide regular donations in equal shares to a local school, a hospital, and a planned home for the elderly and thus helped to ensure continuing local government support for these temples.

In the trees on the hillside below the temple, Mr Huang also installed a tableau in carved stone of Huang Chuping and Huang Chuqi among a number of white boulders depicted as transforming into sheep or just having completed the transformation. Some visitors to these temples also visited this site, and their children played among the boulders-turning-into-sheep. Thus, Huang Daxian's images and worship returned to mainland China near the site where the seventeenth century CE Ming patriot, Huang Gongfu, had lived near the end of his life, writing a poem to commemorate Huang Chuping's achievements, but the temple built by Huang Guang on the mountain represented the deity at the altar as a two-dimensional image in a painting, not as a three-dimensional statue (as in all of the previous temples to Huang Chuping in China), and used the same image of the saint as in the painting of Huang Chuping above the altar in the main Seseyuan temple in Hong Kong. The iconography of the Hong Kong version of the cult was being reinserted into mainland China because of the wealth and devotion of Hong Kong believers.

Meanwhile, villagers in Liang Renan's ancestral village of Rengang in Guangdong, who were also aware of the growing interest among Hong Kong worshippers in visiting such sites, decided to build a new temple to HDX in the village. The large temple which Liang Renan had established in the village around 1901, after he left Guangzhou, had operated more or less continuously up to the 1950s, although it went into a decline during the Japanese occupation of Guangdong in the late 1930s. Despite the fact that Liang Renan had decamped to Hong Kong in 1915 and focused his energies on setting up a new temple in the colony, there were periodic visits between devotees of the two temples until 1949, and the temple in the village survived up to the 1960s.

But the temple did not survive the "Cultural Revolution." When gangs of Red Guards were smashing temples throughout the province, this temple was also destroyed, and the land returned to growing crops. Only a few pieces of the temple remained after the 1960s. Ragvald and Lang visited the village in 1987, and villagers showed us those few remaining pieces, including a slab more than two meters long with the title of the temple and the date of construction inscribed in relief on the slab. It was large and heavy, and villagers told us that by the time they had finished knocking down the temple and carrying away the bricks and woodwork, they were too tired to haul off the slab, so they left it face-down in the grass. But the care with which they placed straw under the slab before turning it face-down again on the ground, after showing it to us, led us to predict that public veneration of the deity would eventually be revived in the village. This prediction was soon proved to be correct.

In the early 1990s, the villagers moved the stone slab into a hut and placed it carefully on wooden planks on the floor. In 1992, a Seseyuan tour group visiting the sites of temples built by Liang Renan in Guangdong visited the village and some of them placed incense reverently in niches in the stone slab. (Photos of the villagers showing Ragvald and Lang the slab in 1987 and of a Hong Kong pilgrim placing incense in the slab in 1992 are in Lang and Ragvald (1993).) Not long after that visit, the villagers built a new but much smaller version of the temple inside the village and installed the stone slab above the entrance to the new shrine. This temple used two statues inside the shrine, rather than just one statue or picture of Huang Chuping.

Thus, two versions of the cult were being revived inside China: variants of the original cult, with statues typically representing the two brothers, Chuping and Chuqi, and a Hong Kong version of the cult, with only a painting to depict the deity, and a focus only on Huang Chuping, now known as "Huang Daxian."

By far the largest and grandest of the new temples to HDX built in China from the 1990s based their icons of the deity not on the original versions of the cult of the two brothers but on the Seseyuan's image and sole focus on Huang Chuping, although these differing versions of the cult existed in several places in Jinhua in close proximity (see Chapter 3). Four grand new temples were built in the Jinhua area in the 1990s (1991, 1995, 1996, and 1998) and one large new temple was built in Fangcun, a suburb of Guangzhou (1999).

There were several other temples or shrines established in Guangdong in the 1990s and 2000s. Some of them were mid-sized or small temples and were relatively obscure, such as a HDX temple in Jieyang, Chaozhou, built in 1994 by a group of local Daoist worshippers who donated three million to build the Longcandong Chisong HDX temple in Jieyang. But there are several other much larger new temples or shrines in Guangdong built in the 1990s.

The grandest of these was a large "Huang Daxian park" in the Pearl River Delta at the foot of Xiqiaoshan, an extinct volcano on the plains about 60 kilometers south of Guangzhou. This mountain was a site for Daoist shrines and herbal medicines for many centuries, with venerable Daoist and Buddhist temples on the mountain. Liang Renan, the founder of the major HDX temple in Guangzhou in the late 1890s, came from Rengang village near Xiqiaoshan. In the mid-1990s, an entrepreneur acquired some 400,000 square meters of land at the base of the mountain within the Xiqiaoshan National Geopark and built a kind of theme park devoted to HDX which opened in early 1996. The park included a giant 28 meter outdoor statue of the deity modeled on the image of Huang in the Hong Kong Seseyuan temple. Some members of the Seseyuan visited and gave donations to support the project. The park, called Huangdaxian Shengjingyuan, advertised itself as offering "comprehensive scenery combining Daoist culture, the culture of Lingnan [an older name for the Guangdong/Guangxi region] and artistic gardening". It also featured a "Daxian footprint" in the rock, an "immortal cave," and a low building adjoining the large plaza in front of the statue with a smaller indoor statue of the deity and stalls for fortune-tellers and for the sale of religious paraphernalia and souvenirs.

It was evidently designed to attract tourists, particularly from Hong Kong, but provided divination sticks at the base of the statue and fortune-telling for visitors inclined to seek the saint's advice or help while visiting the park. Lang and Ragald visited the park in January of 2001 and observed groups of visitors periodically arriving by bus and by car. Some bought firecrackers and set them off on a patio below the statue, while a few others consulted the fortune-tellers. They could also buy incense to be kept burning at the temple for varying periods of time, with the following prices and promises: "good prospects for the future," for 30 days: 88 RMB; "whole family safe," for 3 months: 220 RMB; "good business," for 6 months: 460 RMB; "may wealth come generously to you," for 9 months: 660 RMB; and "be rich and lucky," for 12 months: 800 RMB. The park was featured in a billboard designed as a guide for tourists near the entrance to the Geopark, showing a map of the mountain and the locations of the various temples, outdoor statues, and tourist attractions. The builders of the HDX statue-park were clearly aware that nearby Rengang village had once included a major temple to HDX linked to the man who founded the Hong Kong temple in 1921, and they evidently hoped to attract Hong Kong visitors. Of course, they shared this hope with most of the other HDX temples built in China in the 1990s and early 2000s, as we show in the later chapters.

However, we were told by informants that the site was not registered as a "religious activity site" and hence, not a legal site for such observances. Many temples elsewhere are also unregistered for various reasons and continue to operate with the tolerance of local officials, but in this location, the land was very valuable, and as the roads to the area were improved and the local economy flourished, a decision was made to reallocate the land. Meanwhile, a giant statue of the Buddhist deity Guanyin was installed on the top of the mountain, with a much grander plaza and stairway up to the statue than in the HDX statue at the base of the mountain (Figure 2.1).

Figure 2.1 Statue of HDX at the foot of Xiqiaoshan in Guangdong (built in 1996, demolished by 2012).

Some time after 2008, the HDX statue along with the plazas and buildings were demolished and the site cleared. The land was taken over by a film-studio, Xiqiao Dreamworks, which built a Xiqiao Mountain Film Studio complex that was largely completed by 2014. It had a "Huang Daxian temple" within the complex, with a statue of the deity made of solid gold (weighing 52 kilograms, it was submitted for recognition as a Guinness record for a golden statue). The temple is open to the public but is included within the list of "shooting sites" at the Studio along with another temple to a different deity nearby. Both temples are evidently intended primarily as settings for Hong Kong and mainland film crews to shoot scenes which need to be filmed on the grounds of a temple. The other "shooting sites" in the complex included "Shanghai Street," "Hong Kong Street," "Guangzhou Street," "Japan Street," "Ming Qing palace," and "ancient village." The Film Studio complex was also planned to include a theme park with rides, a five-star hotel, performance venues, and other "tourism and amusement facilities," based on the model of Universal Studios in the U.S., and designed to take advantage of the flow of tourists to other attractions on Xiqiao Mountain.[5]

This kind of use of temples as part of the tourist circuit for local economic development and profit has been well-described by scholars for other locations (see, e.g., Dott 2010, Svensson 2010), and the HDX temple in the Xiqiao Mountain Film Studio complex seems to be a similar operation, with the added function of also serving as a film set. But there is a 30 RMB admission fee for entry to the temple, and despite the prospect of seeing a solid gold statue of the deity, it seems that there are few visitors.

More recently in Guangdong, a new temple dedicated to HDX was being planned in Daling village at Panyu in 2014. Daling village was apparently the site of the shrine in Panyu called Peishan Pujitan where Liang Renan engaged in spirit-writing in the 1890s and began to gather a group of devotees of the saint, before they eventually moved to a larger site in the Huadi district across the river from Guangzhou, as described earlier in this chapter. Local authorities had already decided to highlight the village as a model for environmental good practice and as a destination for cultural-historical tourism. The fact that a shrine in the village had played a role in the origins of worship of HDX in Guangzhou, and thus indirectly, in the rise of worship of the deity in Hong Kong, provided a rationale for building a new temple to the deity in the village. The emphasis for official purposes was on developing heritage and cultural/historical tourism for the village. But the temple could also be a site of religious tourism or pilgrimages and of worship for local believers. The Daoist Association was involved in choosing the name—Chisong Gong—for the new temple, and the project was supported by the local government. The plan called for a temple compound of about 20,000 square meters, with about half of that space devoted to the main temple hall, with on-going discussions between local government planners, officials, and villagers about the location of the project and the arrangements for accommodating villagers displaced by the new temple.[6] Whether this temple will become popular as a site of worship for residents in the district around the temple will only become clear in the years after the temple is completed in 2016.

In the following chapters, we explore the revival in worship of this deity at some of the new temples in Guangdong and Zhejiang and the roles of Hong Kong believers and of local government officials and villagers in the two provinces. For Guangdong, we will focus mainly on the big temple to HDX in Guangzhou (Chapter 7). For Zhejiang, where a striking proliferation of new HDX temples occurred within a small area around Jinhua in the 1990s, we provide some information about each of the new temples in the area, along with case studies and comparisons of four of these temples, including some comparisons with the major new temple to the deity in Guangzhou (Chapters 3–6).

In the following chapter, we will discuss the reasons for the revival of worship of HDX and the legitimacy of the construction of a series of temples dedicated to HDX in Jinhua from the late 1980s, the impact of Hong Kong believers and organizations, and the importance of the impending return of Hong Kong to China in 1997.

Notes

1 The first book-length study of the worship of HDX, *The Rise of a Refugee God* (Lang and Ragvald 1993), included an account of the origins of the legends about HDX and an outline of key developments in the history of worship of the deity in Zhejiang, Guangdong, and Hong Kong up to the early 1990s. We refer readers to that book for details, particularly in the Introduction, Chapter 2 ("The origins and fate of the cult of Wong Tai Sin [HDX] in Guangdong, China"), and Chapter 7 ("Offshoots").
2 One could imagine the elderly Chuqi squinting across the valley toward the hillside and seeing those white shapes—perhaps sheep resting quietly in the grass and shrubbery— mistaking them for boulders and informing his brother that there were white boulders but no sheep on the hillside. His brother then called out to the sheep, and they rose from the grass at the shepherd's call, magically transforming themselves (in the eyes of the credulous Chuqi) from white boulders into white sheep. In fact, on one of our trips into the hills at Jinhua, Lang saw a sheep or white goat about two hundred meters away across the valley, and with its limbs hidden in the grass, it was nearly indistinguishable from a white rock except when it occasionally moved as it nibbled on the grass.
3 As noted in Lang and Ragvald (1993: 160, fn. 5): "it is likely that the writer of this 'autobiography' was aware of attempts to merge the two figures, or of confusions between them."
4 See also Dean (1998: 265) on the large gap or "black hole" in the records of the Three-in-One sects from the mid-Qing period to the late nineteenth century.
5 See http://www.nationalarts.hk/Dreamworks?lang=en, accessed April 30, 2014.
6 See http://roll.sohu.com/20140411/n398067641.shtml, accessed April 30, 2014.

3   Making religious places

Memories and transnational ties

Introduction

Unlike the popularity of HDX in Hong Kong, HDX and the associated religious beliefs were unknown to most Jinhua people before the 1980s. It is however amazing to note that HDX has now become widely known by locals and tourists in Jinhua and there are altogether 8 temples dedicated to HDX in different places (Table 1.1).[1] How and why have HDX become so popular over the past few

Table 3.1 Jinhua temples: location, construction, and financing

Names of temples	Location	Year	Construction	Finance
Jinhua Guan	Next to the Double Dragon Cave (mid-levels of Jinhua Mountain)	1991	Cadres from the Double Dragon Cave Scenic Park Management Team	Double Dragon Cave Scenic Park Management Team
Chisonggong	Chisong	1993	Villagers	Villagers
Yuan Yuan Yuan	Lanxi	1995	Township cadres	Seseyuan from Hong Kong
Xianyiguan	Muchenyuan, Lanxi	1995	Villagers	Villagers
Lingyangci	An island in Lanxi	1995	Hong Kong investor and later rebuilt by investors from China	Private investors
Zugong	Top of Jinhua Mountain	1996	Cadres from Municipal government	Local companies
Chisong Daoyuan	Chisong (on top of the peasants' temple)	1998	Chisong Huangdaxian Research Association	Investors from Hong Kong and Taiwan
Erhuangjunci	Xianqiao at Chisong	1996 (renovated)	Villagers	Villagers

decades? What are the roles of different groups of overseas Chinese in reawakening memories and reviving religious beliefs in HDX? What kinds of social memories of HDX have been evoked in Jinhua?

Social memories are known to be manifested in many forms, including myths,
narratives, legends, and stories (Fentress and Wickham 1992; Halbwachs 1992;
Misztal 2003). This chapter will investigate social memories of HDX through
examining publications and oral narratives of HDX legends and stories. We demonstrate how legends and narratives of HDX have become an important source
of legitimacy for temple-building projects in Jinhua. Our studies on the revived
memories of HDX are not concerned with the historical accuracy of events or legends, or the authenticity of those memories.[2] In fact, social memories often contain elements of fabrication because details and accuracy could be pushed aside
to accommodate present and future interests (Schwartz 1991; Zelizer 1995: 217).
Like Feuchtwang and Wang (2001: 28), we also believe that an understanding of
how and what memories have been presented and recalled is more important than
the historical truth because the narratives of memories are more helpful for understanding the current sociopolitical and economic concerns of people. Memories
are taken not only as "a general category of knowledge" (Zelizer 1995: 217, 219),
an "expression of collective experience" (Frentress and Wickham 1992: 25), and
visions of the past but also as aspirations for the present and the future (ibid., see
also Halbwach 1992). This chapter therefore investigates why and how certain
narratives of HDX are selected, revived, and constructed to suit the interests of
various parties. It analyzes the process in which individuals and various groups
are involved in awakening memories of HDX through connecting to global and
transnational networks. This chapter will show how the recollection of stories of
HDX is constructed, reconfigurated, and related to the present and future interests
of the government and locals in Jinhua. It will examine how legends of HDX are
revived, selected, and promoted for temple-building projects and place-making
purposes.

Transnational ties and the awakening of HDX memories

In a number of studies, the connections of overseas Chinese with their hometown in the Southern part of China are of particular importance in the revival
of temples and religious practices there (Woon 1984; Dean 1993; 1998; Kuah-
Pearce 2000). In the present case, hometown connections of the overseas villagers are of no importance in reviving religious beliefs of HDX. Instead, various religious groups from Hong Kong and Taiwan went to Jinhua to search for
the hometown of their deity and subsequently triggered the awakening of religious memories there. In our research in Jinhua, we found that several religious
groups from Hong Kong and Taiwan have played a significant role in evoking
memories of HDX which subsequently led to a number of temple-construction
projects.

The largest and the most prominent religious group of these overseas pilgrims is SSY, the organization that manages the major Hong Kong HDX temple
(see Chapter 2). The second group of pilgrims is from Yuan Qing Ge (YQG)
(see Chapter 2). The third group is Chisong HDX Association, which was established in 1994. The key founder is a Hong Kong resident and a HDX worshipper,

Mr Chow, whose native place was at Dongyang, Jinhua, and who came to Hong Kong in 1955 when he was five. In 1994, Mr Chow formed the Chisong HDX Association in Hong Kong together with a Taiwanese woman, Ms Luo, who was also a resident in Hong Kong (see Chapter 5). The Association included about a dozen members only—with some religious specialists such as fengshui experts and Daoist priests—but later expanded to include cadres, intellectuals, and businessmen from Jinhua (see Chapter 5).

In view of the imminent return of Hong Kong to China following the Sino-British Joint Declaration in 1984, members of these three religious groups from Hong Kong started visiting Jinhua and came into contact with various officials at different counties in Jinhua. Indeed, it was also the return of Hong Kong to China in 1997 which created the opportunity for the return of the refugee god HDX to his birth place in China. The visits of three religious groups have brought "new" information to the locals in Jinhua, who then became aware of the overwhelming popularity of HDX in Hong Kong. These visits by overseas pilgrims create interactions, connections, circulations, and transfers of ideas and knowledge between various places, actors and institutions.

Among all these Hong Kong visitors, the Hong Kong pilgrims from SSY were the first group to visit Jinhua in the 1980s. The visits provided SSY with opportunities to cultivate networks with cadres in the Chinese government, thus strengthening their confidence that their rights to religious freedom in Hong Kong beyond 1997 would be preserved. More importantly, the trips were for SSY to search for the roots of HDX in Jinhua. The cadres in Jinhua prefectural-level city government received these Hong Kong pilgrims with enthusiasm. They were very surprised to learn that HDX, as a native of Jinhua, was so popular overseas. Like most people in Jinhua, they had been ignorant of HDX at that time. However, that 1984 visit by SSY sparked a wave of interest in HDX among cadres in Jinhua, who were very impressed with the enthusiasm of the Hong Kong pilgrims in searching for the roots of the immortal. The Jinhua cadres saw HDX as an unusual opportunity to connect with the Hong Kong people, who would be wealthy visiting pilgrims with strong spending power and were also potential investors for temples or businesses. This was a timely opportunity for the cadres at that time because Jinhua's economy had been depressed following the decline of manufacturing in the 1980s. Subsequently, the cadres became active in reviving religious memories and in searching for historical sites related to HDX.

Similarly, another group of HDX worshippers, YQG, subsequently went to Jinhua in 1988 to search for the roots of HDX. In addition to that, these businessmen from YQG also had the intention of exploring business opportunities in Jinhua. They were approached by the Jinhua cadres to invest and build a temple near the national grade scenic park, Double Dragon Cave (see Chapter 4). To the cadres, a new temple should complement the Double Dragon Cave as an additional attraction for tourists. The investment proposal, which cost 10 million RMB, was however declined by the visitors from YQG. In 1991, the Double Dragon Cave Management Team built a temple, Jinhua Guan (see section on "Transnational Ties and the Awakening of HDX Memories"). In 1994, together with other members of

Chisong HDX Club, Mr Chow and Ms Luo visited Chisong. Since then, they have been working with local historians and the local government to revive memories of the immortal in Chisong and to build a temple there (see Chapter 5).

Apart from the visits of various religious groups, some Jinhua locals also learned about the popularity of HDX in Hong Kong by word of mouth and other means. Mr Shou, a village intellectual from Zhong Tou village in Chisong, read about HDX's immense popularity in Hong Kong from a magazine *Hong Kong Scenic Spots*. He associated the inundated temple (Chisonggong) in his village, with HDX. He recalled that Chisonggong was inundated after the government built a reservoir next to the village in 1958. Like the cadres who were excited by the immense popularity of HDX in Hong Kong, Mr Shou was also proud that HDX was a native from Jinhua. Mr Shou wrote to SSY in Hong Kong and informed them that HDX was a native of his village. Around the same time, another Zhongtou villager, Mr Jiang, heard from his boss, Mr Du from Zhejiang Jianfeng Group, who had visited HDX temple in Hong Kong, that HDX was a popular god in Hong Kong.[3] He also drew the connection between the inundated temple (Chisonggong) in his village and the one in Hong Kong.

Having heard from Mr Du that the SSY pilgrims were visiting Jinhua in 1990, Mr Jiang went to the hotel where these Hong Kong pilgrims were staying and invited them to come and see the temple at the reservoir. With the help of the Jinhua prefectural-level city government, SSY pilgrims visited the inundated temple at Chisong where they were greeted with villagers playing horns and children waving flags. At the time of their visit, the water level of the reservoir was low enough for part of the temple to be visible. We were told by the villagers that the visitors from SSY knelt down at the bank of the reservoir to worship for almost half an hour. Upon witnessing the visit of the Hong Kong pilgrims, the villagers were very touched and started planning to build a temple (Chisonggong). Reviving the old temple for themselves and the overseas pilgrims is a legitimate justification for the construction of Chisonggong. In 1993, the Chisonggong was built at the bank of the reservoir with donations from fellow-villagers. The cost of the temple was 160,000 RMB. A few years later, the Chisong HDX Club came to Chisong and decided to further develop that area. A bigger temple dedicated to HDX (Chisong Daoyuan, hereafter CSDY) was constructed in 1998 (see Chapter 6).

Meanwhile, another transnational connection brought news of HDX as a Jinhua native to a local intellectual in Lanxi, which is around 20 kilometers west of Jinhua city. It was in 1986 when a Jinhua intellectual, Mr Zhao, came to learn that HDX was a popular god in Hong Kong from a scholar from the Chinese University of Hong Kong while attending an international conference on Chinese drama and poems in Shanxi. He was excited to know that such a popular god in Hong Kong was from Jinhua and yet was not well-known by Jinhua people. Later, he searched for legends and historical documents and argued that Huang Peng village in Lanxi was the hometown of HDX. In 1987, he worked closely with the Lanxi county government and formed an informal research group on HDX. He started a series of activities which helped revive memories of HDX in Huang Peng village. Based on this historical evidence, villagers in Huang Peng then made a request to build a temple to HDX (see Chapter 5). It was supported enthusiastically by Lanxi county government because the cadres wanted to develop temple tourism. The Lanxi county government approached SSY, successfully solicited a donation of 1.3 million RMB, took over the temple-building project, and built Yuan Yuan Yuan (YYY) in 1995 (see Chapter 5).

Almost 30 years after SSY's first visit to Jinhua, today HDX and his reputation in Hong Kong is well-known by everybody in Jinhua. HDX's name even appears on the official tourism website. Various legends of HDX, such as about how he lived in the area as Huang Chuping, his visits to different places along Jinhua Mountain while practicing Daoism and how he achieved immortality were recorded on different websites (e.g., http://www.chinaypages.com/zhejiang/jinhua/jg/english2.html, accessed on August 14, 2012). It is therefore interesting to examine how memories of HDX were so quickly revived, what legends were reawakened, and how the cadres have supported the popularization of memories of HDX. To understand how and what memories are retrieved, oral narratives given by villagers, cadres, intellectuals, and entrepreneurs, as well as publications on HDX in Jinhua will be analyzed in the following sections.

Remembering Jinhua as the native place of HDX

Shortly after the visits of these overseas groups, different local governments decided to enhance the connections with them through investigating historical texts relating to HDX. In Jinhua, there are four books altogether (published in 1993, 1995, 2003, and 2007), one magazine (1998), and one journal (five issues in 2005, 2006, and 2007) dedicated to HDX research since the 1990s. All these materials were published with the support of different local governments—the Jinhua prefectural-level city government, the Jinhua county government (the present Jindong district government), and the Lanxi county government.

The first book about HDX was published in 1993 although data were claimed to be collected since May 1986. Apparently, the efforts to search for data relating to HDX began with the support of the Jinhua prefectural-level city government after the first visit of Hong Kong pilgrims from SSY. These efforts in the 1990s were perceived by the officials at the Religious Affairs Bureau under the United Front Office and cadres at the prefectural-level city government as a means to keep "overseas Chinese satisfied." An important provincial cadre who was in charge of religious affairs even mentioned HDX in his report at a seminar for religious work at the provincial level in 1995. He stressed that HDX enjoyed a high status in Hong Kong and Macau. The revival of HDX in his home area and the acquiescence to commemorating the immortal were a friendly gesture toward Hong Kong Chinese. In fact, mutual respect and warm ties were of particular importance during that time as a prelude to a smooth reunification of Hong Kong with China in 1997. Moreover, the potential of attracting pilgrims to visit the local area and to develop Jinhua's economy was the key motivation behind the reawakening of religious memories. This aim of reviving memories was in fact mentioned from time to time in different publications. Memories of the HDX are therefore closely linked to the present and especially to economic development. Memories of the past are imagined by a social group for present purposes.

All publications have provided a description of various legends of HDX in different places in Jinhua. They have a similar coverage of landscapes, poems, and legends relating to HDX. Places where HDX went were revered as sacred sites to be commemorated together with the legends recalled. Poems relating to HDX were cited, as were famous landscapes, mountains, rivers, and huge rocks associated with him. Some temples, pavilions, and even caves in Jinhua were highlighted with their specific association to HDX.

HDX was recalled in different historical texts to demonstrate that he was born in Jinhua and also lived in different places there. Oral narratives from informants and legends collected in different publications suggested that HDX was a shepherd who wandered to different places in Jinhua while practicing Daoist immortality. These publications show memories and knowledge of HDX legends have become conventionalized and are meant to be transmitted to a wider group of the reading public.

Memory of the past is not only meaningful in the present but also effective in framing the perception of the present to be in line with the past. This may lead to the invention of new legends and the creation of new ways of commemorating the past. A new legend of HDX and his sheep was invented in 1991 when Jinhua Guan was built. Several huge pieces of white rocks were discovered in the process of building Jinhua Guan. These stones were said to look like the sheep and were therefore associated with HDX who was once a shepherd in Jinhua Mountain. These "sheep stones" were interpreted by the cadres and workers as a sign of approval from HDX for building this new temple. The "sheep stones" were preserved by the cadres and displayed at the temple to commemorate HDX's life as a shepherd at Jinhua Mountain before becoming an immortal. Thus, a new legend was created to perpetuate memories of HDX's life as a shepherd.

Memory politics of HDX's hometown

Cadres at different local government offices, local intellectuals, and even villagers believe that HDX could be used as cultural capital to promote the growth of tourism and hence the local economy. Knowledge and memories of Jinhua as the hometown of HDX were believed to be helpful for developing Jinhua's economy. Different versions of memories were proposed in various areas around Jinhua, providing a rich pool of cultural resources which may attract economic development of specific local places. Cadres, intellectuals, overseas members, and villagers explore stories and legends of HDX at their own local places and utilize them for place-making and temple-building activities. In particular, Jinhua, Lanxi, Yiwu, and Dongyang county governments all claimed to be the specific hometown of HDX with reference to different interpretations of historical documents. As a result, there was a controversy among these local governments in the early 1990s about the exact location of the hometown of HDX. To settle the controversy over HDX's place of origin, the deputy provincial mayor made the statement, "HDX was born in Lanxi, became a saint in Jinhua city, and became popular in Hong Kong" on September 19, 1995 (*Huangpeng Cunzhi* 1997: 209). In other words, it is the government which creates a sense of interconnectedness between various places (Huang Peng in Lanxi, Chisong and Jinhua Mountain) in Jinhua while institutionalizing the diversity of local communities' imagined connections to HDX.

Lanxi county government has then become active in reawakening memories of the immortal while Jinhua, Dongyang, and Yiwu county governments have since turned quiet. The Lanxi HDX Research Association was set up by the county government to take up the task of reviving HDX memories. The association was chaired by Mr Zhao, with members including local historians, intellectuals, and government officers from Lanxi, and it was financially supported by the county government. It meets several times a year to discuss organizational matters, such as attracting new members, and disseminating findings and achievements in research through publications and conferences. Historical records and legends were collected in the book compiled by Lanxi HDX Research Association in 1995 and highlighted that Huang Peng village was the hometown of HDX. Such memories invoked through legends are clearly politicized as they are in line with the provincial government's objectives. In the following, we will examine how the Lanxi county government supported their assertion that Huang Peng village was the birthplace of the immortal through searching for and promoting local memories and how local villagers narrated the stories of the immortal to us.

First, Huang Peng village in Lanxi was confirmed as the hometown of HDX through archaeological relics collected by intellectuals in the Lanxi HDX Research Association under the leadership of a local, Mr Zhao. He cited the Lanxi county gazette which has recorded that Huang Chupin was a native from Huang Peng village in Lanxi (*Huangdaxian Zhiliaoxuanbian* 1995: 8, 18). With the support of the local government, the HDX relic renovation committee was formed together with the Lanxi county HDX Study Association in September 1992. Villagers were mobilized to re-excavate a well which, according to historical records Mr Zhao had traced, was first excavated by HDX and his brother. Through much searching, and after digging for about 1.5 meters, the villagers discovered the well and a broken piece from a plaque with the characters *xianjing* (the well of the saint). This served as a further proof of HDX's existence at the village. Subsequently, Mr Zhao and his research group promoted memories of HDX in Huang Peng village through writing articles in magazines and newspapers. He also published an article on HDX in an officially sanctioned Chinese newspaper *People's Daily for Overseas Chinese*. In 1993, a research seminar on HDX was conducted by Lanxi HDX Research Association to promote memories of the saint in the village as well as in Lanxi. The Lanxi government formally labeled the "Two Saints Well" as a piece of protected antiquity. The lane next to the Two Saints Well was also renamed as "Saint Well Lane."

In addition to the renovation of the "Two Saints Well," Huang Peng villagers also commemorated HDX and his brother by restoring a house next to the well, claiming that was the house where HDX's parents stayed. Villagers placed the saint's picture and the relevant historical description of him in the house. A plaque, "HDX Former Home," was erected at the entrance of Huang Peng village, with an inscription written by the Vice President of the National People's Congress and became the new landmark of HDX in 1995. Indeed, old relics were preserved and displayed while a new house and a new plaque was built to make Huang Peng village as the historical landmark of HDX's birthplace. Relics, such as Huang's house, and the plaque further objectify the memories of HDX's hometown in Huang Peng village. The process of digging up the well, searching for and promoting legends, as well as erecting a plaque consolidated Huang Peng as the home village of HDX. Indeed, Huang Peng as the hometown of HDX is constructed as a result of both transnational and local forces. The making of Huang Peng as the hometown of the immortal reflects "local relations within the place and those many connections which stretch way beyond it" (Massey 1999: 200; Brickell and Datta 2011: 6) and "wider geographical histories and processes" (Burawoy 2000; Brickell and Datta 2011: 3).

A village gazette published by the Huang Peng village also devoted a section to HDX and recorded associated legends and stories as collected from villagers. In other words, villagers in Huang Peng have now generated a new understanding of local identities through making memories and recognizing HDX to be the saint who was born in their village. Nevertheless, all these historical narratives did not consistently and conclusively prove that HDX was born in the village, although it does show a strong connection between the place and the immortal (see more at the end of this section).

A strong connection between the local place and HDX was enhanced through recalling local legends recounting his magical powers in healing different Huang Peng villagers.[4] Villagers told us that the water from the Two Saints Well was for healing. At the time when it was first rediscovered, villagers queued to fetch its water due to its supposed healing effects. One legend in Huang Peng village claimed that Huang Chuping made a "dragon bed" for healing purposes (see Appendix). Villagers who were sick would be healed after lying on this "dragon bed." It was said that the emperor was furious upon hearing the existence of a "dragon bed" in the rural village, because the "dragon bed" was commonly used to refer to the bed of the emperor. The emperor therefore wanted to kill HDX. Huang and his brother fled down the well and found their way out to the river, where they re-emerged and later disappeared into the Jinhua Mountain, never to return to Huang Peng village.

Another legend recounting HDX's healing power was related to the invention of a local vegetable, "luotangqing," that was found in Jinhua. A legend recorded in the Huang Peng gazette said that HDX saw a girl crying in the field while picking vegetables (*Huangpeng Cunzhi* 1997: 245–247). HDX was told that the girl's mother had to eat vegetables all the time as there was no other food available. Upon eating nothing else but vegetables, her feet became swollen. HDX therefore invented a special type of vegetable called "luotangqing". It was said that "luotangqing" could be eaten in bulk without causing swollen legs. In the late 1990s, during our fieldwork, this vegetable was renamed as "Daxian" (the saint) vegetable and could be found on the menus of many restaurants. Stories of this vegetable as an invention of HDX were fondly narrated by informants to us. During that period, the same vegetables were marketed as Daxian vegetables in Shanghai too. Indeed, memories of HDX were enhanced through everyday practices of consuming vegetables and could be found in menus at various restaurants. Besides, another legend suggested that HDX invented a yellow color ceramic vase, which was used to store food and prevented it from turning bad (*Huangpeng Cunzhi* 1997: 185). In sum, through various stories narrated by Huang Peng villagers, the locality of Huang Peng was portrayed as the home village of HDX, where he was born, lived, healed, and helped his fellow-villagers.

Apart from Huang Peng village in Lanxi, Muchenyuan in Lanxi was also highlighted as a place to demonstrate HDX's healing powers. Legends suggest that it was a place where HDX made herbal medicine and played chess with other immortals. A piece of stone in the shape of a wok was found in the mountain and said to be the wok used by HDX to make herbal medicine (*Huangdaxian Zhiliaoxuanbian* 1995: 61). In the publication compiled by HDX Research Association, it was also noted that the Lanxi county gazette mentioned the existence of this special "stone wok" and a temple that was found next to it during the Qing dynasty. However, there was no mention of whether the wok or the temple is related to HDX in the gazette. Apparently, new ways of appropriating relics were found in narrating stories of HDX in the present. Indeed, the locality of Muchenyuan was constructed through the association of the "stone wok" and HDX.

Subsequently a villager at Muchenyuan, Mr Yang, began building the temple Xianyiguan in the 1990s. Mr Yang was born into a religious family in which his father was a spirit medium who conducted healing services for villagers when he was alive. He became a devoted worshipper of local goddesses, "seven fairies," after a narrow escape from an accident when he was 18. He then became a devoted worshipper of the seven fairies. In the 1990s, he received an instruction from the seven fairies to build a temple for HDX in a dream.[5] Mr Yang managed to solicit donations from villagers and started building Xianyiguan since then. When we were there in 2007, the main hall of the temple was completed, while the other halls were still in the process of construction.

To the local government, historical legends of HDX in Muchenyuan are legitimate grounds for temple construction. To the cadres, the historical existence of a temple along the mountain track also justified the choice of having Xianyiguan built on the same site, although that earlier temple was not related to HDX and was demolished. Most importantly, the local cadres believe that the project would increase the attraction of Lanxi as the homeland of HDX and thus supported it. Xianyiguan is located along the steep slope of a mountain. It took us more than an hour to hike up there. The construction project was extremely tough because workers had to carry all the construction materials up the hill using poles.

Furthermore, HDX was also remembered as a helpful saint. In Lingyangdao, an island near Huang Peng village in Lanxi, villagers recalled that the island was often flooded. Legends said that HDX used his whip (for shepherding the sheep) to support the island so that it did not sink when the flood came. In 1995, a Hong Kong investor was invited to develop the island into a resort, and a temple dedicated to HDX, named as Lingyangci, was also built. Again, temple construction was justified by HDX legends associated with Lingyangdao. Most important of all, the project was supported by the local government as the government wanted to turn Lanxi into a tourist site. Nevertheless, transport to the temple or the island was rather inconvenient because visitors could only reach there by special-chartered ferries with reservations. In 2011, the Hong Kong investor went bankrupt and sold the temple and the resort island project to Mao, a retired cadre, for an amount of more than 10 million RMB.[6] Mao rebuilt the resort area, renovated, and expanded the size of the temple. In 2014, there were 80 villas, a yacht pier, a boat restaurant, and a hotel with one complex which accommodates around 100 guests. Another complex of the hotel which accommodates up to 300 guests, as well as some additional villas, is still under construction. Several priests live in Lingyanci and training programs for Daoist masters were conducted in 2012. Upon the invitation of Mao, members of YQG also went there and discussed possible ways to strengthen the religious aspect of Lingyangci in 2013. In 2014, plans for refinement of Daoist rituals for Daoist priests were under discussion by YQG and Mao.

Although memories of HDX were actively recalled by Huang Peng villagers as a result of the encouragement of intellectuals and the Lanxi government in the mid-1990s, the Lanxi government has become less active in promoting memories of the immortal since the late 1990s because the senior cadre who was keen on supporting this project left office. In 2011, there were claims that Yiwu was the true hometown of HDX. It was reported by the Yiwu local media, after another round of reinterpretation of historical texts, that Yangyingcun (literally meaning sheeps' footprints village) at Chian in Yiwu was the genuine hometown of the immortal. The escalation of the hometown controversy was due to two reasons. First, the economic influence of Yiwu county has risen because the city has now become famous for its "small commodities market" and lots of traders from different parts of the world come every year. There was in fact speculation that Yiwu was about to gain independence from the Jinhua city government soon. Yiwu would therefore also desire to develop its heritage tourism industry further. Second, the efforts of both the overseas Chinese and the local investors were keys to this move. A group of visitors from Chisong HDX Association and Taiwan Chisong HDX Association went to Yiwu under the leadership of Mr Chow to search for the hometown of the immortal in 2011.[7] In fact, two local investors in Yiwu, the boss of a local wine factory and a resort developer, were active players behind the controversy of HDX's hometown. The resort developer was developing the area near Yangying village, where it was said to be the place where HDX kept his sheep. It would therefore be in his interests to argue that Yangying village in Yiwu was the hometown of HDX. As for the boss of the local wine factory, he would like to enhance the reputation of the local brewed wine through promoting the local place. Indeed, it was the boss of the local wine factory who brought Mr Chow to Yiwu Local Gazette Office to meet with the researchers. According to the researchers' investigation of historical data, Yiwu should be the hometown of HDX. During Mr Chow's visit in

2001, these two investors invited and arranged the media to make more reports on this "new" discovery. New historical narratives were invoked to show that Chian in Yiwu is the place where HDX was born. Such a process has demonstrated how memories were revived differently in response to the changing political and economic environment. As Fentress and Wickham (1992: 86) have pointed out, "the process of reinterpretation reflects real changes in external circumstances as well. The past could always be recreated and reformulated into different versions from the standpoint of the changing emergent present." Whether this memory could be popularized or not very much depends on the efforts of local investors and overseas Chinese.

Connecting local places with HDX through different legends

In 1995, the Lanxi county government successfully obtained official recognition from the provincial government as the hometown of the immortal. The governments of other counties therefore turned to draw other links between the immortal and the local place through different legends. Nevertheless, it is interesting to note that all these legends told by villagers and recorded in publications focus on HDX exclusively, although the inundated temple at Chisong was actually dedicated to both HDX and his brother. Villagers at Zhongtou village in Chisong recounted the spatial map of the inundated temple and various legends relating to HDX to us enthusiastically. They associated the name of their county to HDX, who was also called Chisongzhi, which means son of Chisong. It was said that pine trees were widely found in Chisong (literally meaning pine tree) in the past although there are none there today. Some villagers told us that the pine trees turned red when HDX was transformed from an ordinary man into an immortal.

Legends also recorded that HDX saved villagers from the harassment of the emperor in snatching the red color pine tree from their village. It was said that there was one particularly beautiful giant pine tree in Zhongtou village in Chisong county. The bark is red in color and the leaves are gold in color. One day, the emperor saw the image of a beautiful pine tree in a pond at the imperial garden (Shi 1995: 155–156). After checking with officials, the emperor was told that the image could be that of the special pine tree from Zhongtou village in Chisong county, Jinhua. The emperor sent the soldiers to chop down the tree and intended to ship it back to the capital city. On the way to the capital city, the boat sank and the emperor was not able to see it. To commemorate this special pine tree, the villagers built a temple dedicated to HDX and his brother and called it "Chisonggong" (also named as Two Saints Temple) (Fang 1995: 156). Another related legend also mentioned that the emperor wanted to come to see the special pine tree at Zhongtou village (Huang 1998: 24). In order to prepare for the arrival of the emperor, the local government officials built roads, planted trees, recruited more taxes, and snatched treasures from the local village. Villagers were very upset by these policies and therefore sought help from HDX. HDX set up rocks and other obstacles on the routes approaching the village, so that the emperor had difficulty reaching there. One of the officials therefore suggested cutting down the special tree and replanting it at the imperial garden so that the emperor could enjoy it alone. Villagers were shocked and asked HDX for help again. Huang then turned the red pine tree into an ordinary pine tree. The emperor and his troops could not find the tree and so they left. Despite different versions of the stories of the pine tree, a connection between HDX and the red pine tree was drawn and the link between the immortal and the local place at Zhongtou village in Chisong has also been created

Besides, legends of HDX could also be found in Xianqiao town in Chisong county. Different legends addressed HDX's contribution in building the bridge to fight against the flood. It was believed that a few bridges built at Xianqiao collapsed in the flood because an evil dragon destroyed them. Eventually, HDX and his brother killed the dragon, and therefore the new bridge could stand firmly (Ma 1993: 55–62).

Another version of the legend highlighted the miraculous contribution of the immortal and his brother in a different way. It was said that villagers prayed to the immortal in Zhongtou village before they started building the new bridge (Qian 1998: 22–23). After they prayed, they discovered statues of HDX and his brother at the cornerstone of the remnants of the bridge destroyed by the dragon. This was regarded as a sign that HDX and his brother had responded and promised to protect the bridge. A few days later a flood hit again, but it stopped right in front of the bridge. After the water receded, villagers discovered lots of stones in front of the two statues. These stones were perfect for building the bridge and villagers believed that they were sent by the two gods. After the new bridge was completed, it was named as "Erxianqiao"—literally Two Saints Bridge—in order to commemorate the contribution of HDX and his brother (Qian 1998: 22–23). A similar version of this legend was narrated by the local villagers to us. It was said that HDX and his brother placed their bodies in front of the cornerstone and stopped the flood, thereby rescuing the villagers by sacrificing themselves. With that courageous act, they turned into immortals and flew to the sky. According to the villagers, the temple Erhuangcunci (Two immortal temples) was subsequently built by them to commemorate the good deeds of the two immortals.[8]

In sum, different places have made connections with HDX through different narratives of memories in the form of legends and stories. Xianqiao town in Chisong is remembered by the villagers as the place where HDX and his brother died and became immortals while fighting a natural disaster. Zhongtou village in Chisong is the place where HDX planted pine trees and helped villagers resist a possessive emperor. Huang Peng in Lanxi is considered as the home village of HDX, where he was born and grew up.

Old temples remembered and new temples constructed

Apart from legends, historical evidence of temples dedicated to HDX was also cited to highlight that Jinhua was the hometown of the immortal. Two books (1993, 1995) took a special interest in emphasizing Jinhua as the place where HDX was born and achieved immortality through tracing the origins of two temples there. The first book was published in 1993 with the support of Jinhua prefectural-level city government, which tracked down two HDX temples located at Double Dragon Cave scenic park in Jinhua Mountain and Chisong county. Double Dragon Cave scenic park covers 79.9 square miles in a mountainous landscape and is managed by the Double Dragon Scenic Park Management team under the Jinhua prefectural-level city government. The second book provides a detailed discussion on Chisonggong in Chisong county and was published with the support of Chisong county government in 1995.

The first temple, Jinhua Guan (also named as Chisong Xiaguan), is located somewhere between the top and mid-level of Jinhua Mountain. This temple was dedicated to HDX and his brother, and it was believed to have existed as early as the Tang dynasty although it was unclear when the temple was first built. It was known that the temple was rebuilt many times, including in 1110 and 1934 (Ma 1993: 207). During the 1950s, the temple was abandoned and torn down. Although the history of the temple was recorded clearly in the book, locals seem to be rather ignorant of this and none of our informants recalled anything about this temple. A new Jinhua Guan was constructed next to the Double Dragon Cave by the Double Dragon Scenic Management Team from the Jinhua prefectural-level city government in 1991. The legitimacy for building the new temple was based on the historical existence of Jinhua Guan in this mountain. Representatives from YQG in Hong Kong attended the opening ceremony of the temple. To further develop tourism and to capitalize on the devotion of overseas Chinese to HDX, another grand temple dedicated to HDX was built by the Double Dragon Scenic Management Team under the leadership of Mao Gengzhi by the Jinhua prefectural level city government in 1996 (see Chapter 5).[9] The justification was also based on the past existence of Jinhua Guan in Jinhua Mountain. Although a new Jinhua Guan was already built in 1991, it was considered too small. A grand temple, Zugong (literally meaning ancestral palace) was built on the hilltop in 1996, a year before the reunification of Hong Kong to China, symbolically representing the return of the refugee god from Hong Kong to the ancestral land in Jinhua Mountain. Indeed, the local cadres had expected more frequent visits of Hong Kong pilgrims in Jinhua. These temples are projects taken up by the Double Dragon Cave Management team, which is under the Jinhua prefectural-level city government, primarily for tourism and economic development.

The second temple is Chisonggong, which was located at Chisong county (Ma 1993: 209). The temple was said to be first built in the Jin dynasty (265–420 AD) and was rebuilt in Song dynasty (960–1279 AD) and was renamed as Baojiguan (ibid.). It was then rebuilt in 1477 and 1582 in the Ming Dynasty, as well as in Qing dynasty in 1821 (Ma 1993: 209). It was destroyed in the late Qing dynasty in late 1800s and reconstructed in 1917 and renamed as Chisonggong. The temple was known to be dedicated to HDX and his brother. Memories of old temples were promoted by invoking historical documents and oral recounts by the Daoist priest Chen Jinfeng, who stayed at the temple until October 1949 (Shi 1995: 132). Chisonggong was said to be the biggest temple in the Yangtze Delta during the Qing dynasty (ibid.: 133). It was said that the temple was rather powerful and even owned landed property of around 20 mou in the early Republican period (ibid.: 134). The temple was destroyed in May 1942 during the Japanese war and was rebuilt in 1945 after the war (ibid.: 132). It was however inundated when a reservoir was constructed there in 1958. It was clear that villagers in Chisong had vivid memories about that. Villagers fondly recalled the structure of the temple to us during our visits. It was a big temple with two courtyards and some of the villagers used to play there when they were children.

The "forgotten" temple and the "forgotten" god

Erhuangjunci, which exists in Xianqiao at Chisong, was largely ignored and almost completely forgotten by the cadres in the 1990s. Although two publications in 1993 and 1995 briefly mentioned that villagers there once built an Erhuangjunci while narrating the legends of HDX bridge, one publication did not mention the present condition of the temple while the other simply noted that the temple was destroyed in the late Qing dynasty (Ma 1993: 217; Shi 1995). All through the years in our interviews with different cadres and villagers in Chisong since 1999, none of the officials and cadres mentioned that there existed an old temple called Erhuangjunci in Jinhua although they were keen to tell us stories of other temples. Lately, we tried to ask temple managers and officials about Erhuangjunci and the response was either ignorance or denial of its connection to HDX.

During our fieldwork in summer 2007, we decided to search for Erhuangjunci in Xianqiao, Chisong and eventually visited it. Erhuangjunci was indeed an old, and run-down temple run by the villagers. It was basically closed, except on the first and the fifteenth of each month as well as on the birthday of HDX. When we arrived there, we asked around and realized that the person who ran a store next to the temple was holding the key to the temple. He brought us into the temple and explained the details to us. We saw broken plaques lying in different corners of the temple. From these old plaques, the temple was identified as "Erhuangjunci" and "Guerxianci" (literally meaning Old Two Saints' Temple). Although it is unclear when the temple was built, a piece of stone plaque at the temple dated 1752 and another carving on the stone incense stove dated 1810. Local villagers told us that the temple was abandoned during the Cultural Revolution and it was converted into a restaurant in the 1970s. In 1996, the temple was renovated by the local villagers and statues of HDX and his brother were installed. However, this temple has always been locked and has only been visited by local villagers in the community.

The year 1996 was the time when Zugong was built and members from both SSY and Yuanqinge (YQG) attended the opening ceremony. These Hong Kong pilgrims were brought by the cadres in Jinhua prefectural-level city government to visit Jinhua Guan and even YYY in Lanxi. Nevertheless, none of them were told about the existence nor the renovation of this ancient temple, although this temple was about a 10-minute drive away from Chisonggong. To the cadres in Jinhua prefectural-level city government, it is clear that temples built by the governments (Jinhua city government and Lanxi county government) need to be introduced and promoted to the Hong Kong pilgrims so that possible investment in these districts could be solicited in the future. To these cadres, the local temples which were managed by villagers could be ignored as they could be competitors to the government-operated temples.

At this point, it would be interesting to investigate why the inundated temple was remembered while the other temple in Xianqiao was "forgotten" despite the fact that these two temples were both located within the Chisong township. First, this is due to the efforts of the villagers who actively informed SSY about their inundated temple and thus pilgrims from SSY arrived. In contrast, villagers at Xianqiao did not seem have contacted SSY and did not actively pursue any development plan for their temple in the early 1990s. Second, we speculate that it also has to do with the location of Xianqiao and Zhongtou village. Xianqiao village has always been a business centre as the market is located there and public transport to other places in Jinhua is also readily available. Xianqiao villagers have therefore always had many employment and business opportunities. In contrast, Zhongtou village is located in a relatively inconvenient place with no public transport before 1997 when a new temple (CSDY) dedicated to HDX was built. Villagers had less employment opportunities and were desperate for development opportunities.

Only until 2007 did local villagers at the Xianqiao start to work together with intellectuals and local government to pay more attention to their temple. Like all others villagers in other counties, these villagers attempted to draw a special connection between their village and HDX. During our visit there, the villagers also told us legends about HDX and his brother. It was said that their village was the place where the two brothers played chess. Upon seeing the villagers having difficulties in getting fresh water, HDX threw a chess piece onto the ground and it magically turned into a well. Moreover, villagers also reiterated the legend that the bodies of the immortal and his brother were found at the cornerstone after their attempt to save the village from the flood. Thus, villagers built a tomb for the two brothers and a temple dedicated to them. Villagers interviewed expressed disappointment at the fact that there was no Hong Kong investor at this temple even though this site is a "genuine" HDX heritage. Indeed, a detailed narration of this temple and legends of HDX's tomb only appeared in the publication in 2007 together with a discussion in the appendix on the potential to further develop HDX heritage (Wang 2007). The book mentioned that this site should be fully explored for economic development.

Besides, it is also important to note that the revival of religious memories focused largely on HDX and not his brother although historical evidence found in two peasant temples (Chisonggong and Erhuangcunji) seems to indicate that both brothers were equally important to the locals in the past. In fact, it is clear that both HDX and his brother were worshipped in Jinhua. Statues of two brothers were found in the inundated temple at Chisong and Erhuangjunci at Xianqiao. The names of the two old temples (literally meaning Two Saints' Temple) and "Erhuangjunci" (literally meaning "Two Gods' Temple") suggest that both brothers were worshipped.

Although it was mentioned in one of the publications that HDX became immortal first and only later did his brother join him (*Huangdaxian Zhiliaoxuanbian*

1995: 9), legends recorded in the publications and oral narratives recalled by villagers tended to downplay the elder brother.

For instance, the legend of "Erxianqiao" (Two Saints' Bridge) focuses on HDX exclusively and neglects the contribution of his brother. Such memories may however not be "naturally recalled" but could well be affected by the present socioeconomic environment. Forgetting is a prescriptive act which is believed to strengthen the link between Jinhua and Hong Kong. The forgetting of the brother was clearly related to Jinhua locals' knowledge of the fact that only HDX is worshipped in Hong Kong. This was also reflected by the fact that various publications carried a small section that narrated the popularity of HDX in Hong Kong and overseas. It was recorded that HDX and not his brother was brought by migrants from Xiqiao in Guangdong to Hong Kong in 1915 (Shi 1995: 141, 143). It was mentioned by the local scholars in Lanxi that HDX has gained popularity through fighting against plague in Hong Kong and finally a temple dedicated to HDX was built (Zhao and Zhao 1995) (see Chapter 2). Meanwhile, the message by pilgrims from SSY, YQG, Chisong HDX Association, and other individuals from Hong Kong has also clearly indicated that only HDX has been widely worshipped in Hong Kong, but not the brother. Therefore, it was natural that only the memory of HDX was revived in Jinhua, given that he is a household name in Hong Kong. Thus, neglecting the brother and focusing on HDX is a kind of prescriptive forgetting, one that is shaped by the transnational connection. It is to acknowledge the ultimate objective of boosting the Hong Kong connections, which serves to attract pilgrims and promotes economic development. Indeed, the transnational ties and the Hong Kong connection have shaped the content of remembering and forgetting.

Finally, another part of largely omitted religious memories was the absence of any revival of religious practices directly relating to HDX. None of the publications mentioned religious festivals relating to HDX in the past or described ritualized celebrations. All villagers interviewed were delighted to share the legends with us as these were apparently very important in making local places. Different places have been marked through legends which highlight the special connections with HDX. When it came to religious practices related to the immortal, very little was recounted. These memories could possibly be suppressed because ritual practices could be easily considered as superstition by the government. And more importantly, these memories are not as useful as those of the legends in justifying temple construction projects and in striving for tourism and economic development.

Conclusion

The visits of various groups of Hong Kong pilgrims at different places have created various degrees of impact at several places in Jinhua, which led to the subsequent search and revival of memories of HDX in these areas. It is however the local governments which take on the leadership role to mobilize the intellectuals and local historians, to reawaken legends, and to compile stories of HDX. This is rather different from existing studies which suggest that it was the locals who took the initiative in reviving religious memories and reconstructing temples (e.g., Jing 1996; Mueggler 2001).

Narratives and legends recalled about HDX in Jinhua since the 1990s are more diverse than the stories produced in Guangdong in the late 1890s, which formed the basis for the worship of the deity in Hong Kong from about 1915 (see more legends in the Appendix). Both the Jinhua and Guangdong versions recounting the saint's life indicate that he had magical powers deriving from Daoist cultivation and that he devoted himself to help others, particularly through Daoist medical arts and healing. However, the Jinhua legends go far beyond this simple formula, providing examples from the saint's life which illustrate his cleverness, compassion, and courage, as well as his Daoist powers. Living in an agricultural society, HDX responded to the problems and troubles of villagers, displayed human compassion as well as human emotions, and also demonstrated his virtues. Eventually, he achieved extraordinary powers as a "perfected human." Almost all of these Jinhua stories about the activities of Chuping were completely unknown among Hong Kong believers up to the early 1990s, even among the inner circle of members and directors of the SSY, whose texts were limited to the nineteenth century spirit-writings from Guangdong and the semicanonical "autobiography" of HDX received through spirit-writing by the original founder of the SSY, Liang Renan.

In Jinhua, memories of HDX were revived in the form of legends and promoted under the leadership of different local governments with the aim of pursuing local economic development. This contrasts with existing studies on social memories in China, which highlight unsanctioned remembrance recalled by people to resist state hegemony (e.g., Watsons 1994). Jing (1996) has suggested that temple-related memories are related to collective traumas of forced resettlement and the traumatic memories are a form of local protest against the state. Similarly, Mueggler (2001: 9, 2007) also provided an analysis of how the remembering and forgetting of the famine and the Cultural Revolution are ethical struggles against the state, calling for justice and reconciliation in the present and future. Our research on religious memories on the worship of HDX does not reveal a confrontational relationship between state and society. Instead, selected distant memories are awakened and re-invented as symbolic, economic, and political resources for the present and the future under the leadership of different local governments. Memories of HDX in the form of legends are recalled and promoted as symbolic capital with the aim of soliciting overseas investment and developing religious tourism. They are recalled and used as a tool by local governments for economic development through temple-building projects.

Cadres from different counties, the city and provincial government, intellectuals, businessmen, and locals in different counties and communities have both commonalities and differences in their agendas for triggering this reawakening of religious memories. Various parties are engaged in the process of remembering, revising and inventing but also in selectively forgetting and contesting memories. Different legends and stories were invoked as a result of the competition between different local governments in utilizing HDX as symbolic capital for economic development. The controversy over the true hometown of the immortal in the 1990s and 2011 reveals that memories are continuously changing as the present changes all the time. We have explained why some memories are chosen to be remembered while others are allowed to be forgotten. The "forgetting" of the temple at Xianqiao and the brother demonstrates that memories are indeed a result of a power struggle in the present. Memories are selectively recalled, recorded, and promoted in response to the continuously changing present.

To the local governments, their aim is to justify Jinhua as the original hometown of HDX, a deity who has acquired overwhelming popularity overseas, especially in Hong Kong. To achieve this they therefore set out to revive legends, oral narratives, and historical relics related to HDX and have these documented in various publications. To the villages at Chisong and Lanxi, recalled stories of HDX have different themes, such as the healing power of HDX in Lanxi and his helpful personality in fighting against the emperor and natural disasters in Chisong. New identities of local places are made through different narratives of HDX, drawing a unique connection between the immortal and local places. Huang Peng village has become the birthplace of HDX and Lanxi, Chisong, and Jinhua Mountain are places where HDX healed people, helped the general public, and achieved immortality. In sum, the making of places linked to HDX—Lanxi, Chisong, and Jinhua Mountain—has resulted from the circulation and transfer of people, goods, ideas, symbols, and various narratives of HDX from different groups.

Most importantly, memories of the deity HDX as well as historical evidence of HDX temples at Jinhua Mountain form legitimate grounds for building or reconstructing temples dedicated to the immortal. Three temples were constructed by the local governments with the aim of developing tourism and stimulating the economy (YYY, Zugong, Jinhua Guan, Table 1.1), while two other temples were built by private investors also share similar goals (CSDY, Lingyangci, Table 1.1). Three temples were built or renovated by local villagers mainly with the hope of reviving and reinventing religious life (Xianyiguan, Chisonggong, Erhuangjunci, Table 1.1). The construction of each of these temples is the result of the unique combination of narratives of HDX in local places, the efforts of individual villagers or intellectuals in the local community, financial support from the government, investors, overseas pilgrims and locals, and the dynamics among different local governments. After these temples were constructed, it would be interesting to see how they survive and what strategies the governments and temple managers have adopted to attract visitors. In the following chapter, we will turn to investigate how the Jinhua-prefectural level government promotes HDX as a cultural heritage to visitors and how various types of visitors received them.

Notes

1 From 1988 to 2000, Jinhua as a prefecture-level city administered nine county-level divisions, which were termed as city, district, or counties. The lower county-level divisions were Lanxi City and Wucheng district, and 7 counties: Jinhua county, Yongkang county, Wuyi county, Dongyang county, Panan county, Yiwu county, and Pujiang county. From 2000 onwards, an administrative restructuring exercise was conducted. Jinhua as

a prefecture-level city still includes nine county-level divisions, but these county-level divisions are mostly changed; they now include Wucheng district, Jindong district, Lanxi city, Yongkang city, Yiwu city, Dongyang city, Wuyi county, Pujiang county, and Panan county. County-level administrative divisions are further divided into township-level divisions, which are in turn subdivided into village-level communities. Also note that the Chinese term for "city" can be of various levels: provincial-level, prefecture-level, or county-level.

2 Frentress and Wickham (1992: 26) pointed out that whether memories are historically true are less important than whether people accept them as true.

3 Zhejiang Jianfeng Group is a company which manufactures and sells cement, produces pharmaceutical products. It is listed in the Shanghai Stock Exchange Market. The boss of the company visited Hong Kong in the late 80s and was entertained by Mr Chow. Chau brought him to visit the HDX temple operated by SSY in Hong Kong. He later became a devotee of HDX and made donations to different HDX temples (see Chapters 5 and 6).

4 It is possible that memories of the healing power of HDX is a learnt memory brought by transnational ties as HDX was known to be famous as a healer in Hong Kong (see Chapter 2).

5 Local peasants and soldiers have been credited as initiators of temple reconstruction projects (see, e.g., DuBois 2005, Jing 1996; Feuchtwang and Wang 2001).

6 Mao was in charge of the construction of Zugong in Jinhua Mountain (see more in the next section and Chapter 5)

7 Taiwan Huangdaxian Association was set up in 2011 by Mr Chow. Members include worshippers of HDX in Taiwan.

8 It is unclear when the temple was first built, see more in the next section.

9 Mao later retired from the government. Since 2011, he began to invest in the Lingyandao project, see earlier section.

4 Heritage and temples

Authenticity, tourists, and pilgrims

Introduction

After delineating how memories of HDX were revived and how eight temples were constructed and renovated in Jinhua since the 1990s, we now turn our attention to examine how the local government promoted HDX and the temples dedicated to him after their construction. This chapter will investigate the process in which HDX has been portrayed as an important part of religious heritage and more importantly, an authentic cultural heritage in Jinhua by the local governments. It will also examine how religion has been represented as an authentic local, national, and transnational cultural heritage predominantly by the Jinhua prefectural-level city government and the temple management teams at various temples, as well as how that portrayal attracts pilgrims and tourists from various places.[1]

We suggest that the sociocultural aspects of HDX have been highlighted by various governments and temple management teams while the religious facet has been downplayed. This is partly due to the fact that religion was suppressed during the Cultural Revolution and therefore official accounts of the transmission of Daoism were either nonexistent or fragmented. Religion is a sensitive issue and hence the government officials are careful not to be seen as fostering superstition[2] (see also Palmer 2009; Goossaert and Palmer 2011). Turning religion into a cultural resource is however a common strategy used by local governments or/and government-related tourism companies (see also Lang and Chan 2005; Sutton and Kang 2010: 113; Svensson 2010). For instance, the national ideology of building a harmonious society and the emphasis on tourism are highlighted in the recent establishment and promotion of a cultural (religious) festival at Wutaishan in Shanxi province for tourists (Ryan and Gu 2010: 171). Similarly, the "secularizing" strategy of a religious site is also found in Mount Tai where revolutionary heroes were highlighted by the state Dott (2010: 40).[3] In the post-reform era, the state often exploited the market value of the temple and reduced it to folklore (Sutton and Kang 2010: 122; Kang 2009b). Indeed, the construction of the HDX temples is an example of using local cultural resources to attract overseas investments and foster economic development. Moving beyond existing studies which merely mentioned the fact that temples were exploited as cultural resources, we examine the general promotional strategy adopted by the government officials, as based on the case of Jinhua. We analyze how the government presents HDX as an authentic cultural heritage to attract visitors. Authenticity of HDX cultural heritage is taken as a discourse in which particular views, beliefs, perspectives, or powers are constructed.[4] This chapter considers how different actors and institutions involved in constructing HDX cultural heritage are motivated by multiple and sometimes conflicting agendas. The authenticity of HDX heritage in Jinhua will be analyzed to understand how the state, the local governments, entrepreneurs, and the media draw knowledge, authority, and credibility from historical, cultural, and legal practices. HDX cultural heritage will be viewed as discursive practices produced by various institutions and through different sources. As Goossaert and Palmer (2011: 320) correctly argued, "discourses on religion in the People's Republic of China should be seen in the context of the broader economy of discourse production and circulation between various official and unofficial actors, including Party leaders and organs, government departments, academic institutions, religious leaders and followers, and the media."

We suggest that different agents, who are closely related to the Jinhua prefectural-level city government, play important roles in constructing the image of HDX through cultural festival and creative cultural media. Such a process is also considered as authenticating and relocalizing HDX in Jinhua. The way in which branding has, through various media and cultural strategies in the recent decade, constructed a sense of authenticity on HDX will be investigated. We will also demonstrate how the authenticity of the cultural heritage of HDX is further enhanced through the state's recognition of HDX legends and oral narratives as national intangible cultural heritage.

The second part of this chapter intends to examine how these representations of HDX constructed by the Jinhua prefectural-level city government are being received or consumed by pilgrims and tourists. We will examine how pilgrims and tourists bring their own cultural, religious, or identity orientations to these sites and how these beliefs and expectations relate to the constructed representations of HDX—Jinhua as the hometown of HDX, the positive moral virtues of HDX as a local cultural heritage, and HDX as a symbol of Chinese identity.

Authenticating HDX temples and heritage, branding Jinhua city: media and cultural advertising strategies

Shortly after the establishment of initial contact with HDX worshippers from various Chinese communities abroad, the immortal's fame climbed rapidly in Jinhua, and HDX soon became widely remembered by Jinhua people (see Chapter 3). Today, one could find HDX legends and cultures being considered as an important part of Daoist religious heritage in the Jinhua prefectural-level city government website. The authenticity of the immortal HDX as a Daoist god is directly certified through tracing the Daoist volume known as *Ge Hong's Shen Xian Zhuan* (*Biographies of Immortals*). The immortal was believed to be a person who lived there 1,600 years ago and was said to have performed many good deeds and also left traces of his existence at various places in Jinhua (see Chapter 2). Legends and oral narratives related to HDX construct Jinhua as an authentic homeland for HDX, who as an immortal originally from Jinhua has gained popularity in Hong Kong and other Chinese communities abroad.

As for the authenticity of these HDX temples, it is not marked by the physical structures of the temple buildings. Historical authenticity of the temple is not an important issue for the tourists or pilgrims or governments to decide which temple to visit or to promote. Erhuangqunci, which is the oldest temple among those dedicated to HDX, is largely forgotten and neither the Hong Kong pilgrims from SSY and YQG nor the local tourists visit it because they are not even aware of its existence (see Chapter 3). In contrast, newly built temples—Zugong, Jinhua Guan, Chisonggong, CSDY, YYY, Xianyiguan, and Lingyangci—attract more visitors.

Among all these newer temples, CSDY, Jinhua Guan, Zugong, and YYY were the temples built by investors or local governments with the primary aim of promoting tourism (Table 3.1). These temples are "genuine fakes" (Brown 1996: 33) because they are newly built and are intended to arouse deep and genuine feelings in the visitors. The authenticity is partially based on the fact that these new temples (Chisonggong and Jinhua Guan) were built on sites where the original temples linked to HDX were previously located. Meanwhile, the authenticity of Zugong, CSDY, Xianyiguan, Lingyangci, and YYY is also derived from the fact that these places are associated with legends and stories of HDX (see Chapter 3).

In this connection, it is worth noting that while CSDY is promoted as a cultural heritage relating to HDX through legends in Chisong, an authentic historical site left over from the Southern Song Dynasty—the graveyard of prime minister Wang Huai (1126–1189 AD), who was a Jinhua native in the Southern Song dynasty (1127–1279 AD)—and which lies within the scope of CSDY has not been similarly mentioned. Visitors did not know about its existence there until they came and were hence rather surprised. Neither was this genuine historical heritage promoted by the government or media. Instead, legends of HDX and his reputation overseas are the focus of the government's efforts in promoting Jinhua's cultural heritage.

Indeed, the deputy secretary in the Lanxi county government claimed that HDX could be utilized as a cultural resource to promote tourism and economic development as early as 1995. Another cadre from the Jinhua prefectural-level city government whom we interviewed also commented, "It is important to take advantage of 'cultural resources,' such as the famous deity HDX. HDX could be a 'brand name' for attracting tourists." In fact, all local cadres interviewed claimed that religious heritage should not be suppressed but should instead be managed efficiently for the country's advancement, namely economic development. The local governments were also candid in their explanation to the provincial authorities that temple buildings were a means to attract overseas Chinese pilgrims from Hong Kong and Taiwan to the hometown of the immortal, as well as solicit foreign investment, foster tourism, and promote economic development (see Chapter 3).

Transforming HDX from a religious icon to a cultural symbol is largely due to HDX's immense popularity in Hong Kong, a cosmopolitan city as compared to Jinhua, which was still a small, quiet town by the mid-1990s. Hong Kong's prosperity is what the Mainland Chinese have aspired to since the inception of the Open-Door Policy. While most mainlanders could not travel freely to Hong Kong, they are relatively free to tour within the rest of China, which includes Jinhua.[5] It was indeed the uniqueness of this immortal who established his fame in Hong Kong which has transformed HDX from a country bumpkin to a semiforeign cosmopolitan being. Local in origin, and yet being transnational and hence possessing a foreign and mysterious side, the immortal appeals to the domestic tourists' curiosity. To the Jinhua prefectural-level city government, the appeal of HDX temples in Jinhua lies in its symbolic link to the outside world as they may draw overseas pilgrims to visit these temples and also to invest in Jinhua.

More importantly, HDX is being presented as a Jinhua cultural heritage and is not only authenticated through historical evidence but also through authoritative media-based cultural branding strategies, such as reviving and promoting legends in cartoons, drama series, and the organization of the HDX cultural festival. Indeed, after the market reforms began, every city in China now competes with one another to attract tourists and promote economic development. The branding of cities has therefore become an important and popular strategy in China for attracting domestic and international tourists. Such a branding process focuses on constructing the uniqueness of a city and therefore differentiates it from others. Four government organizations—Jinhua prefectural-level city government, Jinhua Tourism Bureau, United Front at Jinhua prefectural-level city government, and Double Dragon Cave Scenic Park Management Committee—are heavily involved in branding the city of Jinhua through promoting the moral values of HDX legends, mobilizing new and creative cultural production of HDX, as well as organizing touristic activities related to HDX.

With the encouragement and financial support of the Double Dragon Cave Scenic Park Management Committee, Jinhua HDX Cultural Research Association was founded in 2005. The objective of the Association was to promote HDX culture through historical research. It published an occasional magazine, entitled *HDX Culture*, that promoted academic research on the legends of the immortal and teased out the moral virtues of HDX (*Jinhua Huangdaxian Yanjiuhui Bangongshi* 2006: 44; Wang 2007: 19). In 2007, Zhonghua HDX Cultural Exchange Association (Chinese HDX Cultural Exchange Association) was set up with the encouragement of the Jinhua prefectural-level city government and the United Front. The Association has been responsible for promoting HDX culture through organizing seminars or conferences at Jinhua's HDX Cultural Tourism Festival, when international participants were also invited (*Jinhua Huangdaxian Wenhua Yanjiuhui* 2007: 4).

Indeed, historical and cultural practices of HDX heritage are discursively authenticated in repetitive research on legends conducted by the above associations. Legends recount HDX's experience of becoming an immortal by narrating how he turned stones into sheep (see Chapter 2). Some legends gave accounts of how HDX went to the mountains to collect herbal medicine for healing different villagers who were suffering from various kinds of diseases (see Chapter 2).

Other stories narrated how HDX helped to save people's lives from danger (e.g., flood, tiger) and helped farmers by giving them seeds and fertilizers. Different legends also depicted how HDX helped the local villagers by tricking the authorities or greedy wealthy people who oppressed them with unreasonable demands or requests. Some stories illustrated how HDX lent a helping hand to ordinary people who were cheated by dishonest villains and punishment was meted out to these villains with HDX's witty tricks (see Appendix).

Nevertheless, the magical aspects of these legends have been downplayed as they are considered superstitious by the state (Chen 2006: 30; Peng 2006: 2–3; Shi 2007: 23–24; Wang 2007: 19–22). Instead, the secular values and moral values of HDX legends have been promoted, especially after these legends have been declared as Jinhua intangible cultural heritage in 2006 (ibid., see next section on intangible cultural heritage). The moral virtues of these legends were claimed to highlight how HDX cured sicknesses and saved lives (zhibingjiuren), averted danger and relieved hardship (fuweijikun), practiced kindness and suppressed evil (xingshanzhie and furoujiping), as well as promoted virtues and discouraged vices (yanshanchene). These moral virtues have now also been objectified as the personality of HDX.

Traditional cultures, including legends such as those about HDX, were suppressed during the cultural revolution and have now not only been revived but also promoted to build a harmonious socialist society. The concept of a harmonious society was first raised by the government during the National People's Congress meeting in 2005, as a response to the conflicts brought by social injustice and inequality from the rapid economic development since the market reforms. It is important to note that these legends should not simply be analyzed as a revival of local traditions. Instead, their new meanings have to be understood in the post-reform context. Unintended consequences—such as inequalities, corruption, and individual-centered morality of rights—have created a "moral vacuum" that has challenged the state authority and moral values (Eng and Lin 2002: 1265; Yan 2011: 43).[6] Not only is there a decline in the moral authority of officials but an authoritative set of moral meanings for any cultural form is also absent (Fischer 2012: 368). Moral virtues in HDX legends presented by the local officials could be perceived as a way in which the local government struggles to formulate a new moral order. HDX's moral virtues as recounted in legends were asserted by the Jinhua prefectural-level city government to shine a positive light on Jinhua and construct a brand name for the city. Recently, these moral virtues found in HDX legends have also been claimed to be an important part of the heritage of Confucianism and Buddhism (*Zhongguo Jinhua Shuang Long Jing Qu Guan Wei Hui and Zhongguo Chengshi Jingzhengli Yanjiu Hui* 2010: 44, 69) because they are indeed not much different from the virtues of these Chinese philosophies. This slight modification in its presentation was intended to let HDX appeal to a much larger number of Chinese from all over the world.

Apart from publishing articles and organizing cultural festivals to promote the HDX culture, the creative cultural industry is also mobilized to popularize the connection between HDX and Jinhua. In 2006, a 22-episode drama series with a focus on HDX, "Chisonghun" (the spirit of Chisong), was filmed. The drama series was initiated by the Jinhua prefectural-level city government and the script was jointly written by representatives from the Jinhua HDX Cultural Association and the Double Dragon Scenic Park Management Team, together with the Jinhua Daoist Association (*Miaoxie Huangdaxian De Dianshiju* 2006: 27). A team of writers set up four guidelines in drafting the script of the drama series. First, the story of HDX had to be based on legends and narratives, while emotions and martial arts should be added for elaboration (*Miaoxie Huang Daxian* 2006: 27). Second, the story had to be set in the context of Jinhua Mountain in line with historical evidence. Third, various landscapes in Jinhua should appear in the drama series. Fourth, shots of the various HDX temples at Jinhua and Hong Kong had to be included as well (ibid.: 27). The first two guidelines emphasized the historical authenticity of HDX in Jinhua, while the last two connected HDX with Jinhua's landscapes specifically and temples in various places. In addition, a cartoon show entitled *Chisong Weilong* was also made with HDX as the main character. Both the cartoon and the drama series were modifications of legends related to HDX.

In addition, the Double Dragon Cave Scenic Park Management Committee also provided financial support to a traditional Wu opera performance on HDX legends at the HDX Cultural Tourism Festival (*Jinhua Huangdaxian Wenhua Yanjiuhui* 2007: 5). Similarly, the traditional opera was modified from the legends reported in "HDX Legends" by the Jinhua HDX Cultural Research Association and the moral virtues of HDX have also been highlighted (ibid.).

The Cultural Tourism Festival is another classic activity that was promoted to bolster cultural tourism relating to the Daoist HDX temples and is also a common branding strategy used by many other Chinese cities to enhance Chinese identity among Chinese living within and outside China. Earlier, Siu (1990: 790) noted that the chrysanthemum festival in Guangdong was organized by the town's party committee and attended by the heads of native place associations from Hong Kong and Macau, with wide media coverage. At Wutaishan in Shanxi province, Ryan and Gu (2010: 171) narrated how the cultural festival is an event where various people get together with the common purpose of seeking economic returns and reinforcing personal and group identities.[7] This occasion also lets "dominant groups seek to legitimize themselves even as subordinate groupings seek recognition of their own identity and aspirations" (ibid.: 173). Similarly, Jinhua HDX Cultural Tourism festival is also utilized by the Jinhua prefectural-level city government and the Jinhua tourism promotion bureau to develop tourism and to cultivate and invent relationships between themselves and HDX pilgrims within and outside mainland China. This festival provides an opportunity for the state to construct economic and cultural practices of HDX heritage.

In 2006, Jinhua HDX Cultural Tourism Association and Jinhua Tourism Bureau held a press conference at Miramar Hotel in Hong Kong. It was hosted by the deputy mayor of Jinhua prefectural-level city government together with 23 representatives from HDX-related organizations in Jinhua. The seminar was attended by participants from representatives of various sectors in Hong Kong. It included members from SSY, YQG, Chisong HDX Association, representatives from Hong Kong's Jinhua native place associations, more than 30 tourist agencies from Hong Kong, as well as reporters from the media. At the press release conference, the deputy mayor of Jinhua's prefectural-level city government announced that a series of HDX-related cultural tourism activities would be held in Jinhua. Tourists are encouraged to visit Jinhua and temples of HDX, which are claimed to be like fairyland located in beautiful scenic sites.

In 2010, the Double Dragon Cave management team organized a Jinhua Mountain HDX Cultural Festival. During the festival, HDX's life as portrayed in legends was displayed in 40 pieces of carved-jade screens with a total length of 33 metres. The Jinhua prefectural-level city government paid 1.6 million RMB for the jade-carved screens, which was ¼ of its cost. The rest of the cost was absorbed by the artist who carved the artwork. The government intends to sell this artwork for eight million RMB. Until 2014 when this book was written, a buyer for the artwork had not been found in China. Plans for finding a customer from Hong Kong or Taiwan were under consideration by the government.

In the last 15 years, HDX has also been actively presented as one of the important brand narratives of Jinhua city and has been used to highlight the uniqueness of Jinhua city and its differentiation from others. These efforts were also reflected in a seminar on Brand Promotion Strategy of Jinhua Wong Tai Sin (HDX) Harmonious Culture in 2010. The seminar was jointly organized by the Jinhua Double Dragon Scenic Park Management Committee and the Chinese Cities Competitiveness Association. A research report was published afterwards and suggested that HDX should not only be identified as one of the key cultural attractions in Jinhua to tourists but should also be highlighted further in branding Jinhua city and developing tourism (*Zhongguo Jinhua Shuang Long Jing Qu Guan Wei Hui* and *Zhongguo Chengshi Jingzhengli Yanjiu Hui* 2010: 27). Suggestions such as longevity resort tours with HDX Daoist longevity exercises and Daoist healthy cuisine, tea, and wine were mentioned.

Moral virtues of HDX have been presented by the Jinhua prefectural-level city government to highlight the uniqueness of the city and its cultural heritage through various creative cultural industries. These are indeed repetitive advertising strategies and are deployed to socialize the public and potential tourists on the immortal and the connection between him and Jinhua. The cultural festival, cartoons, drama series, and traditional operas are like what MacCannell (1976: 81) suggested that the cultural festival, cartoons, drama series, and traditional operas were made or invented on the basis of the original with modifications to suit the present society. They could be considered as "authentic" cultural productions because they are enacted by the locals according to tradition and are positioned as signifiers of the past (MacCannell 1976: 81, Chhabra, Healy and Sills 2003: 705). These new ways of representing legends of HDX are conducted through commodifying the past in novel forms. This is a common way of conducting heritage tourism (see Urry 1995).

From local heritage to national intangible cultural heritage

In 2006, the petition for a legal and official recognition of HDX legends as a Jinhua cultural heritage and a national intangible cultural heritage sought to further substantiate its authentic status on authoritative grounds. Such a process of gaining recognition from the Jinhua prefectural-level city government, provincial, and central governments has also transformed and authenticated HDX from a local heritage to a national cultural symbol via legal practice.

The Jinhua Prefectural-level City Intangible Cultural Heritage Preservation Office and the Experts Advisory Committee approved the application of HDX legends and HDX Daoist music as an intangible cultural heritage at the city-prefectural level in 2006 (*Huang Daxian Chuanshuo Yu Huangdaxian Dao Jiao Yinyue Bei Lie Ru Jinhua shi Shou Pi Sheng Feiwuzhi Wenhua Yichan Daibiaozuo Minglu* 2006: 49). In 2007, the Double Dragon Scenic Park Management Committee and Jinhua HDX Research Association applied for HDX legends to be declared as an intangible cultural heritage at the provincial level. First, historical authenticity was invoked to support the application. HDX legends and oral narratives were claimed to have a history of 1,600 years, beginning from the Eastern Jin dynasty (Huangdaxian Wenhua Secretariat 2007: 47). HDX is a Daoist god, and this Daoist association creates a linkage to an indigenous religion in China which has a long history. Second, the sociopolitical, cultural values of HDX as embedded in the moral virtues were highlighted in the application for the status of intangible cultural heritage. It was proposed that legends and oral narratives of HDX reflect the universal search for truth, kindness, and beauty in all human beings, which is also a part of Chinese traditional culture. As stories of HDX also appear in traditional literature, poems, and recent local drama series and cartoons, HDX is therefore also deemed to have rich educational value, especially in instilling the right social values in young children. In terms of its political value, HDX's positive traits were claimed to help construct a harmonious society in China, which is in line with one of the key missions of the State (ibid.: 47).[8] Legends and stories are now identified as intangible cultural heritage with moral values, which are suitable for the appropriation of state ideology. Such processes of linking local cultures to state ideology is a common practice found in today's China. For instance, the traditional values associated with Confucius have been highlighted in representing his hometown at Qufu. These values are considered "social utility" that may help provide support for the state hegemony as the state attempts to solve the problem of a "moral vacuum" that resulted from the fast expansion of its economy (Yan and Bramwell 2008: 985).

Third, the popularity of HDX among various transnational Chinese communities is also a reason to justify its application for official heritage recognition. It was noted that HDX is widely worshipped in various places, including Jinhua, Guangdong, Hong Kong, Macau, Taiwan, Singapore, Malaysia, Australia, Paris, Chinatown in New York, San Francisco, and Canada (Huangdaxian Wenhua Secretariat 2007: 47). The widespread popularity of HDX narratives at various places is claimed to be a unique phenomenon. It was even claimed that worshippers of HDX from all over the globe could well exceed 20 million Chinese (ibid.: 48). In 2014, the Jinhua prefectural-level city government contracted a historian to write a book which includes information about worship of HDX in different parts of the world. The promotion of HDX heritage is thus seen to be beneficial in attracting overseas Chinese, thus supporting tourism development and religion-related cultural activities.

In 2007, HDX legends were officially recognized as intangible cultural heritage by the Zhejiang provincial government. An application to the central government for the status of national grade intangible cultural heritage was submitted in 2008 by the Double Dragon Scenic Park Management Committee and the HDX Cultural Research Association. The fact that the application was initiated and handled by the Double Dragon Scenic Park Management Committee shows that heritage tourism is an important motivation. In the process of preparing for the application, the Double Dragon Scenic Park Management Committee and the Cultural Research Association had solicited advice from scholars and experts at the evaluation team, as well as relevant institutions in Beijing. Finally, they compiled a DVD together with a detailed description of HDX legends in their submission. On June 14, 2008, HDX legends were officially recognized as National Intangible Cultural Heritage (ibid.).[9]

Such a process of institutionalizing the status of HDX legends as intangible cultural heritage has certainly enhanced the authenticity of HDX culture in Jinhua. The registration of HDX legends as intangible cultural heritage also pronounces the legitimacy of HDX religious tradition and its value for nationalism and tourism development. The next goal of Jinhua government officials is to put in an application, together with other worshippers of HDX in Hong Kong and Guangdong, for HDX to be recognized as UNESCO intangible cultural heritage.[10]

From Jinhua HDX to Chinese (Zhonghua) HDX: appeal to transnational Chinese

In 2011, the Double Dragon Scenic Park Management Committee and Jinhua HDX Cultural Research Association created a website named as Zhonghua HDX Wenhua (http://www.huangdaxian.org/). HDX has been narrated as an important Daoist immortal on the website. The Daoist historical religious tradition and stories of HDX in Jinhua were posted on the website and the status of legends as national intangible cultural heritage was also highlighted. Besides, HDX is also used to promote transnational Chinese identity. Not only have five temples in Jinhua (Zugong, YYY, CSDY, Chisonggong and Jinhua Guan) been introduced, but temples dedicated to HDX in Guangdong and overseas are also narrated.[11] Promotion of HDX temples is conducted through narrating its importance both locally and globally. A migration history of HDX to Hong Kong has been summarized to highlight its popularity overseas. The latest spreading of HDX culture to Guangdong and Taiwan has also been noted. In 1997, a temple dedicated to HDX was opened at Swatow in Guangdong (ibid.). In 1998, Jinhua HDX Taipei Daoist Hall was founded in Taipei and a Taiwan HDX Association was also set up. Besides, the recent development of HDX in the United States, Canada, and Australia has also been noted. In 1983, a Chisong HDX Temple was set up in the Chinatown of New York (ibid.). In 1990, Chisong HDX temple was built in San Francisco (ibid.). In 1997, an Australian WTS (HDX) temple was built in Sydney while in 2002 another Wong Tai Sin (HDX) Temple was set up by a group of Hong Kong pilgrims from YQG in Sydney (ibid.). The detailed account of the existence of temples relating to HDX overseas was provided to demonstrate the local and global dimension of HDX culture. HDX as a cultural heritage has therefore been represented as a symbol of transnational Chineseness. On the one hand, Jinhua's HDX legends, oral narratives, and temples were objectified as roots of HDX culture (*Zhongguo Jinhua Shuang Long Jing Qu Guan Wei Hui and Zhongguo Chengshi Jingzhengli Yanjiu Hui* 2010: 4). On the other hand, the translocal HDX culture in Jinhua (Lanxi, Jinhua Mountain, Chisong), Hong Kong, Guangdong (Luofushan, Fangcun, Foshan, Xinhui, Donguan), Australia, and the United States has been highlighted to emphasize the transnational Chinese identity.

While the Chinese government has presented HDX as a Chinese cultural heritage and translocal ties of HDX have been highlighted, a page in the Chinese (Zhonghua) HDX Wenhua website has been designated for worshippers living in different places inside and outside China to enjoy a religious tour of HDX temples in cyberspace. The virtual religious and touring experiences allow a further linkage between different HDX temples to be drawn in the Internet networks (http://www.huangdaxian.org/newsdetail2.aspx?id=37, http://www.huangdaxian.org/newslist.aspx?typeid=21). Spectacular pictures of Zugong and Jinhua Guan are posted with a narration of their histories, locations, and uniqueness. It is now possible to get a preview of visiting the HDX temples through seeing spectacular pictures of some of these temples in Jinhua and Hong Kong, as well as reading the stories, legends of HDX, and its development globally on the Internet. In addition, drama series of HDX were uploaded so viewers could understand more about HDX and watch these videos any time and from any place. In essence, this is to experience HDX vicariously, as a simulacrum through cyberspace. Such an experience in cyberspace has rearranged our sense of space and time as Harvey (1990) suggested. What is real is not necessarily the actual visit to the temple and the reading of Daoist scripts related to HDX, but the virtual visit conducted through the Internet.

The virtual visitors are now not only allowed to shuttle from one link to another but are also invited to recite prayer. Indeed, religious services are also available on the Internet—a "virtual" temple of HDX in cyberspace. The website provides a way of showing respect to the deity which is not much different from one made during an actual visit to a HDX temple. First, one could choose to recite or copy Daoist scripts via the Internet, which is a common way for pilgrims to practice Daoism. Second, one could choose to make an offering of water, incense, flowers, or fruits via the Internet. Third, one could make a wish, or ask for blessings, or express gratefulness upon the completion of a wish. While these services are free, donations are no doubt also welcome and could be arranged through the Internet as well. In order to enjoy these services, one has to submit an application by providing some basic personal information in electronic form. We could see from the website that these religious services are occasionally used by tourists and pilgrims.

The most interesting experience is the provision of divination services by pulling bamboo sticks via the Internet. While the "real" divination is conducted through shaking the bamboo cup filled with bamboo sticks gently until a single bamboo stick drops out, the "simulacra" praying activity on the Internet is done through a single click (http://www.huangdaxian.org/Qian.aspx). Interestingly, the simulacrum experience is more "real" than the "original" in two ways. First, a set of instructions is clearly given to the participant regarding the prayers needed before starting with the bamboo sticks. The best time and condition to pray is clearly written, such as between 11 and 1 a.m., at midnight or around noon. There were also instructions to be sincere and to concentrate on the question or prayer for 2 minutes, as well as starting the process after washing hands, if not after a shower (http://www.huangdaxian.org/Qian.aspx). Certain moments are considered forbidden times, such as during a thunder storm, heavy rain, and after sex (ibid.). After reading the instructions, one should then think about the issue that one wants to pray for and then click a button, and a bamboo stick will be selected. The bamboo stick still needs to be certified after a second set of rituals is conducted. In this step, the participant needs to obtain positive results for three consecutive times while casting the moon blocks (shengbei) (http://www.huangdaxian.org/Qian.aspx). Such a sophisticated procedure and detailed set of rules are often absent when one conducts the actual process of divination with real bamboo sticks at the temples. This is because most participants do not know the "proper procedures" of divination. If there is a specialist at the temple, the instructions regarding the proper procedure for divination would likely be brief. Most participants would just be told to kneel down and focus on the issue at hand before shaking the bamboo cup. Nevertheless, a detailed set of rules in cyberspace has encouraged participants to go through standardized rules and rituals before pulling the bamboo sticks. This has made the cyberspace experience of divination more elaborate and rule-bound than the actual divination experience at temples which is more casually conducted. Once the bamboo stick has been certified through the second step of casting the moon blocks, the original scripts of the text for the selected bamboo stick would appear in classical Chinese language together with an interpretation delivered in modern Chinese. Thus, with the development of Internet technology and its popularization in China, praying activities conducted in cyberspace have also become a clear experience of replication at a real temple. Upon checking on the profile of the users of these services, it is noted that some have claimed to be tourists while others appear to be pilgrims and claimed to be HDX worshippers. Nevertheless, the visitors who consume this service are from the Lower Yangtze Delta and not overseas Chinese from different parts of the world as intended by the government.

Hometown of HDX and transnational ties as attractions

It is clear that the officials at Jinhua have been working tirelessly in asserting Jinhua as the authentic homeland of HDX through various cultural media strategies and appropriating HDX as a cultural resource to attract overseas visitors and investment. Today, temple visitors in Jinhua have fostered the development of tourism. Nevertheless, the majority of the visitors to these temples are domestic visitors, and not overseas pilgrims as intended by the government. More importantly, substantial investment was not brought to Jinhua by the overseas pilgrims as expected by the government. This section examines why domestic visitors are motivated to visit the temples. It investigates the various ways that visitors appropriate the temples and how they are related to the government's promotion of HDX heritage and temples. It examines how Jinhua as the authentic hometown of HDX and HDX as the symbol of Chineseness have been received or negotiated by pilgrims and tourists in CSDY and Zugong.

Before we analyze how domestic pilgrims and tourists respond to the representations constructed by the Jinhua prefectural-level city government, we will first consider the respective features of pilgrims and tourists. Tourists compare new sites with other sites of attractions while pilgrims commit to religious sites because of their spiritual power and have a narrower frame of comparison (Oakes and Sutton 2010: 9). Nevertheless, the boundary between domestic tourists and pilgrims is not always clear because their experiences often overlap (Oakes and Sutton 2010). Both pilgrims and tourists came when they were free from work and to enjoy the experience during the holidays (Naquin and Yu 1992, cited by Oakes and Sutton 2010: 9). Tourists imitate the ritual of pilgrims at religious sites while pilgrims join the tourists to appreciate the aesthetic aspect and to conduct sightseeing activities (Oakes and Sutton 2010: 9–10). Pilgrims and tourists can be understood in a continuum rather than in oppositional categories (Oakes and Sutton 2010: 9). Although pilgrims and tourists conduct similar activities at temples, pilgrims were motivated to visit religious sites primarily for religious reasons while tourists did so mainly for sightseeing and leisure.

It is clear that the best-received message by visitors is that Jinhua is the authentic hometown of the Daoist immortal, HDX. Many tourists came primarily because of the reputation of HDX in Jinhua and overseas, as well as the beautiful scenic surroundings.[13] Almost every domestic visitor we interviewed mentioned that Jinhua is the hometown of HDX, a famous god in Hong Kong or overseas. This is a dramatic change from the situation 30 years ago when SSY first went to Jinhua and found that almost nobody in Jinhua had heard of HDX. Thus, it is clear that narratives constructed by the Jinhua prefectural-level city government through various media strategies have successfully socialized the public into believing that Jinhua is the hometown of HDX, thus helping to turn HDX temples into popular tourist sites. Today, temples most frequently visited by pilgrims and tourists were newly built ones—Zugong, CSDY, Chisonggong (which is within the jurisdiction of CSDY), and Jinhua Guan (which is next to the Double Dragon Cave).

Visitors at Jinhua Guan and Zugong include few domestic visitors (see Chapter 6).Most tourists come to Jinhua Guan after their visit to the Double Dragon Cave as the two places are located right next to each other.[14] Some of these tourists also went to Zugong, which is located on a hilltop, after they went to the must-visit national-grade Dragon Double Cave Scenic Park in the middle of the hill and the Jinhua Guan next to the cave (see more in Chapter 5). Recently, more visitors went to Zugong after touring the Dragon Double Cave because the management team started issuing admission tickets for both sites as a joint and discounted package. Most tourists went with the aim of sightseeing though they also bowed and prayed at the temple.

In CSDY and Chisonggong, the tourists were primarily from Jinhua and nearby provinces. Organized groups were also sent by schools or various associations involving senior citizens, especially during the spring and autumn seasons. It was not unusual to see tours of over 100 senior citizens arriving in several big buses. School children were also brought here on school excursions. We also found families spending their vacations and employees holding their companies' recreational activities at CSDY, with a key attraction being that the temple does not charge admission fees. We also saw domestic tourists from nearby areas driving to CSDY, most of whom were middle-class people on holiday. Touring around, consuming fresh air, gazing at the scenic environment and exotic translocal HDX cultures are experiences of modernity for these tourists in Urry's (1995) terms. It is modernity brought by market reforms that "pulls people away from home in a quest for pleasure in other places, due to advances in technology, living standards and 'pushes' people away from home to tourist destinations for relaxation, recreation, the experience of change, novelty, fantasy, and freedom" (Wang 2000: 215). These outings to the temples on weekends and public holidays provide pleasure and a break from working life and are what Graburn (1989) called a modern pilgrimage, which combines religious pursuit with a refreshing and soothing experience for the tourists.

In addition, there were also pilgrims who visited CSDY regularly. These pilgrims were from different backgrounds and occupations and came from nearby places in Zhejiang province. Pilgrims came to express gratitude for good life and prayed for a wide range of wishes, such as better business opportunities, specific business deals health, family harmony, and special issues (see Chapter 6). There were businessmen who sealed their contracts at temples after praying together. Indeed, religious practices address needs in the present situation with a strong emphasis on this world orientation. The concerns expressed by the pilgrims are rather similar to those found elsewhere in China. In Chaozhou, villagers expressed concerns over "how to get ahead" in the market economy, "marriage, child bearing, health, and relational harmony" (Eng and Lin 2002: 1273). In Beijing, Fischer (2012: 348–349) also found that different religious practices at the temple are coping strategies that deal with morality issues brought about by market reforms.

In Chisonggong, CSDY, Jinhua Guan, and Zugong, we observed that most tourists bowed and some prayed while enjoying the scenic environment around the temple. All pilgrims also seemed to enjoy and appreciate the spectacular environment around the temples while praying. Both pilgrims and tourists often praised the quality of fresh air and the beautiful scenery surrounding Zugong and CSDY.[15] Pilgrims went through the experience of spiritual enhancement by praying while tourists enjoyed scenic sights through exploring the exotic sites in their leisure time (Oakes and Sutton 2010: 9–10).

In addition, part of the attraction of HDX temples to tourists is predicated on the transnational flow of capital, information, and religious beliefs. This knowledge is successfully constructed, presented, and promoted by entrepreneurs, government, media, and temple management teams and are observed by visitors. Indeed, the transnational links mark HDX temples out as distinctive and remarkable, thus becoming an important differentiator for HDX temples. The transnational attraction involves the inflow of financial support, information, and knowledge from Taiwan and Hong Kong. Tourists pay attention to the donations of pilgrims from Hong Kong and Taiwan, as well as those from mainland China, which was recorded in the plaques at CSDY and Zugong. Tourists and pilgrims also look at the exotic icon of HDX at CSDY, which was derived from the interaction of local and overseas religious cultures. The icon of HDX at CSDY was a painting, which was said to be a self-portrait of the god and was modeled closely on its counterpart at a small temple in Hong Kong run by YQG. However, many elderly pilgrims did not really like the paper icon because it was too exotic for them.

In 2007, the temple manager finally replaced the paper icon with a bronze statue. Consequently, the design was changed to a younger-looking version of HDX in CSDY. The new icon was originally designed after the one at SSY. However, the design was claimed to be rejected by HDX through *fuji*—a type of spirit medium-ship that is supposed to relay the thoughts of a deity through spirit-writing (see Chapter 2)—at YQG in Hong Kong. The reason, according to spirit-writing (*fuji*) in Hong Kong, was that Huang became immortal when he was young and there-fore his image should be younger (see Chapter 5). Eventually, the icon followed the instruction given by *fuji* (spirit-writing) at YQG in Hong Kong. Interestingly, original iconographies at old temples (Chisonggong and Erhuangjunci) did not play an influential role in shaping the icon at CSDY. In contrast, we found the influential leadership role of the "peripheries" (Hong Kong) in determining the iconography of HDX. Thus, networks of localities linked with a transnational orientation seem to be more important in temple-building and iconography.[16]

Some tourists also paid attention to the huge notice boards at the temple dis-playing information and pictures about the free medical services and charitable activities offered by the temple (see Chapter 6).

In fact, charitable activities of different kinds were displayed and narrated in detail (Figure 4.1). The amount of money donated and the number of benefi-ciaries or schools benefiting from CSDY's charitable activities were also noted. While these charitable practices were claimed to follow SSY's approach of *puji-quansan* (to act benevolently and to teach benevolence), which reveals the Hong Kong influence, they also enable CSDY to create an attraction in the eyes of its visitors (see Chapter 6). Charitable practices conducted by CSDY reveal civic concerns. To visitors and residents in local communities, they are also an impres-sive gesture to foster morality. Such activities have therefore generated goodwill and moral authority for the temple (see Chapter 6).[17] These are also unintended consequences not anticipated by the Jinhua prefectural-level city government.

Negotiating moral virtues embedded in HDX legends

After understanding why domestic visitors went to Zugong, Jinhua Guan, CSDY, and Chisonggong, this section will further analyze how they responded to HDX legends and the embedded moral virtues which were promoted by the Jinhua

Figure 4.1 Notice board displaying charitable scholarships for underprivileged girls.

prefectural-level city government. We will also examine how legends became popularized in ways not expected by the local government, as well as how HDX has enriched the religious life of devoted pilgrims, both of which were not the intended consequences of the Jinhua prefectural-level city government's promotion efforts.

Legends of HDX being a healer have been popularized and well-received in many regions. This led to many informal domestic pilgrimage tours organized to visit CSDY. These tours were run by spirit mediums, who claimed to have healing powers when possessed by HDX. Some spirit mediums claimed to have healing powers when possessed by other Daoist or Buddhist gods. These spirit mediums attracted followers who believed that they had received or could receive healing after sessions with them.

By 2013, there were around a dozen spirit mediums from Jinhua who had claimed to be possessed by HDX. These spirit mediums and their followers usually came to CSDY during the birthday of HDX.[18] In addition to them, there were many such spirit mediums living in other parts of the Lower Yangtze Delta, such as Shanghai, Hangzhou, Nanjing, and Wuxi. Some other spirit mediums and their followers were from even further places, such as Dalian, Henan, Beijing, Xian, Guizhou, and Xiamen, and came all the way to CSDY.[19] These spirit mediums and their followers came in groups from as large as a few dozen to a few hundred on the first or fifteenth of each lunar month. Some of these pilgrims stayed overnight at the resort hotel while others came on day trips.

Most of the members on these informal pilgrimage tours were elderly women. These women often conducted various pilgrimage tours to different Daoist and Buddhist temples, especially during the respective birthdays of the various gods.[20] At CSDY, these pilgrims prayed and chanted but did not perform possession-trance rituals. These pilgrimage trips, including those to CSDY, reflect how these elderly pilgrims spent their leisure time. Besides, the pilgrimage tours have enriched their religious life. Nevertheless, these religious practices and gathering activities at CSDY would be easily considered as superstitious and retrogressive by the state.

Apart from pilgrims, many of the local domestic visitors were drawn to CSDY because of its reputation for charitable activities, such as free medical services and financial support to underprivileged children[21] (see more in Chapter 6). These charitable activities reveal positive moral virtues, which are widely applauded and appreciated by the public and the visitors. In contrast, the moral virtues of HDX put forward by the government through cartoons and drama series were hardly mentioned by any visitors.[22] Instead, many domestic visitors interviewed were particularly impressed by the generosity of CSDY in supporting charitable activities in Jinhua. To them, the charitable practices of the temple were really rare when most people in post-reforms China are desperate to make money only for themselves. As Yan (2011: 40) wrote, "despite the continued insistence of socialist civilization and collective ethics in the official discourse, the most important thing in the popular discourse and moral practice has been a shift away from an authoritarian, collective ethics of responsibilities and self-sacrifice towards a new, optional, and individualistic ethics of rights and self-development." It is indeed under this current sociopolitical environment that CSDY's charitable activities have gained moral authority for the temple to attract visitors (see more in Chapter 6).

One of the most striking things was found among the primary students who came during school excursions when we were there in 2007. These children drew petition pictures and hung them on the bushes in a corner of the temple. The idea of hanging their wishes on wishing trees has its origin in Japan and has also spread to Taiwan. The Taiwanese temple manager of CSDY introduced this practice to the temple. We discovered that many of the pictures drawn by the students conveyed positive moral virtues, such as praising honesty, and denouncing corruption and greed. In one picture, the author claimed to be drawing a new version for the popular Chinese comic series—*Black Cat Detective* (Figure 4.2). The original series was about the black cat detective wandering around and stopping villains in the forest. In the picture the black cat detective actually committed corruption by accepting illegal gifts in the form of cash and luxurious banquets. Eventually, the black cat detective was jailed. The picture denounced the corruption of officials, which has been a serious social problem brought by market reforms in contemporary China. The message behind the drawing reflects the social discontent over the breakdown of moral virtues and urging moral reconstruction. In some ways, these children's petitions correspond symbolically to the efforts of the Jinhua prefectural-level city government to highlight the moral virtues of HDX through legends.

HDX as a symbol of multiple identities?

Although overseas visitors to HDX temples do not constitute the major group of visitors, it should still be interesting to analyze why they come to the HDX

Figure 4.2 A primary school girl drew the picture. In the picture, the black cat detective
committed corruption by accepting illegal gifts in the form of cash and
luxurious banquets. He was jailed later.

temples in Jinhua. We also analyze how Daoism or HDX roots-searching trips
grant different meanings to them and how are they different from or similar to the
projection of the Chinese government in enhancing Chinese identities. The initial
visits of these YQG and SSY pilgrims in the 1980s were to search for the roots
of the Daoist immortal in Jinhua (see Chapter 3). For these visitors, most of them
were curious to see the hometown of HDX while a few also attempted to explore
business opportunities in China. This search for roots brought together Hong Kong
visitors and officials in the city and county governments, via the United Front
and Federation of Returned Overseas Chinese. Jinhua has been conceptualized
as an authentic homeland of HDX where pilgrims from Hong Kong attempted to
reconnect with China. Pilgrims' knowledge of the development of Daoism and the
HDX heritage in China has been raised. The roots-searching experience has also
improved pilgrims' understanding of Chinese religion and China's development.

Hong Kong pilgrims' attitudes toward Jinhua have also changed over time as
interactions between them and officials at Jinhua increase. Pilgrimage tours on
behalf of YQG and SSY to HDX temples started to dwindle and have become
rather infrequent in the last two decades though some individuals from SSY and
YQG visited Jinhua and participated in the HDX Cultural Festival in 2007 and
2010. Neither YQG nor SSY were strongly attached to any of the HDX temples in
Jinhua. This is different from the situation at the Mazu temples in Fujian, where

pilgrimage trips to Fujian were important for worshippers in Taiwan to enhance their status and prestige back home (see Dean 1998: 265). Pilgrims from Hong Kong SSY or YQG neither speak the dialect in Jinhua nor have any kinship connections with the locals and hence lack good reasons to visit on a regular and frequent basis. It is unrealistic to expect overseas pilgrims to make the journey regularly to Jinhua merely to see the exotic "authentic hometown" of the immortal without them becoming integrated into the networks of the local communities on a long-term basis, even though honorary citizenships were granted to some members of SSY who donated to build YYY in Lanxi. In fact, pilgrims from SSY were rather disappointed at YYY's development after having donated to its construction. In contrast to the HDX temple managed by SSY in Hong Kong, which is a successful temple in many aspects (Lang and Ragvald 1993), YYY is far away from the Hong Kong model and has not developed as planned (see details in Chapter 5). Hong Kong pilgrims' intention of reviving worship of HDX in the Jinhua through the temple of YYY was overly idealized and romanticized. Subsequently, pilgrims from SSY became rather cautious about making further donations and commitments to any HDX temple in Jinhua.[23] Such an experience allows the Hong Kong pilgrims to draw a distinction between the practices of managing HDX temples in HK and in China and thus between Hong Kong people and Mainlanders.

Similarly, the roots-searching and touring experience of Taiwanese visitors also provides them with a better understanding of Chinese religion as well as its latest cultural and economic development. These pilgrims visit several famous Daoist sites in various parts of China, with Jinhua being one of the stopovers. They stayed at the resort hotel in CSDY and visited both CSDY and Zugong. To them, these temples in Jinhua were authentic Daoist heritage sites where HDX practiced and attained immortality. Their trips were partly to search for the roots of the authentic Daoist heritage in China and also partly to enjoy the exotic landscape in China.

The visits of Taiwanese to Daoist temples in China offer them a sense of familiarity because of their similarity to those found in Taiwan. Some informants claimed that the trip allowed them to witness religious freedom in China, which was different from what was heard in Taiwan. Other Taiwanese were amazed by the number of high-rise buildings and the rapid development of the Chinese economy. One Taiwanese actually pointed out that Jinhua had more tall buildings and the city looked even better than Tainan in Taiwan. This is significantly different from their stereotypes of China. During a religious tour organized by CSDY for the Taiwanese pilgrims in 1998, senior officials from the Religious Affairs Bureau in Beijing and Zhejiang, as well as representatives from Baiyunguan (the most prestigious Daoist temple in China), entertained them with banquets and welcome speeches. Officials from the Jinhua prefectural-level city government hosted banquets and touring activities at HDX temples for these visitors. These gestures have earned positive comments from the Taiwanese pilgrims. Indeed, the banquets and entertainment activities in the religious tour have also drawn the Taiwanese closer to the mainland Chinese. They also found comfort in similarity, such as the drinking and toasting culture, which is a familiar Chinese hospitality culture to the Taiwanese. Such a process of Chinese religious and cultural exposure in mainland China thus enhanced the ability of these Taiwanese visitors to identify with the Chinese cultural identity. Meanwhile, the Taiwanese visitors were aware of the difference between HDX temples in Jinhua and other Daoist temples in Taiwan. Daoist temples in Taiwan often have a longer history while HDX temples in Jinhua were newly constructed because of the suppression of religion during the Cultural Revolution. In sum, the distinction between themselves as Taiwanese and the mainland Chinese was drawn at one level while the identification with Chineseness was also enhanced through cultural exposure at another level.

In addition, the Jinhua Hometown Association in Hong Kong also arranged for its members to visit CSDY and Zugong during the HDX Cultural Festivals in four of the years between 2006 to 2011.[24] This is indeed a response to the prefectural-level city government which would like to have more pilgrims from Hong Kong to support the HDX Cultural Festival and to explore investment opportunities in Jinhua.[25] The management team and members of the Hometown Association in Hong Kong usually have a pro-China political stance and are seen to identify closely with China, which explained why they took the initiative in organizing these tours. In each of these tours, there were more than 100 people. In 2010, members from Jinhua Hometown Association formed a "Hong Kong Jinhua Hometown Association Economic Exploration Group" to conduct a Jinhua HDX Cultural Tour. The tour only costed around HK$1,200 per person. The local governments in Jinhua not only subsidized expenses on local transport, food, and lodging but also provided sumptuous gifts of precious Jinhua ham and other local souvenirs to these participants.

In the four-day trip, there were few activities planned on the first and the last day. On the second day, the tour attended celebrations of the HDX Cultural Tourism Festival at CSDY and Zugong, which are temples managed by the Double Dragon Cave Management Team under the Jinhua prefectural government. On the third day, the tour took a trip to Yiwu, which is famous for its small commodities trade. On the fourth day, the tour was dissolved and individuals were then free to visit their respective hometowns in Jinhua for a few days or weeks before returning to Hong Kong. From the perspective of the participants, they joined the tour because it was an attractive and cheap package, as well as a good opportunity to visit relatives and families at their hometown, to conduct some sightseeing activity in Jinhua, to explore possible investment opportunities, and to pray at HDX temples.

It is however important to note that the primary interests of those visitors were neither to conduct cultural religious activities related to HDX nor to explore business opportunities although these were the primary motives of the Jinhua prefectural-level city government. In fact, these members did not know about HDX in Jinhua before moving to Hong Kong and neither were they regular worshippers of HDX in Hong Kong. Although they are aware of the popularity of HDX in Hong Kong, many of them did not know that HDX was from their hometown—Jinhua. The trips to temples of HDX in the god's hometown at Jinhua have caused them to feel proud of their own Jinhua ethnicity, an ethnicity which is the same as that of the popular god HDX. As mentioned by an informant, he felt proud of the Jinhua ethnicity because HDX as a god from Jinhua had been widely worshipped by Hong Kong people who are predominantly Cantonese. In addition, these visits to Jinhua were also opportunities for them to enjoy reunion with relatives back in their hometown. Thus, the visits to Jinhua have also renewed the visitors' Jinhua identity although they had lived in Hong Kong for decades and also identified themselves as Hong Kongers at the same time.

During these tours, visitors were very pleased by the hospitality of the government. Upon the completion of the tour, various local governments sent cars to fetch these people from Jinhua and sent them to their home village at different counties. During the banquets and sightseeing tours, the Hong Kong visitors were able to catch up with the development of Jinhua and China. Indeed, they were all very delighted by the rapid development of China and felt proud of their motherland. Such an experience therefore enhanced their Chinese identity. Meanwhile, the special treatment that they received was also due to the fact that they were Hong Kongers. Thus, these trips during the Cultural Festivals have allowed the Hong Kong visitors to renew and affirm their Jinhua ethnicity, Hong Kong identity, as well as Chinese identity.

Conclusions

This chapter has demonstrated how the Jinhua prefectural-level city government took the lead in reviving and constructing the HDX cultural heritage and promoting temples for economic development and tourism purposes. Authenticity of HDX heritage is entangled in various discursive historical, legal, and cultural practices. HDX has been represented as an authentic cultural heritage in Jinhua through cartoons, drama series, traditional opera, branding strategies, and cultural festivals by the Jinhua prefectural-level government, temple-management team, and media. HDX legends as a cultural heritage have also been institutionalized as a provincial and a national intangible cultural heritage. HDX has been used by cadres and officials to create a common identity or imagined community of Chinese living in different places, especially those outside the mainland in Hong Kong, Macau, and Taiwan. It is used as a symbol which aims to consolidate nationalism and reinforce a Chinese identity that transcends boundaries, both geographical and ideological. Indeed, HDX has been portrayed as an important symbol of local and transnational cultural heritage, which enhances both the Jinhua local identity and the transnational Chinese identity.

Apparently, the secular aspects of HDX have been promoted in various branding strategies, such as promoting the moral values of HDX legends, mobilizing new and creative cultural production of HDX and organizing touristic activities relating to HDX while the religious and magical aspects of HDX have been downplayed. Indeed, the Jinhua prefectural-level city government has framed the newly revived heritage relating to HDX with the objective of enhancing economic development within the socioeconomic settings of post-reform China. This is in line with Siu's (1990) earlier analysis in which the revived traditions, festivals, and rituals have new meanings because they are both framed within the new social and institutional structure and are reflective of the local political economy. Economic, cultural, legal, and historical practices of HDX heritage have been analyzed discursively through the domestic and transnational dynamics, local and provincial forces, as well as the interactive flows of overseas and local resources. The complex meanings of the revived, recycled, and reinvented symbol of HDX were also delineated through an analysis of how the power of state and local governments has been received and negotiated by tourists and pilgrims.

It is clear that the knowledge of Jinhua as the hometown of HDX is well-received by all visitors. Nevertheless, tourists and pilgrims appropriate and consume other representations constructed by the government in different ways. Instead of enhancing the transnational Chinese identity as predicted by the state, a complex, multifaceted process of identities is formulated and negotiated by overseas pilgrims in their respective roots-searching and pilgrimage experiences. The connection of these pilgrims and visitors to the mainland is being renewed from time to time through the increased interaction and flow of information, finance, and cultures between them and their counterparts in China.

Although the local government intends to authenticate HDX as a cultural heritage and downplay its religious meanings, domestic pilgrimage tours were attracted to CSDY primarily for religious reasons. To these pilgrims, legends of HDX have not attracted public attention to the moral virtues as the Jinhua government had intended but have instead popularized HDX's magical healing powers. Meanwhile, the touring and praying experiences have enriched the pilgrims' religious life. Through diverse ways of using the symbol of religion, some visitors seek leisure while others seek spiritual support or guidance to handle general moral issues. To different types of visitors, the meanings of HDX and the trips to temples have numerous and diverse meanings. Multiple ways of appropriating HDX and the temples have been considered as responses to both the official discourse constructed by the local governments and the unexpected reactions creatively appropriated by different visitors.

Notes

1 This chapter mainly focuses on the development of temples in the Jindong county-level division, which has been directly under the Jinhua prefectural city government.
2 Yang (2008: 17) also mentioned that villagers in Wenzhou were troubled by the distinction between religion and superstition.
3 In Mount Tai, the secularization process is done through revolutionizing the sacred space (Dott 2010: 41) while the people who visited Mount Tai paid little attention to the revolutionary sites. Instead, they focused on the sunrise and natural scenery.
4 A discourse is considered as groups of ideas, images, representations, conventions, and practices, which are ways of discussion that define the scope of knowledge with specific historical and cultural meanings (Hall 1997: 6).
5 In 2003, the Chinese government introduced the "individual visit scheme" which allows residents of some cities in China to travel to Hong Kong and Macau on an individual basis with simplified procedures. This is different from earlier times when Mainlanders were only allowed to travel to Hong Kong and Macau on business visas or group tours.

Since 2007, residents from 49 cities have been allowed to travel to Hong Kong under this scheme (http://www.tourism.gov.hk/english/visitors/visitors_ind.html).

6 On the withering of state authority and power, see Siu (1990).

7 Cultural religious festival is also an occasion where the Buddhist monks and nuns from Thailand, China, and Tibet get together to learn and share their studies (Ryan and Gu 2010: 175).

8 In fact, there is a wide range of stories and legends about HDX and many are related to different aspects of his life as a shepherd and an immortal (see Chapter 2).

9 Mazu religious ritual in Meizhou in Fujian has been recognized as a national grade intangible cultural heritage in 2006, when China first started offering official recognition to intangible cultural heritage.

10 As early as 2007, the Deputy Mayor of Jinhua already mentioned that the hosting of the HDX Cultural Tourism Festival is an important preparatory activity for getting HDX temples in Guangdong, HK, Macau, and Jinhua ready for official consideration as intangible cultural heritage in the future (*Zhongguo, Jinhua Guoji Huangdaxian Wenhua Luyoujie Xinwen Fabu Hui Zai Xianggang Juxing* 2007: 19). Hong Kong SSY has however not been keen for a joint application and, at the time when the book was being written in 2013, SSY had instead submitted an application for Hong Kong's HDX folk beliefs to be recognized as intangible cultural heritage in Hong Kong as well as intangible cultural heritage at the national level.

11 Other temples relating to HDX in Jinhua are not mentioned because they are built by peasants and local investors who are not closely related to the local government.

12 On Internet religious experience, see Apolito 2005.

13 Zugong and CSDY are highly recommended by various travel brochures or tourism-related websites.

14 Jinhua Guan does not have any religious specialist and is contracted to a local villager who has good connections with the cadres managing the Double Dragon Cave. This villager is from Lutian village, which is located on the hilltop.

15 Both temples were chosen to be built on those two sites partly because of their beautiful surroundings.

16 The paper "self-portrait" of HDX has been moved to the administrative office for the temple management team, while the bronze statue is now placed at the main altar for tourists.

17 Indeed, SSY has always actively supported secular welfare projects in Hong Kong, such as building schools.

18 In fact, there were two or three spirit mediums in Chisong village. Others are from the local area.

19 Spirit mediums from Xiamen and Nanjing were men while others were women.

20 We met a group of women together with a spirit medium while attending the inauguration of HDX god at Gunglu temple in Huang Peng village. These women also visited CSDY and Xianyiguan on various other occasions.

21 For details of the charitable activities, see Chapter 6.

22 Instead, some villagers from Lanxi accounted for the peace and order through improved morality as resulting from the worship of HDX in YYY. One informant told us that worshippers of HDX would perform proper deeds because they know that the god was watching them.

23 Some members of YQG and SSY know each other and members of YYY heard of SSY's experience in Lanxi.

24 Mr Chow from Chisong HDX Association is the key figure who organized the trip. He himself is also a key member at the Dongyang Hometown Association and a member at Jinhua Hometown Association in Hong Kong.

25 Most hometown associations in Hong Kong have received annual financial subsidy from United Front to organize activities for members since the last decade.

5   Two grand temples in Jinhua

Introduction

After having shown how the Jinhua prefectural-level government has promoted and utilized the symbol of HDX for tourism and economic development, we now would like to investigate the details of the development of two temples, YYY and Zugong, which were constructed and managed by government-owned or government-linked companies. Zugong falls within the geographical scope of a national grade Double Dragon Cave Scenic Park, while YYY is located in Lanxi, a small town which is not near any scenic site. The development strategies of Zugong and YYY are similar to those found at scenic or ethnic heritage sites with governmental support where the secular aspect of the temples has been promoted. The scenic beauty as well as historical and cultural significance of the sites have been highlighted through media and branding strategies as well as cultural tourism festivals (see Chapter 4). Zugong and YYY are promoted by the local governments as temples in HDX's homeland, based on legends of the immortal (see Chapter 4). Temples are represented as a symbol of commonality between local and transnational Chinese in Hong Kong and Taiwan.

The sacred aspect of temples has been downplayed in the promotion process. This is very much due to the fact that the temple management teams are from the local governments. This characteristic is also found in many other government-managed temples in China. In Mount Tai, shrines and temples were renovated and monks and nuns were returned, nevertheless, religious and ritual elements were ignored officially in the promotional strategies. The state tries to use secular features, such as the addition of revolutionary sites to attract tourists and to overwrite the "superstitious" religious aspect of Mount Tai (Dott 2010: 34, 38–39). Similarly, the old Middle Temple was rebuilt by the Huanglong administration in Sichuan as a tourist attraction while the ritual components were omitted (Sutton and Kang 2010: 106–107). Although the local governments downplay the religious features, temples in those studies did not seem to have difficulty attracting visitors. Our analysis, however, shows that the temples we examined were unsuccessful in getting visitors. The beautification of the temple building, the provision of transport facilities, the promotion of the historical reputation of the immortal, and the location of Zugong in the scenic park all do not seem to be able to attract tourists and pilgrims. Why are they not successful in attracting visitors? Why and how have different strategies been consciously adopted by temple management teams at different times?

How do religious specialists, local people, and temple management teams play their respective roles in attempting to popularize the temples?

The building of YYY: turning overseas connection into economic capital

YYY was constructed by the Lanxi county-level government in Huang Peng village, which adjoins the town of Lanxi, a county 15 kilometres northwest of Jinhua. The total cost of YYY was around 1.5 million RMB, of which 40,000 RMB was contributed by villagers, and US $20,000 was donated by a Singaporean business man, who was a Daoist worshipper with business connections to one of the villagers. Indeed, it was the villagers who initially developed a plan to build a temple to the deity near the village, after they rediscovered that HDX, before he became a Daoist hermit and immortal was born in the village and lived there for some time (see Chapter 3). According to the villagers, the idea of building a temple to HDX was initiated by a female villager, who responded to the reawakened memories of him by claiming that the immortal had "possessed" her. It was after recovering from a serious illness that she made this claim, at which point she also became a spirit medium.[1] From that time onward, she began to call for a statue of HDX in the village temple. Evidently, she was talking about this for several years after being "possessed" by the deity. She claimed that HDX wanted to come home and would like to have a temple built for him.[2]

Subsequently, villagers started soliciting donations to build the temple. However, the-then Lanjiang township government soon took over the project because they believed that HDX's immense popularity in Hong Kong would draw pilgrims and tourists to the immortal's hometown at Lanxi.[3] This move also integrated the temple into the state's official Daoist religious establishment and the village into the national policy of economic development. The township government wanted the temple to be grand and spacious so that it would have the capacity to develop religious tourism and to receive thousands of pilgrims from Hong Kong and elsewhere. Ignoring the original plan of the villagers to build the temple on a small plot of land at the center of the village, the township government decided to locate it on a larger site at the edge of the village. The location of the temple was also decided by township officials because this spot was believed to be the place where the immortal and his brother had farmed. There were plans to build entertainment sites, restaurants, a hotel, and a charity school to support hearing-impaired children in the area.

The construction of the temple began in 1994, and was completed on 28 June 1995. Ms Hu was recruited by the Lanjing township government to work in the temple management committee.[4] She graduated from a university in Beijing and was recruited partly because of her English proficiency, which the government believed was an advantage given that this position requires frequent contact with foreign visitors. Ms Hu landed this job immediately after graduating from the university, and therefore did not have many social connections to call upon in managing the temple. She had no independent sources of wealth with which to cultivate and entertain visitors. She relied very much on the local government's open support in promoting the temple. As an employee of the township government, she was rather vulnerable to variability in the township government's support and also had to follow different development directions given to her by the government at various times.

For the establishment of YYY, various types of networks are utilized by Ms Hu and her team on behalf of the-then Lanjiang township government. Overseas connections with Hong Kong SSY were also tapped by the township government (see Chapter 3).[5] The Lanjiang township government solicited a donation of 1.3 million RMB from SSY to construct YYY. The donation was partly due to SSY's devotion and loyalty to HDX, and partly because of their curiosity over the native place of this deity. This interest in Jinhua created inflows of ideas and resources, and also triggered economic and religious exchanges between people in the "hometown" of the saint and those overseas. This is different from most other cases of temple renovation or reconstruction, in which overseas Chinese contributed funds to their hometowns as a sign of lineage unity or loyalty to their native place (Aijmer and Ho 2000: 126).

The township government constructed YYY with great enthusiasm. It was opened in September of 1995 amid great publicity and attracted thousands of visitors for the opening ceremonies, including a large contingent from the SSY and important officials from the city and from the county. They had the ambition of developing the local economy through attracting tourists, especially Hong Kong pilgrims. The township government promoted the reputation of the immortal in the local region through working together with the Lanxi HDX Research Association to provide historical evidence of his existence (see Chapter 3). Ms Hu worked closely with the Association to organize seminars and to promote historical findings regarding the legends and stories of HDX (see Chapter 4).[6] Her position in the local government enabled her to mobilize various government-related offices to support the revival of HDX histories, which has enhanced the reputation of the temple. Such acts of reviving history, local legends, and folk customs relating to the immortal, as well as connecting with overseas Chinese, are in close compliance with the state's religious policy (see Chapter 4).

At the same time, the management committee, headed by Ms Hu, also had great support from the Party Secretary of Lanxi at that time, Zheng Yueming. He joined Lanxi's office in January 1994, and paid special attention to cultural tourism. In particular, he encouraged the use of local cultural resources, such as HDX, to develop tourism. From 1995 to 1997, some tours were therefore directed to YYY from Shanghai through his connections. According to Ms Hu, those were the best years, and the temple managed to get a regular flow of visitors and pilgrims. Some of these pilgrims have been keen supporters of YYY till today. These pilgrims include several Hong Kong investors in Zhejiang, as well as some worshippers from Nanjing, Zhejiang, and Wenzhou.

The decline of YYY

Opened with high hopes, within 3 years YYY was attracting few visitors, and the buildings were beginning to deteriorate. The township government managed to bring in some tour groups from the nearby region through its connections in the initial years when the temple was first built, but these tourists were neither enough to create employment nor were they sustainable. A few years after the completion of the temple, the local government was no longer interested in promoting this temple to tourists after the key official, Zheng, who was in charge of it left office. YYY faced much difficulty in retaining the support of the government officials to promote the temple. There were no more organized tour groups mobilized by the township government from nearby areas. YYY is also not able to get any spill-over tourists because it is not located next to any major sightseeing spot in Lanxi. Later, the local government transferred the responsibility for overseeing and promoting the temple to the local Tourism Bureau, with the hope that their expertise in promoting the city outside the region might increase the number of visitors to the temple. But this had little or no effect on the temple's fortunes.

Meanwhile, Ms Hu also tried hard to maintain close contact with SSY, hoping to attract more tourists from Hong Kong. Members in the committee visited SSY almost every year at the beginning. When Huang Yuntian, the then-chairman of SSY, passed away in the late 1990s, Ms Hu and other members in the management team attended his funeral in Hong Kong. Nevertheless, these visits were not able to draw them closer to the members of SSY.

After 1997, the reunification anxiety faded away in Hong Kong, and the nostalgic sentiment to visit the immortal's native place also subsided. This is very different from the Taiwanese who have remained keen on praying regularly at revived temples in their hometowns (e.g., Dean and Zheng 2010). The Taiwanese also had the added incentive of visiting their kin when they come to pray at the revived temples. Although key members of SSY were given the titles of honorary citizens at Huang Peng village, they did not visit Jinhua frequently because none of them had even distant relatives living in the area. In fact, there were fewer and fewer visitors at YYY. The YYY temple was not well maintained and developed despite the donations by the SSY. There was not enough money to sustain any local charitable activity as was planned earlier. Thus, SSY was disappointed with the development of YYY. As the trust between SSY and the management committee weakened, the ties and exchanges between the two organizations waned. SSY did not respond positively when YYY requested for further donations from the SSY to renovate some of the temple buildings, which had begun to deteriorate within a few years after their construction due to a lack of proper maintenance. SSY also stopped visiting YYY regularly, and there were also very few organized tours from SSY members later.[7]

We visited the temple in 1996, 1999, 2000, 2003, and 2007, but noticed fewer worshippers or visitors in our later visits. There was only one fortune-teller and one woman—the ex-village head's wife—selling incense and candles for praying. Inside the one-hectare temple compound, there were often no more than two or three worshippers during our visits. Sometimes, there were none (Figure 5.1). There were priests, but we hardly saw any ritual performances at the temple. The temple was rather quiet most of the time. The large paved plaza in front of the temple compound—designed to accommodate an anticipated stream of buses and taxis

Figure 5.1 Empty courtyard in front of YYY.

off-loading worshippers—was always empty. The spacious parking lot in front of the temple became a place that was sometimes used by peasants to dry their crops. The shop spaces on both sides of the lane leading to the temple, which was supposed to be filled by shops selling souvenirs or incense, were empty. In fact, they were never opened as there were insufficient visitors to support these businesses.[8]

The temple was rather vacant most of the time when we visited there. It soon began to show signs of disrepair due to poor maintenance, which probably reduced visitor numbers further. Few ritual performances were conducted by the religious specialists. We found priests and priestesses hanging around at the temple, chatting, or watching us. In 2000, we received further confirmation of the decline from villagers whose business dealings with the temple also had declined sharply since the first year of its operation.[9] For example, we met a villager whose business included buying used candle wax from the main temple which he melted down, re-cast into candles, and then sold back to the main temple for resale to worshippers (Chan and Lang 2007) (Figure 5.2). In the first year of the main temple's operation in 1996, he had been able to buy between seven and eight tons of wax from the temple. By the late 1990s, he was able to buy only two or three tons from the temple. In 1999/2000, he had been able to buy only one ton of used candle wax. While a villager's estimates of his purchases of used candle wax are obviously not a methodologically rigorous means of determining a temple's income, the interview reinforced our conviction that the temple had suffered a serious decline in the stream of worshippers.

Figure 5.2 Worshippers lighting candles, with used candle wax collected underneath the candles (Zugong temple, Jinhuashan).

Due to the lack of visitors and income at the temple, YYY even had difficulty paying the salaries of the priests on a regular basis in 2000. At that time, the temple had a priest and seven priestesses living in a row of huts behind one of the buildings. The priestesses had come as a group, after the Lanxi city government asked the provincial Daoist Association to help them find some Daoists to perform ceremonies at the temple. But their incomes were much lower than they expected. In Hangzhou, the priestesses had been paid a monthly base salary of about 200 RMB, and with additional money earned from performing rituals for visitors, they said they earned 500–600 RMB. In Lanxi, they evidently did not get a share of the funds which visitors paid to the temple for special ceremonies to supplement their base pay of 160 RMB. They felt they had been deceived about the prospects of the Lanxi temple, were eager to leave, and intended to do so as soon as they completed their one year contracts. During our visit in 2000, they complained that they had not been paid for several months because the temple had received few visitors.

Meanwhile, the priest tried to increase his income by spending much of his time visiting other towns to provide various services to clients (traveling to these towns on his motorcycle, and receiving requests for his services on his cell phone). This nominally temple-based priest was increasingly resorting to (and no doubt learning from) the same kind of "private practice" as the so-called *sanju daoshi* or non-temple-based Daoists (see Yang, 2003: 193–197). This was evidently more profitable and interesting than waiting for the few visitors inside the temple. On our fourth visit in 2003, the priest and all the priestesses had left because of the lack of decent salaries.

Since 2000, the YYY was entering a period of quiet crisis. The SSY hardly came and did not offer additional financial support to the temple, local visitors were sparse, temple income was low and probably declining, the priest and the priestesses had decamped, and some of the temple buildings were becoming decrepit (as we observed during one of our visits).

Popularization of HDX belief: disillusioned villagers

Although YYY has not been able to attract visitors, religious and cultural practices relating to HDX have been popularized in Huang Peng village. A traditional festival that was held during Chinese New Year—known as the Dragon Parade—was revived by the Huang Peng villagers and renamed as HDX Lungyouhui (HDX Dragon Parade). The parade was terminated during the Cultural Revolution but was revived in 1995. This festival is held annually on 15th day of the lunar calendar in January.[10] It is meant for the purification of the community and also for seeking the blessings of HDX as well as other gods in Gunglu temple at the village. The parade now starts from YYY and ends at Gunglu temple, which is a small village temple at Huang Peng village. The annual participation by over a hundred villagers in this parade has turned out to be an engaging experience for them, and that has helped to strengthen the appeal of the deity in the village. Nevertheless, villagers had no recollection of any worship of HDX in this parade in the past. The renaming of the traditional festival to honor HDX highlights the growing importance of the deity in local religious and cultural life. As a recycled traditional festival, this festival has been reinvented by local villagers to bless the community in purification rituals. Indeed, the (re)popularization of religious symbols (such as HDX) often involves a process of recycling tradition. As was also found in the case of Mount Tai, locks were introduced to enhance conjugal relationships through granting new meanings to the fertility goddess Bixia Yuanjun (Dott 2010: 34). As at Mount Tai (Dott 2010), our studies at Huang Peng demonstrate a process of inventing new practices and meanings through recycling rituals.

While Huang Peng villagers have increasingly identified with HDX, they were also frustrated by the fact that the township officials had maintained complete control over the temple. They tolerated it in the hope that these officials, with their further plans to build supporting facilities such as restaurants and entertainment spots, would deliver on these promises to stimulate economic development. Upon the final completion of the temple, the villagers were however infuriated that they had to pay an entrance fee to visit it, feeling that it should have been waived for them. To appease them, the temple management first agreed to waive the fee for villagers who arrived at the temple before 7:30 in the morning, and decided to waive the fee altogether without any time restriction in 2007.[11]

Although the township government initially promised to arrange jobs for villagers whose lands were sold to build the temple, it failed to deliver on this promise. Only a few villagers managed to get jobs in temple-related businesses, such as in fortune-telling and selling incense at the temple. The villagers in Huang Peng were well aware of this decline, discussed it freely, and attributed it to poor management. Some villagers suspected that part of the donation from SSY was used to purchase a new car for local cadres. In addition, the villagers also complained that the financial records of the temple were not open to the public. They also said that admission fees were charged and donations were received without records or receipts.

Meanwhile, the villagers at Huang Peng were also skeptical about the religious specialists. According to them, the priests did not do their job well enough, and the temple was unfrequented most of the time. While villagers expressed understanding on some behaviors of the priests, such as meat-eating for health reasons, they could not tolerate other forms of misconduct which violated the moral expectations of priests.[12]

Apparently, the residents in the local communities near YYY did not develop a sense of cultural self-identification with the temple because the temple seemed to have little (*xianghuo*) "incense and fire" and religious specialists did not seem to conduct their duties properly. Nevertheless, villagers are still devoted to HDX. It is clear that the villagers did not give up on their interest in religion or temple-related activities. They largely abandoned the large state-run temple on the outskirts of the village. Instead, they went more frequently to a small but convenient Gunglu temple located within their village, and in due course they also raised sufficient funds to install a new statue of the deity HDX in that temple.

On 13 December 2000, villagers installed the statue of HDX at their own village temple, Gunglu Temple,[13] and ignored the larger statue of the same deity in YYY. The villagers had collected funds for several days of opera performances to coincide with the event and had hired an opera troupe from the province. Local opera was performed to entertain the god (and villagers) for 5 days and 6 nights at a total cost of 8,000 RMB. Villagers donated over 300 catties of rice, vegetables as well as other food, and the whole ceremony cost around 13,000 RMB.

We attended the installation and "dotting the eyes" ceremony for that statue, before sunrise, along with the opera performance in the village held to mark the event. The ceremony took place at 5 o'clock in the morning, but the temple was crowded with villagers, worshippers, and beggars from nearby areas. Neither Ms Hu nor any government officials were there. Many voluntary helpers from the village participated in praying activities on that day, and we saw village women cooking food for the opera performers and worshippers. The crowd had dutifully gathered in front of the statue of HDX when the installation ceremony began. Inside the temple, the atmosphere was intense and joyful. The statue-maker was also responsible for the rituals on that occasion and he began by spraying water on the statue before wiping it away (Figure 5.3). A local spirit medium was present who is periodically possessed by the deity, offering advice and remedies. The villagers sacrificed a chicken, dripped the blood into a basin of water, then used a branch with some leaves to dip into the water and then sprinkled it over the worshippers.

The statue-maker then recited some scriptures to the deity. When the red cloth over the statue was uncovered, villagers lit firecrackers outside the temple. The crackling sound of firecrackers lasted for several minutes. A male villager holding a bunch of joss sticks divided and distributed them to the crowd. The crowd, mainly women, rushed forward to grab their share, and there was consequently a lot of pushing and jostling. This was a joyous occasion for them. The noise, the laughter, and the crowds found at the village temple are such a contrast to the quiet and empty YYY. We were struck by the lively and joyous atmosphere in the temple that morning.

Indeed, the installation of the statue of HDX at Gunglu temple was a reflection of the villagers' disappointment with YYY. In such a process, locals have also

Figure 5.3 At the installation of a new HDX statue at Gunglu temple, the statue-maker sprayed sacred water to the crowds.

attached new meanings to temples where the statues of HDX were placed. Gunglu temple continues to be the site of the religious life of villagers in the community, while YYY has become the corresponding site for outsiders and tourists.[14] YYY contributes to the popularization of religious beliefs although it does not seem to be able to draw regular visits from villagers.

New strategies to promote the temple: cultivating good relationship with female villagers

Knowing that it would be unrealistic to continue trying to attract more Hong Kong visitors to YYY, Ms Hu decided to rely on the resident priests and priestesses to popularize the temple through promoting the religion to locals. During the period from December 2001 to December 2002, the temple was "contracted" to the head priest through the "contract–responsibility" scheme. The head priest was free to keep all the revenue except for a submission of 60,000 RMB to the management committee.[15]

Although affiliated with the temple, the priest spent most of his time else-where, studying and evidently practicing Daoist arts in other cities. The temple staff said they had no idea where he was located most of the time. The head priest lacked the business skills to run the temple and did not adopt many new mea-sures to attract worshippers to the temple. This "contract–responsibility system" experiment failed to generate improvement in the number of visitors for which the committee had hoped. There are many possible reasons for the failure. One of the reasons is that the priests themselves are often not particularly committed to attracting visitors to their temples, but are instead keen on attracting clients to whom they could provide ritual services that generate income for them personally. The priests are hence more interested in using temples as sites to meet potential clients for ritual services such as funeral rites, rather than having them come so that visitor numbers could be boosted.

During this period, YYY started offering small illuminated spaces on conical towers, about four to six feet high, which are placed near the main altar. They are called "bright lamps" (*guangmingdeng*).[16] There are fewer niches near the top of the conical towers and more near the bottom; so the upper niches are considerably more expensive to rent than the lower ones. The worshipper's name is inscribed over the niche, which contains a small gold-colored statue of a deity, and there is a small electric motor which slowly rotates the conical tower near the main altar. Thus, worshippers get a special place near the altar, and presumably benefit from the radiant benevolence issuing forth from the god-statue on the main altar, or gain the deity's special attention. In fact, "bright lamps" or light towers became popular during that period in Zhejiang. These "bright lamps" increase the tem-ple's income. It was also assumed that those who bought the light towers would also come to the temple more often; and therefore, the temple would become part of the villagers' everyday life. By 2003, more than 500 lamps were sold and a substantial number of them were bought by villagers. The annual charge for a tablet at the light tower ranged from 60 RMB to 380 RMB. When we were there in 2003, the main hall where the light towers were located was quiet and dark because of cost-cutting measures. Once we stepped into the hall, chanting via a tape recording was manually activated by an attendant. The chanting stopped right at the moment when we left the hall. The temple remained quiet most of the time.

After the priest who was contracted to manage the temple left, there was no religious specialist at YYY for a few years. From about 2003, Ms Hu decided to turn increasingly to her local connections to try to mobilize villagers in Huang Peng and residents in Lanxi to visit the temple regularly. Meanwhile, Ms Hu decided to popularize the temple among local villagers by utilizing a localized gendered network. She came up with the idea of utilizing gendered networks to promote the temple by forming a charity group (Chishanxiaozu). The charity group included around 35 women and comprised worshippers of HDX from Huang Peng village and elsewhere in Lanxi. These women were regular worshippers at various temples nearby, including YYY. They were close to each other and went to different temples together as a group to pray for their families during festivals. The key members included a Huang Peng villager, who was the wife of a party secretary, and a spirit medium (Figure 5.4). The wife of the party secretary was a devotee of YYY and many other temples in the local region. She was clearly influential among local village women, and if she and her friends could be induced to spend more time and devote more of their worship to the YYY temple, that would be a considerable achievement and could help to revive the temple. The spirit medium lived in Lanxi city and was known to be possessed by HDX from time to time. When she was possessed by the immortal, she was able to treat patients through the god's prescriptions

Figure 5.4 Spirit medium delivering a message from the deity, with a group of devoted female villagers.

or exhortations, although she did not give out medicine herself. We met her during one of our fieldtrips, and she went into a trance to welcome us on behalf of HDX, speaking the deity's words of welcome in a gruffer tone than her usual speaking voice. She was always surrounded by a group of female villagers.

Although spirit mediumship is classified as a form of "feudal superstition" and "illegitimate" in official discourse about religion in China, and the YYY temple is officially managed by the township, Ms Hu decided to try to use the spirit medium's popularity to draw more villagers to the temple. She invited the spirit medium to come to the temple regularly to meet worshippers, and allowed her to use a room on the second floor of the main building as her "office." The spirit medium agreed, and came to the temple every day except for weekends. The popular spirit medium gave periodic consultations in the temple—hidden away, however, in an office, where her presence was known only by word of mouth.[17] Apparently, Ms Hu turned a blind eye toward activities which could be considered "superstitious" and "illegitimate" by the state as long as they were small scale and under her control. Indeed, the relationship between local society and the state is neither clearly separate from each other nor a dichotomous one. Ms Hu as a representative of the local government is also a local in Jinhua and has expressed sympathy and tolerance for villagers' needs in conducting "superstitious" religious activities.

In addition, ritual activities also increased as these religious activities were often encouraged by the spirit medium. Under the leadership of the spirit medium, praying and simple rituals, attended primarily by local women, were conducted at the temple on the first and fifteenth of every month and on the respective birthdays of various gods. Besides, village women in the charity group organized themselves into teams of three and took turns to serve as voluntary workers at the temple. They helped to clean up the temple and also mobilized fellow villagers to donate money for minor temple renovations and for ritual celebrations during festivals. They also mobilized other female villagers to come and attend ritual activities on the first and fifteenth of every month in the lunar calendar, as well as during the birthdays of other deities in YYY. This of course is a pattern familiar to researchers who have studied the activities of women at many other small local temples in China (e.g., Kang 2009a), but it was a considerable innovation at this large temple, which had been designed and promoted originally, with its grand size and admission fees, to attract and profit from the visits of overseas pilgrims and tourists. Apparently, there has been a shift in management strategy. The management team is now no longer promoting the secular aspects of HDX, such as generating tourism through translocal connections. Instead, an emphasis on sacred religious life has been observed at the temple.

In June 2003, the women in the charity group thought that the scripture hall in YYY was rather empty and, therefore, proposed to place three Buddhist statues there because many residents in Lanxi and Huang Peng were also Buddhists. It was approved by Ms Hu, who was evidently keen to add features to the temple which would further enhance its appeal to local women. Indeed, she is aware of the fact that another obvious way of increasing the appeal of a temple is to add additional deities to which visitors might wish to worship during a visit even if the principal deity is the main attraction. The charity group then solicited 70,000 to 80,000 RMB from other female fellow villagers in the local community to construct the statues and have them placed at the scripture hall. Unfortunately, it raised a controversy because many male villagers thought that it was inappropriate and illegitimate to have Buddhist statues in a Daoist temple. The three Buddhist statues—incongruous in what was supposed to be officially a Daoist temple—were eventually withdrawn at the request of the Religious Affairs Bureau, which found it difficult to defend three Buddhist statues in a Daoist temple. Subsequently, the statues were moved to a small temple at Huang Peng village known as Gunglu temple. Elsewhere, in Longwanggou, a similar effort to expand the temple's attraction by adding new halls for various gods was observed. The temple manager had also suggested adding a "God of Wealth" hall to the temple to make it more attractive to businesspeople and those seeking greater wealth, but was persuaded by his associates that this was unnecessary, since the main deity of the temple, Heilongdawang, had *already* become a "god of wealth" in the eyes of local people as his powers expanded beyond his original "rain god" function to accommodate the strivings and ambitions of the emerging "petty-capitalist" society of Shaanbei (Chau 2006: 120–121).[18]

These concessions to popular religiosity had only a small impact on the flow of visitors to the site. Eventually, the spirit medium stopped coming to the temple. Her health was failing, but she had also begun to charge much higher fees for her medium sessions, partly no doubt because of gambling losses, which had been noticed and discussed among her clients. In any case, giving her an "office" in the temple had also failed to bring more people from the village and the town into the temple.

Although the charity group comprising village women continued to function, it became less active. The temple returned to its earlier state of relative emptiness and decrepitude, subsisting with only a trickle of worshippers and few regular pilgrims. In order to improve the condition of YYY, Ms Hu believed that the temple should be renovated and the number of gods should be increased so that more visitors would be attracted to come. Consequently, she solicited a substantial part of the needed expenses through donations from several regular and devoted pilgrims, whom she has known since the temple was built. In 2012 and 2013, two halls were added to YYY through donations collected from few pilgrims from Hangzhou, Wenzhou, Guangzhou, and Hong Kong. Some of them are businessmen from Hong Kong who ran factories near Lanxi and have all along been worshippers of HDX. They have been the supporters of YYY since it was built. These halls are dedicated to Dragon King and Medicine King, with the aim to attract a wider group of worshippers. To improve the credibility of YYY, Ms Hu also managed to invite religious specialists to stay at the temple, and there were five priests in 2013.

In sum, Ms Hu developed several strategies to try to appeal to locals, especially women, and to draw them more firmly into the religious activities and upkeep of the temple, but was only partly and temporarily successful. While the religious belief takes off in the local area, the worship of HDX at YYY has not been popularized. Ultimately, these strategies did not seem to work well, despite Ms Hu's best efforts.

In fact, the temple's funds were so depleted that it could barely support a small-scale school in the village for hearing-impaired children, as was promised in the original agreement with SSY, which had provided funds to build the temple as well as to support an affiliated charity. The school was operating when we visited it in the early 2000s, but was closed a few years later partly because it was an illegal construction, and also because there were no funds to maintain it.

In 2007, Ms Hu estimated that for most of each month, there were only about 15–20 visitors to the temple each day, for an average of not much more than two per hour. Since more visitors come in the early morning or late afternoon, this large temple with its extensive spaces and plazas would be completely empty for much of each day. The meager income from sales of admission tickets and incense sticks was not enough to cover expenses. The occasional donations from business-people and overseas visitors was substantially larger than the yearly income from admissions and selling incense, but still not enough to carry out needed repairs and upgrading of the halls and statues.

By 2013, there was a restructuring exercise and the YYY management committee came under the direct control of the Religious Affairs Bureau at the United Front. Under the instruction of United Front, religious exchanges among priests from YYY and elsewhere have been promoted. At the time of writing this book, she was hoping to gain greater support from the Religious Affairs Bureau in raising the quality of the Daoist priests at YYY and enhancing cultural exchange of priests at YYY and YQG in Hong Kong.

Besides, Ms Hu also hoped to draw support from two newly built temples, Xianyiguan at Muchenyuan and Lingyangci at Lingyang Island within Lanxi, but has not been actively coming up with any strategies (see Chapter 3). In particular, she hoped that the development of Lingyangci could produce positive spillover effects on YYY. Lingyangci was first built in 1995 by investors who were developing a resort in the area. It did not attract many visitors as it was not well managed and could only be reached by a boat which had to be reserved in advance of a visit. In 2012, the resort area was redeveloped together with an expansion of Lingyanci. The project was financially supported by local investors and a retired cadre, Mao Gengzhi, who was the key planner of Zugong when he was working in the Jinhua prefectural-level city government. Through Mao's connections with cadres at different government offices, a road was built to connect the island to Lanxi where YYY is located. Ms Hu hopes that the three temples in Lanxi could form a temple tour circle revolving around HDX and draw visitors in the future. At the time when this book was written, none of these three temples managed to attract many visitors.

A struggling rural mountain-top temple: Zugong

The second major HDX temple in the Jinhua area was built near the top of Jinhua Mountain in 1996, at a cost of about 23 million RMB. Like YYY, this temple,

Zugong, was also initiated by officials in a state-linked company which managed a local tourist park (Double Dragon Scenic Park management team) at the base of the mountain, with participation in the project also by five other companies, each of which would contribute funds and share subsequent revenues. One of the key partners was Zhejiang Jianfeng Group. The boss of Jiangfeng Group, Mr Du, got to know HDX through one of his earlier visits to Hong Kong, when Mr Chow brought him to Hong Kong HDX temple and led him to become a worshipper of HDX (see Chapter 3). This temple was also intended to take advantage of the "cultural capital" of Jinhua Mountain—the legend that HDX had become a saint and immortal on the mountain. As in nearby Lanxi, the local authorities in Jinhua hoped that the temple would attract Hong Kong tourists and investors. Indeed, the management team believed that with the imminent return of Hong Kong to mainland China in 1997, the year 1996 was an excellent time to "welcome Hong Kong's return to the motherland" by building a temple to what they believed was the principal god of Hong Kong people.

Zugong opened in the fall of 1996, accompanied by a festival to celebrate the 1,168th birthday of the god. There were a large number of visitors for the occasion from Hong Kong and Southeast Asia, most of whom had been invited by the organizers, and some tourists also arrived from Shanghai, Hangzhou, and other nearby cities. Around 110 people from YQG came as a group. Each of them donated 1168 RMB to commemorate the birthday of HDX. However, when the crowds at the opening ceremonies went home, and the initial visits by curious locals and overseas visitors were not followed by any steady flows of either locals or tourists, the organizers began to realize that the temple was not doing very well relative to their expectations temples. From the point of view of convenient access to large numbers of worshippers, Zugong was one of the worst locations among the Jinhua HDX. It is inconveniently located on the hilltop, and the management team had to build a road to connect it to the middle of the hill, where the popular Double Dragon Cave is. Zugong can be reached only by an infrequent shuttle bus service. The bus departs from the Cave, and there is no public transport going from the town center directly to Zugong. The temple's one advantage is its setting, on a picturesque wooden hillside that falls within the vicinity of the National Double Dragon Scenic Site. Some people do make the long journey from the city for the aesthetic experience, particularly if they have visitors from other cities and want to take them sight-seeing. In general, Zugong was not appealing enough to induce a lot of visitors to undertake the journey up the mountain on the narrow winding road, even after that road was paved and widened. However, the temple does draw a steady trickle of visitors from the city, particularly on weekends, including mainland Chinese tourists and people visiting Jinhua on business. But for most tourists it is too inconvenient, and not attractive enough compared to other local parks, such as the famous Double Dragon Cave at the middle of the mountain, for them to make such a long and troublesome journey to the top. We learned during our earlier visits that local officials were considering a proposal to build a cable car up the mountain to the summit near the temple. There are several other tourist sites on or near the mountain, and the authorities are keen to promote tourism using temples, caves, waterfalls, and whatever else might draw visitors. But by 2003, the local authorities had given up the idea of a cable car (at least for the near future) because the costs were prohibitive.

To the Lutian villagers who stay next to Zugong, the building of Zugong is to bring the hope of development to them. In fact, the residents of the village next to the temple had been promised that the flow of visitors would provide many benefits, including jobs of selling incense, religious souvenirs, and snacks to the worshippers and tourists, and that this would compensate them for giving up village farmland for the temple, and for the loss of the income and work from farming on that land. A series of stalls had been built along the road in front of the temple to accommodate the villagers who would sell such items. Like the case of YYY, none of the stalls were successfully rented to anybody. On most days during the year, only a trickle of visitors journeyed up the mountain by car or van or bus.

Upon the completion of Zugong, one of the costs to the Lutian villagers was the loss of a reservoir which had been built nearby, with the help of the county government just a few years earlier, but was filled to provide additional space for the grounds of the temple, disrupting local irrigation. Many villagers lost most of the agricultural work around the village, but some villagers managed to continue to grow tea, and eventually began to grow ornamental plants for sale in urban markets. In one of our fieldtrips, villagers also complained to us that the relocation compensation for more than 70 mou of land had not been fully paid by the management team.

Realizing that the temple will not generate good job opportunities for them, villagers started exploring working opportunity in the city. The improved road up to the temple, which passed by the front of their village, had made it easier for villagers to go out to work in shops and restaurants at the base of the mountain and in Jinhua City, leading to increased income in many of the village families. Some of the villagers had been growing decorative plants and shrubs for the urban market, and the road made it easier for them to transport these plants into the city for sale. This improved transportation link to employment and marketing in the city had led to improved household income for some families. Roads which are constructed as a result of temple-building bring economic development and are "very concrete embodiments of hope" of modernization (Flower 2004: 651–652).

The elderly who were left at home started sell incense as hawkers in the public area outside the temple. This inevitably led to animosity and disputes among the dozens of hawkers from the village competing for the attention of those few visitors. Eventually, the village headman organized the hawkers into teams, each of which would be allocated a separate day during the week. This reduced the strife among the hawkers. But some villagers still complained: the informal rule was that only village women would serve as hawkers; and hence, families with several daughters or daughters-in-law could gain a disproportionate share of the income, while families with no daughters gained no income from the temple's visitors. Meanwhile, the temple management team was also unhappy with the behavior of hawkers in pestering the visitors.

The village headman opened a restaurant in the village which catered especially to officials and managers visiting the temple or the mountain on business. Several other small restaurants in the village also occasionally attracted visitors. Most of the time, there was no patron at the restaurants. However, business was better during public holidays, especially during the golden week holidays covering both National Day and Labor Day.

It is rather clear that the villagers have tried to use Zugong largely for raising their incomes. Villagers have not turned the worship of HDX into an important part of their religious practices, although some Lutian villagers may bow and pray at Zugong on the first and fifteenth of every lunar month. Neither has Zugong become a community temple, nor has it become an important site for the community's religious life.

Most of the visitors come only after visiting the Double Dragon Cave nearby, and only if they have enough time left over after the trip to the cave. The temple has few tourists during ordinary days, although it has more tourists during the Golden Week holidays around 1 October. However, once the tourists reach Zugong, they usually finish the tour within 20 minutes. Like YYY, it is also a quiet temple, and visitors do not hear any chanting or see any ritual performance from the priests. Apart from bowing and praying, there is nothing much more for tourists. As one informant said, "15 yuan for 15 minutes. One minute per yuan." In fact, there are also no benches for visitors to sit and rest, making it less likely for them to extend their visit. It is rather clear that most tourists do not think about returning for a second visit.

More striking than any change in the flow of visitors, however, was our discovery that a major religious site had been effectively privatized, transferring control from a state-linked company to a large private corporation which has no explicit connection with religion (see also Goossaert and Fang, 2009: 41). By 2003, the Double Dragon Cave Scenic Management Team had sold it (i.e., they sold the rights to operate and manage the temple for 25 years, and to collect and allocate revenues) to a large private corporation active in Zhejiang, which has lots of assets from other successful business ventures. In addition to the management of the temple for 25 years, the company got the use of about 6 hectares around the temple for developing tourist services, with a lease of 50 years. The company paid off the temple-related loans and debts of the original group of companies which had built the temple, and took over the collection and management of all revenues at the site. We should note, however, that the issues of ownership, management, and control are very complex: see, in particular, Putterman (1995). A full treatment of these complexities is beyond the scope of this chapter. We note, however, that the transfer of control over a temple is similar to the leasing of a communal or state-owned property to private operators for a fixed term (e.g., 40 years). While all the rights which normally accompany "ownership" are transferred during this period, the transaction is not identical to the sale of a state-owned company to private investors. The company which bought the temple is one of these ascendant private Zhejiang-based firms. The Zhejiang-based firm, Guangxia, was the largest non-state construction firm in China as of 2002, and was headquartered in Hangzhou.

One of the firm's business strategies was to take over other companies and make them profitable.

The founder of Guangxia had grown up in Dongyang, just east of Jinhua, and his firm was increasingly active in the Jinhua area.[19] He was evidently close to some government officials in Jinhua; and when they asked him for help with their problematic new temple, he agreed to take on the project and paid 13 million. For a complete takeover of Zugong, Guangxia still has to pay another 10 million RMB. As Guangxia has not paid the full amount, the land deeds have not been transferred to Guangxia and are still kept at the office of the municipal government.[20]

It was a small project compared to the company's other major investments, and did not occupy much of the company's major attention or interest. The boss assigned several of his mid-level staff to look after the secular management issues. He evidently believed he could do so with this mountain-top temple. In fact, the company was also active in tourism and the hotel industry, and the scenic area around the temple provided opportunities for further development to draw visitors to the mountain.

With few visitors during most days, the company began to consider how to proceed with further development at the site. By 2003, they were still losing an estimated one million RMB per year operating the temple, according to an official of the company whom we interviewed in that year. With a reported three billion RMB in assets, they could afford to take the long view. But up to 2003, they had not made any substantial changes or additions. They adopted several new methods of raising revenue, including the light towers which are now common in such temples, as well as bringing tour groups from Hangzhou and Shanghai through their other business venture, which is their tour agency. Nevertheless, the site still attracted few visitors, apart from business groups on sightseeing excursions while visiting Jinhua. To cut further loss, Guangxia recently decided to contract the management rights of Zugong to the Double Dragon Cave Management team. In return, they received a lump sum annually. Since then, Double Dragon Cave management team launched an economy package for tourists to tour the Double Dragon Cave, Jinhua Guan, as well as Zugong. Hopefully, the number of visitors increases.

Division of labor between the management team and priests

Being part of the local government or a local enterprise, the management team primarily aims to promote Zugong as a tourist spot through highlighting the legends of HDX in Jinhua Mountain and its reputation overseas. This management team only handles secular affairs of temple management—including promotion of the temple, repairs, construction, and maintenance—while religious matters are left to the specialists. Neither does the temple management team intend to promote religious activities nor does it attempt to improve the religious services at the temple.

To ensure that Zugong is a legitimate temple and a "religious activity site," the management team continues to hire priests to be stationed there. The existence of these clergy is to legitimize the temple by associating it with an officially recognized religion and a religious organization that is properly registered with the state. The Daoist clergy at a temple are supposed to be registered with a branch of the official Daoist Association, to which they report. The local Daoist Association provided a "head priest" at Zugong, who in turn recruited or vetted other priests applying to work there.[21] The head priest's position at this largest Daoist temple in the county led eventually to his appointment as chairman of the Jinhua Daoist Association. Around 2000, the priests were paid an annual sum, reportedly 300,000 RMB, to conduct rituals, provided that the head priest supported at least ten resident priests, and for those costs and expenses he was guaranteed 20 percent of total temple income.

The head priest, whom we interviewed at Zugong, managed 12 priests during our visit in 2000. In recruiting priests for employment at Zugong, candidates have to undergo a trial period. They could arrive at any time from other temples, sometimes even without prior notice, and are allowed to stay for a few days while the head priest assesses them. The assessment is conducted impressionistically rather than through any formal evaluation of their personal qualities and abilities. The head priest monitored and assessed the priests after giving them various tasks for the first 6 months or so, such as selling souvenirs in the temple shops, introducing Daoist culture to guests, and reading palms. Usually, he said, about half of the recruits continued past the 6 month "probation" period, some departing for their own reasons, and some dismissed by the head priest as unsuitable.

The structural division of labor according to religious and secular matters within the same organization has created difficulties for effective temple management. There is little doubt that some temple managers consider the priests to be an expensive item in the temple's staffing budget, relative to their contributions to the temple's activities and success, but they cannot avoid paying for these priests from temple income because this is the only way to gain the necessary legitimacy with the state for a large temple. Complaints about these clergy can be heard among members of the management teams. The manager and staff also observed that the yearly payment to the priests may have made them too "comfortable" in the temple, and there was some discussion of introducing a "commission" system for the priests, to increase their motivation to market the temple and its services in the area and to visitors. The theme of "lazy" priests could often be heard in discussions about the staff in these temples, and some observers thought that some of the priests were just using these positions to have an easy life and avoid hard work in the cities. One of the secular staff commented that the secular staff and the priests sat in some of the halls directly across from each other (with their separate tasks of conducting rituals, and collecting fees), but seldom communicated with each other—the priests were "in their own little world." The priests are a kind of world within a world in the temple—an enclave of expertise in ritual activities who have little impact on the overall success of the temple in attracting worshippers. No doubt the situation is different in some temples in Shanghai and elsewhere that are more directly controlled and managed by the priests (Yang 2003, 2011). In Zugong, like other HDX temples that we have observed, the priests are not the real shapers of the temple's fate or the source of the temple's attractiveness to believers. We also did not see any regular or elaborate ritual performance conducted by the priests at Zugong. The temple is a site of serenity, which is dramatically different from the image of a popular temple which is full of crowds, incense, and noise.

The temple's revenues were one of the key issues between the priests and the secular managers. The head priest's biggest problem was the conflicting interests of the Daoists and of the managers and staff appointed by the management team to run the temple and collect gate receipts. The admission fee of 15 RMB was a source of perpetual irritation between the managers and local villagers, who wanted to be able to bring visiting relatives into the temple without charge (we heard one of these loud disputes during our own entry into the temple), and even the head priest was sometimes embarrassed that he could not bring Daoists visiting from other cities into the temple without paying the admission fee at the gate for each visitor. But the management team was not willing to give up the policy of charging each visitor for an entry ticket.

Like all the priests in other HDX temples, the clergy at Zugong were really only interested in Daoist iconography and Daoist theory. The head priest occasionally gave lectures on Daoism to the novice priests, and sometimes hosted delegations of Daoists or officials from other cities and from overseas. He was keen to experiment with initiatives which could attract followers of Daoism. The head priest's emphasis as a Daoist was on the theory and practice of nurturing the vital forces in the body (toward longevity in particular). His main task and mission had nothing to do with HDX and he was not very interested in the life and works of that particular saint. His focus was on promoting Daoism to Chinese people and foreigners. In other words, he saw his role as promoting spiritual development.[22] In addition, he also wanted to know something about healing practices and pursuing longevity through Daoist cultivation and nurturing *chi*, the flows of energy within the body.

Some of the priests, including the head priest, are entrepreneurial, and have displayed an interest in increasing their income through off-site services to clients. But it does not seem likely that this would lead to any increase in revenue for the temple, since such income goes directly to the priests and is apparently not reported to the temple's secular managers.

With the introduction of Mao Gengzhi—formerly in charge of the construction of Zugong, and currently in charge of Lingyangci—a business man from Macau donated around one million RMB to build a visitor's lodge (*Wuwaixianjing*, Fairyland in the Wonderland) in 2013. The head priest then launched a health and longevity summer camp at the temple, which attracted a few dozen tourists to stay at its newly-built visitor's lodge for 2 weeks. The cost of the summer camp is 3,000 RMB per person. The participants learnt *qigong* and Daoist longevity philosophy and practices, sampled health-promoting foods, and enjoyed the serenity of the natural environment around the temple. It is however interesting to note that the camp was not run exclusively by the priests at Zugong because of their inadequate training. A selected group of priests from CSDY were instead brought over to conduct lessons during this summer camp.[23] It would be interesting to see whether the introduction of a visitors' lodge will increase the number of visitors in future.

Conclusion

While past research has been written about how temples became successful tourist sites and attracted tourists (e.g., Dott 2010, Svensson 2010), few have explored how temples intended as tourist attractions failed to realize the mission of drawing in visitors and developing tourism. In cases of YYY and Zugong, we have shown that the local governments have put in a lot of effort in constructing the hardware, such as the structure of the temple, the buildings and statues, as well as roads and transport infrastructure. Nevertheless, the management teams from the local governments seem to be rather incompetent in popularizing the temple, hence failing to attract sufficient numbers of local villagers as well as domestic and overseas tourists.

The historical reputation of HDX in Jinhua and the fame of the deity among overseas Chinese are emphasized by both temple management teams as a key promotional strategy to draw both overseas and local tourists and pilgrims (see Chapter 4). However, the historical authenticity of HDX in Jinhua does not motivate visitors to visit the temples. Indeed, these temples are new constructions, which are different from temples revived or renovated in the Mount Tai or Sichuan temples where numerous pilgrims and tourists have visited historically. Both temples clearly do not have enough tourists and are not popular temples with lots of *xianghuo* (incense and fire) and are far from being *renao* (full of crowds and noise).

Moreover, both Zugong and YYY neither have exotic objects for tourists to gaze at nor offer interesting activities for tourists to conduct at the temples. This explains why the number of visitors found in these two temples is way below the expectations of the management teams. Both sites do not have many visitors during ordinary days. In YYY, dozens of worshippers could be found on the first and fifteen of each lunar month, as well as on the birthday of some gods. In Zugong, more tourists could be spotted on National Day, Labor Day, and weekends. Zugong is slightly better than YYY in that regard because it is located near the nationally famous Double Dragon Cave and is able to draw some spillover tourists from there, although not many as expected by the local government. YYY is located in a small town of Lanxi and is not close to any popular tourist spot and hence have few tourists. Indeed, both temples fail to achieve their anticipated economic impact because few visitors have come and consequently the local economy has not benefited from the temples as much as expected.

Furthermore, both management teams did not pay particular attention to cultivate good relationships with villagers living in the local community. They have done nothing to address the grievances of the local villagers in failing to attract visitors and improve local economy as promised. Neither were the management teams interested in addressing the religious desires of the locals or the overseas pilgrims because of their positions in the local governments. It was not the original intention of the temple management teams to resonate with the villagers' religious desires in developing temples, although the YYY began to change shortly after knowing that it was unrealistic to expect many tourists to visit. YYY has changed its promotional strategy and attempted to introduce more ritual activities, install new religious statues, and solicit support from female worshippers. However, these strategies were in vain as villagers have already installed the statue of HDX at Gunglu temple and the quality of religious services provided by the spirit-medium or priests at YYY are not appealing enough. The head priest under the "contract–responsibility" scheme was apparently not competent enough to develop creative strategies or strengthen the religious atmosphere at the temple. The quality of priests was also a factor leading to its failure to enhance its religious credibility, thus contributing to the disillusion of the villagers with YYY.

In addition, the division of labor between priests and management teams on sacred and secular matters is not only detrimental to the development of quality religious services for tourists and locals but also impedes the effective management of the temples. Apparently, the management teams are not competent in overcoming the difficulties brought about by this division of labor. The management teams and priests have different motives. While the management team wants to develop temples and attract visitors, the priests are primarily interested in self-cultivation, or in doing their own business activities inside or outside the temple. Indeed, the temple management teams often experienced difficulties in motivating them to work or asking them to improve their job performance. Although religious specialists in YYY are working in a temple which is under the control of the management team, the latter does not possess the religious knowledge to supervise and improve the quality of the religious specialists. In Zugong, the head priest is more qualified and appears to be a powerful leader whom the temple management team has no control over his work or his team. Indeed, the different motives held by the religious specialists and temple management teams and the incompetence of secular managers in managing religious specialists for the provision of better religious services and secular activities are also barriers to the popularization of temples as religious sites.

Notes

1 A similar story about a spirit medium has also been observed in Guangdong, where a woman became a spirit medium after recovering from a nearly fatal disease (Aijmer and Ho 2000: 255).
2 Spirit mediums were often involved in the revival of temples. In South China, villagers claimed that Dei Mou (Dimu) appeared in their dreams and ordered them to rebuild a temple for her (Aijmer and Ho 2000: 204). Dean (1998: 254) also noted that a woman became possessed and thereafter worked in one of the largest three-in-one temples in Xianyou. Indeed, spirit mediums played a significant role in reinforcing the popularity of religious beliefs, as was the case elsewhere in China (Anagnost 1997, Dean 2003, Fan 2003).
3 Lanjiang township-level division is administrated under Lanxi's county-level government.
4 Since 2003, there was an administrative restructuring of the municipal, township, and district government. Those who were responsible for supervising temples thereafter belonged to the Jingdong district county-level government.

5 In Hong Kong, there are two religious organizations that conduct worship to HDX. The biggest one is SSY and the other is YQG (see Chapter 3; also Lang and Ragvald, 1993).

6 Dean (1998) also pointed out that the conferences of gods in Fujian were regularly organized with strong Taiwanese financial support. In Lanxi, it was the management committee who supported the seminar financially and not overseas donations.

7 SSY began to explore other connections with religious organizations and, in particular, have tried to establish warmer ties with the Daoist Association in Beijing in the past decade.

8 By 2007, one of the shops had been converted into a restaurant called "People's Canteen," with a Mao-era nostalgia theme and "revolutionary songs" played through the speakers on the wall. It attracted customers from Lanxi, but they returned to the town after finishing their meals and did not visit the temple further up the road.

9 This information was obtained from the candle supplier who was a villager (see Chan and Lang 2007).

10 In the past, it was held on the eighteenth day of the lunar calendar in January. But the parade stopped during the Cultural Revolution.

11 Occasionally, there were conflicts between the management team and villagers who brought relatives and friends into the temple without paying entrance fees,

12 We were told that a priestess was impregnated by a priest and had twins and, eventually, they all left the temple.

13 Gunglu temple was dedicated primarily to Zhao Gung, but also included icons of Guan Yin, and Cai Sheng, god of wealth and Tudi, Earth god.

14 In the case described by Sutton and Kang (2010: 107), local villagers reserve a small hall at the religious site for their own religious activities, while the main hall is for tourists.

15 Ashiwa and Wank (2006: 350, fn. 27) also reported the contracting out of a temple, in that case to an accountant with the commission administering the temple, who resigned from the commission to take on the contract.

16 Similarly, Gates (1996: 235) noted that pin'andeng—meaning "peace" or "stability" lanterns—are found in temples in Taiwan. Names of individuals or households are inscribed and the associated persons would be blessed by chanting from taped prayers or chanting specialists.

17 On the penetration of *wupo*, known also as *daxian*, into temples in Shanghai, see Yang (2003: 202–204, 212–213).

18 This evolution of a deity's interests and capacities—from a specialist to a kind of generalist—parallels the evolution of HDX's competence in Hong Kong, from healings and moral advice in the late nineteenth century in Guandgong to all of the problems of urbanites in the capitalist metropolis in Hong Kong in the late twentieth century (Lang and Ragvald 1993).

19 On Guangxia, see "China's largest nonstate construction group takes over prestige firm," *People's Daily*, May 12, 2002 (online English edition); on the company's presence in Jinhua: Jinhua Municipal Government: General Information: Industry, at www.jinhua.gov.cn, retrieved from the Web, December 17, 2003. One of the company's holdings in Jinhua was a large private hospital. We interviewed the company manager responsible for overseeing the temple in an office in the hospital.

20 It was noted that only 30 mou of land has been used for developing Zugong although 118 mou of land were bought. The Double Dragon Cave management team initially wanted to develop it into a resort area. However, there was inadequate capital.

21 Daoist priests have their own networks which allow them to move from temple to temple (see Herrou 2011: 111).

22 In Xishuangbanna, Buddhist monks were also seen to lack "market awareness" and are primarily interested in promoting moral and spiritual development, but not economic development (McCarthy 2010: 163).

23 Ms Luo has been thinking of launching a similar camp at CSDY later, and this was a good learning experience for her (see Chapter 6).

6 A female temple manager and the popularization of a temple

Introduction

In Chapter 5, we described the cases of two state-launched temples to HDX in Jinhua. Each was initiated by a different branch of local government, and their locations and development paths differed, but both temples largely failed to meet the expectations and hopes of their backers. In this chapter, we examine a popular temple, CSDY, in Chisong, which is managed by a Taiwanese woman who has extensive business experience in Taiwan, Hong Kong, and Zhejiang. Why is this temple so popular? What is the role of the temple manager and what creative measures and strategies has she come up with? How do these strategies satisfy visitors and help the temple solve its legitimacy problem? And, finally, how does the temple reflect the dynamics between state and society?

We begin by reviewing other studies on the roles of women in temples and folk religion in China, as well as highlighting the extraordinary work that Ms Luo has done in the temple-building project and in temple management. Next, we will analyze how the temple attempts to seek support from local communities and how these strategies help in the popularization of religion. The exceptional devotion of Ms Luo toward Daoism and the way she manages the priests and attempts to provide quality religious services will also be examined. We will also analyze how transnational ties and cultural exchanges have been conducted at the temple, and how it was an effective way to seek legitimacy for the temple from the local government.

Women, folk religion, and temples in China

Studies on gender and religious practices in Chinese societies have highlighted two features of women's religious behavior and practices. First is the observation and common finding that women almost always comprise the largest proportion of worshippers at Chinese temples (see, e.g., Lang and Ragvald 1993: Ch. 5). This predominance of women among worshippers has been observed in other societies, and the possible explanations for this phenomenon of alleged greater female religiosity have received much attention from scholars (e.g., Sullins 2006).

The most common reasons cited for the high proportion of women among worshippers at Chinese temples are that women have lower labor-market participation and greater family-nurturance responsibilities, and hence are often perceived by the men in their families to be primarily responsible for whatever religious observances might enhance the family's good fortune and security (see also Huang, Valussi, and Palmer 2011). It is also noted in some research that retired women find opportunities for socializing, collective activities, and mutual support in some local temples (e.g., Kang 2009a), and in collective rituals such as celebrating Guangyin's birthday (Svensson 2010: 223–224). Small local temples can serve important social and psychological as well as religious functions for older women.[1]

However, this wider participation of women in temple-based religion has seldom been observed to have led to substantial leadership roles for women in Chinese temples, even if they are typically the key participants in providing logistical support for festivals (e.g., in preparing meals for priests and celebrants of rituals). There are also far fewer cases of female leadership at temples reported in the literature as compared to male leadership. One of these was reported in Songpan, in western Sichuan, where a small local temple which provided a kind of local community center for retired local women was also run by those women, with administrative and leadership roles assigned in open meetings by informal voice votes (Kang 2009a: 46). This is a case observed at a small neighborhood temple, and not at large public temples such as those discussed in this chapter. Dean (1998: 264) also mentioned that a capable woman ran a Mazu temple on Meizhou Island although no detail on her management style was provided. Recently, Huang, Valussi, and Palmer (2011: 118) reported that powerful female abbesses were found to be in charge of Daoist temples in China and Taiwan. However, this research has mainly focused on how they negotiate their gender role as higher mothers by negating their roles as wives and mothers, or their efforts in the restoration of Daoist bodies as a heritage for the nation's next generation (ibid.). Indeed, very little on how these women managed and developed the temples has been analyzed.

A second type of religious activism among women in Chinese popular or sectarian religions is the charismatic religious leader of a religious organization, a sect, or an informal group of followers. A small number of these women are the leaders of organizations. The nun Zhengyan (Cheng Yen), leader of the Buddhist Compassion Relief Ciji Association (Ciji) in Taiwan, belongs to this type, and is perhaps the most extraordinary example of this kind of leadership in running temples and pursuing social welfare projects. According to Huang (2009), Zhengyan's personal charisma is the key to understanding the development and popularization of Ciji Buddhism. Her charismatic leadership style involves a "hands-on" engagement with all of the key decision-making processes in her organization (Laliberte 2004), so that the ultimate authority lies with her, while her followers are devoted to her on the basis of her religious charisma, reinforced by her many written works and her active leadership of the organization's charitable and relief programs (Huang 2009).

Unlike Zhengyan who was educated and was from a middle-upper class business family, a more common type of female religious leadership is provided by uneducated women from the lower class. These women are spirit mediums who help in popularizing the worship of a particular deity through close interaction with believers and provision of spirit revelations and healing services (Jordan 1972; Fan 2003). Although these spirit mediums are to some extent charismatic leaders in their local communities, at least for informal groups of female followers, they are mostly not temple managers and are certainly not comparable to Zhengyan with her successfully routinized charisma and management of a large religious organization.

Unlike previous studies, our research of Ms Luo has revealed that she is neither a charismatic leader like Zhengyan, nor a religious leader of informal groups of women in local communities like some female spirit mediums. She is a manager who oversees the everyday management of the temple, including the recruitment of priests and nuns and the arrangement of ritual activities. This is very different from the existing literature devoted to cases in which men have dominated the management of orthodox or mainstream religious organizations. Temple managers were men and were supported by income from the temple's endowments and adopted and trained disciples (Goossaert 2007). In fact, in studies of religion in mainland China, we know little about female religious leadership, the management of convents, or the biographies of those female leaders.[2] Below, our work will illuminate the various ways in which female temple managers have mobilized social capital in their respective local and transnational networks to promote their temples, attract visitors, and popularize HDX beliefs.

CSDY: multiple sources of funds

Ms Luo is a sophisticated, professional business woman who was born in Taiwan and studied in a Catholic school there. She lived in Hong Kong for a while before moving to China. Before she started building the temple at Chisong, she had invested in a garment factory in Jinhua. Ms Luo claimed to be a regular worshipper of HDX at YQG in Hong Kong. Her motivation for building CSDY at Chisong district was also related to her personal experience. According to her, she first visited the site of CSDY accidentally when a taxi driver took her to Chisonggong, which was built by the villagers, instead of her intended destination at Zugong, and she was inspired by the beautiful scenery. She toured Chisonggong and talked with the peasants nearby. She attributed this personal experience, which resulted from a mistake by the taxi driver, as a special mission given to her by HDX. To her, this was further confirmed after receiving messages from spirit-writing (*fuji*) at YQG in Hong Kong which instructed her to build CSDY in Jinhua.

The actual construction of CSDY was conducted by Hong Kong Chisong HDX Limited company, which included two key members, Ms Luo and Mr Chow.[3] Mr Chow and Ms Luo first met at a tour in Taiwan, as organized by the Chinese government for the Office of Overseas Chinese Affairs. Later, they explored and discussed the possibility of building a temple in Chisong district. In 1994, Mr Chow founded the Chisong HDX Association for the purpose of building the temple known as CSDY, and the founding members included himself and Ms Luo, as well as a fengshui master from YQG and several investors from Hong Kong. More importantly, local elites, cadres, and university professors from Zhejiang Teaching University and Taiwan Fengjia University, as well as representatives from prominent local enterprises and enterprises from Taiwan, are solicited to become members at the Chisong HDX Association. At the inaugural ceremony of the Association in August 1994, the chairman, who was then also the chairman of the Jinhua county Chinese People's Consultative Committee in Jinhua, gave a speech and endorsed the promotion of HDX culture. The mission of the Association is to "raise patriotism, promote good culture, discover Chisong HDX historical material, conduct research on HDX culture, expand Cultural Exchange with overseas, and promote economic and social development of Jinhua."

At the initial stage, it was the overseas members who contributed financially to build the temple. The foundation of the temple was laid in November 1996, and the main buildings were completed in September 1997. CSDY is also different from cases of successful temple building described in other studies, which focus on how overseas Chinese utilize kinship connections in their hometown or ancestral district (Dean 1998; Kuah-Pearce 2000; Dean and Zheng 2010). Dean and Zheng (2010: 235), for example, examined how lineage networks from Southeast Asia overlapped with temples networks in the process of reviving religious activities in Fujian. Kuah-Pearce (2000) discussed how the Singapore lineage members in Fujian helped rebuild ancestral halls. These researches mainly examined how connections are drawn by patrilineal ties through lineage networks and, therefore, the main focus is on the active role played by men.[4] In the case of CSDY, a Taiwanese woman built a temple with other partners at a place where she only had business connections but not kinship links.

The project of CSDY was able to take off because it received support from the then chairman of Chinese People's Political Consultative Committee in Jinhua's county-level government. The county government was very keen on the construction of CSDY and saw it as an opportunity to develop the villages within the Chisong community.[5] In 1995, "an agreement to renovate and revive (xiufu) Chisonggong" was signed by three parties: Hong Kong Chisong HDX Limited Company, Chisong county government office within the Jinhua township government, and the Land Management Bureau. This agreement was indeed a strategy which uses the historical existence of the inundated Chisonggong in Chisong to legitimize the building of a new temple there, although a small Chisonggong was already built by the villagers in 1993. Apparently, it is the ambition of the investors and the local government to build a larger temple in order to develop local economy. The contract signed by the CSDY management team and the then Jinhua county government was to ensure that a temple would be built to develop the local area after a certificate of land use and a certificate for religious sites were issued by the government.

Figure 6.1 Foundation of CSDY, 1996, laid by Ms Luo and local cadres.

Mr Chow negotiated with the villagers from Zhongtou village and Shankoupeng village in Chisong and managed to convince them to sell a piece of land to CSDY for building the temple. This land was sought with support from officials from the then Jinhua county government, with whom Chau has good connections. Around 80 mou (5.33 hectares) of land for about 230,000 RMB was sought from the villagers for building the temple and developing Chisong. As for the certificate of religious site, it is indeed a state policy launched in 1994, which required all temples to be registered as either Daoist or Buddhist temples, and to be under the jurisdiction of provincial Religious Affairs Bureaus (Goossaert and Palmer 2011).[6] CSDY obtained it from the then Chisong county government.

Ms Luo in CSDY managed to bring in capital and manpower from her multiple connections with overseas Chinese at different times in the process of developing the temple. In fact, the construction of CSDY involved a long process as buildings were gradually constructed one after another over the years (Figure 6.1). When we first visited CSDY in 1999, it was apparently not complete although it had been opened to the public. Only one main hall, one office building, and several souvenir stores were built at that time, and they were constructed with the funding from members of the Chisong HDX Association in Hong Kong.

Through Ms Luo's connections in Taiwan, the priests from Zhongguo-chongdaohui (Chinese Daoism Association) donated money to build a Hall—*Wanshenge*, "Hall of a thousand saints"—after visiting CSDY several times. The Hall contains tablets of all emperors in the imperial days. Moreover, Ms Luo also utilized her connections with a Hakka association in Hong Kong where she herself was a member and finally obtained sufficient donations to build a pavilion. In addition, a Taiwanese investing in Shanghai and whom Ms Luo had got to know from her business network was persuaded to donate money for some construction works, and later also funded subsequent construction projects, including a resort hotel built from 2002 to 2003. Besides, Zhejiang Jianfeng company, which earlier donated money to construct Zugong, also donated three million RMB for building the charity clinic, although the clinic was never put into use, at least partly because of lack of funds for the expensive medical equipment (see Chapter 5). The latest plan is to convert it into a center for enhancing Daoist longevity practices.

Legitimizing CSDY: cultivating local support and good relationships with local government officials

Unlike those overseas men who were welcomed by the local officials in building YYY, Ms Luo and her team faced pressure from the Religious Affairs Bureau at the provincial government shortly after the initial construction of the temple. During our fieldtrips in 1999 and 2000, it was often hinted to us by different officials from the provincial government that CSDY was an illegitimate temple. A provincial cadre from the United Front, whom the first author interviewed in 2000, told her directly that the temple was not a legitimate one. Although he and other cadres were very aware of the existence of this temple, they refused to go there as they were embarrassed by its illegitimate status. Indeed, this illegitimacy was the biggest problem that CSDY faced at that stage.

It is clear that Ms Luo had obtained an official document from the county-level government which authorized her to build the temple because it was the intention of the county-level government at that time to develop Chisong through building a temple and developing tourism. Nevertheless, the key official from the county-level office who supported this project stepped down soon after the project began. Cadres from the Jinhua prefectural-level city government were against the idea of having too many temples within Jinhua. Understandably, Zugong considers CSDY as a competitor because these two temples were both completed around the same time and are competing to attract visitors. Zugong was in particular planned by the cadres at the Jinhua prefectural-level city government. Similarly, the provincial cadres also thought that there were too many temples of HDX being built or revived in the 1990s (see Chapter 3).[7] During the local government reorganization in the late 1990s, new officials at the Jingdong county-level government became responsible for issuing the certificates for religious sites. These new officials did not want to recognize or renew the certificate issued for CSDY by the previous county government. The government officials asked Ms Luo to return the certificate to them temporarily, supposedly so they could "have a look at it." Ms Luo, however, suspected that they would confiscate the document and subsequently deny that her temple had any official authorization. According to her, she sought advice from HDX through *fuji* at YQG in Hong Kong and was advised to be cautious. She therefore sent the document to Hong Kong, where it was stored in a bank's safety deposit box. Therefore, although Ms Luo did in fact possess an official document with a local government stamp authorizing the construction of the temple, she was faced with new local authorities who wished to cancel or withdraw that authorization. It was not until 2003 when Luo finally received a religious certificate from Jingdong county-level government claiming that CSDY was a legitimate temple. Throughout the years since the establishment of the temple, Ms Luo and her management team used different strategies to obtain legitimacy for the temple. Sources of legitimacy for the temple are constructed through soliciting support from a wide range of people and organizations, both locally and overseas. They were villagers where CSDY is located, residents in Jinhua, officials and retired officials at county-level and prefectural-level, intellectuals and cultural workers in Jinhua, reputable enterprises in Jinhua, different government organizations, public service and welfare organizations such as hospitals and women's associations, as well as visitors from Taiwan and Hong Kong.

One of the important steps is that CSDY has created and enhanced relationships with local government officials by inviting them to various activities at the temple. As early as 1994, when Chisong HDX Association was first set up by Mr Chow in preparation for building CSDY, government officials from Jinhua were invited to be members. While key members included several investors from Hong Kong, the chairman of Chisong HDX Association was the-then chairmen of the Chinese People Political Consultative Committee in Jinhua county-level government. The majority of the members at Chisong HDX Association were government officials from the cultural bureau, the Religious Affairs Bureau, the local gazette office, the overseas Chinese office, and cadres at the local village where CSDY is located. Meanwhile, chairpersons from reputable local companies in Jinhua and a few Taiwanese from different sectors also became members of Chisong HDX Association. The incorporation of a wide range of officials, local entrepreneurs, and local cadres implies their patronage and support. At the same time, Ms Luo and Mr Chow also invited a few retired cadres from the district government to serve as honorary advisors and to provide advice to the temple management committee. This has allowed CSDY to tap into the networks of these cadres at the relevant government offices despite the allegedly illegitimate status of CSDY. Ms Luo also utilized her networks with government officials built up during her earlier business ventures in the county, while Mr Chow drew upon his networks with officials at various county and city governments, inviting them to join various temple activities on various occasions.[8] Different government officials were invited to attend the ceremonies at the beginning of the construction and at the completion of the halls, buildings, and temples. Pictures were taken by the management team as proof of the attendance of these officials and served as evidence of informal recognition by these officials. Meanwhile, the CSDY management team frequently narrated incidents of government officials praying at their temple to various visitors. One of the incidents which was fondly narrated by the management team was the quiet visit of a group of PLA army soldiers at dawn. The narration is intended to show how popular HDX was in Jinhua. The attendance of PLA soldiers at the temple shows for the management team a kind of informal approval from the "officials."

Furthermore, Ms Luo and her management team tried their best to obtain local legitimacy for the temple through gaining support from local Jinhua residents.[9] When the temple was first opened, a local opera troupe was invited to perform at the temple for 3 days, and a lot of villagers and local residents were drawn by it. Besides, CSDY did not charge an admission fee since it was established, which is very different from all HDX temples and most temples in mainland China. In fact, for a number of years, this was also the only HDX temple in Jinhua, which required no admission fee. This decision was apparently greatly appreciated by many local villagers, residents, and the economically marginalized groups in Jinhua. In addition, Ms Luo also invited members from various organizations, such as school students and elderly people, to visit the temple in spring and autumn.

More interestingly, CSDY also attempted to attract local worshippers by actively expanding her engagements with various local networks through conducting charitable activities. The first attempt in 1997 was to attract worshippers who regularly visit the nearby market. Flyers announcing the launch of free medical services on certain dates were given to shoppers and hawkers at the local market. Free medical services were offered again at the temple for around a week in subsequent years. Around 10 doctors from the Jinhua People's Hospital were employed at the cost of 90,000 RMB. The majority of these people who came for free medical services were women, the elderly, as well as poor and marginal members in the local area. In the initial years when free medical services were provided, local operas were invited to perform on the same days so that bigger crowds would be drawn to the temple.[10] In the subsequent years, there was a period when medical services were offered regularly at the temple every Wednesday to the elderly, disabled, and those classified by the state as poor. In 2003, a Charity Medical Services Building (Ichendalou) was completed with the hope of providing long-term medical services to the poor people in the region. For a few years, six to seven doctors from Huimin Hospital come on the first and the fifteenth of each lunar month to treat elderly, poor, and handicapped patients at the Charity Medical Services Building.[11] Up to 2007, more than 140,000 people had benefited from the medical services provided by the temple. A large number of patients also had cataracts removed (Chan and Lang 2011).[12] The beneficiaries were largely poor, elderly folks and marginal members in the local community. Many of them subsequently became devotees of CSDY. In other words, free medical services have also created new networks which attract worshippers.

Meanwhile, the temple also sent medical teams to poor villages and provided donations to poor students selected at the discretion of Jinhua City Women's Association and Jinhua City Handicapped Persons' Association. Up to 2002, there were over a hundred students in Jinhua who had received substantial financial support from CSDY. In addition, a primary school was built with a major donation from CSDY. Since 2001, the temple further sponsored the school fees of 400 students from various primary, secondary and high schools.[13] On the one hand, various kinds of charitable activities have enhanced CSDY's reputation and attracted worshippers in the local region. These charitable practices of CSDY created new local networks in the form of social capital to attract pilgrims and worshippers. On the other hand, the organization and implementation of these activities has created an opportunity for CSDY to cultivate good connections and trust with various government units.

During the first few years after CSDY was built, there were many notice boards displaying these kinds of charitable work conducted by the temple in Jinhua. These activities were also widely reported by the media. Today, it is likely that everyone in Jinhua has heard about CSDY and its reputation for charitable work. Even the Chinese popular internet search engine, Baidu, has an entry on the charitable activities conducted by Ms Luo and the temple. Through conducting such morally applaudable acts of kindness, Ms Luo has become a famous person who possesses a high moral standing in the local community.

In sum, the charitable practices of CSDY have established the moral authority of Ms Luo. They formed invaluable political resources for her legitimacy as temple manager despite her being an outsider (non-mainlander). Similar findings were also observed in Shaanbei where the temple manager enhanced the legitimacy of the temple by building better roads, irrigation systems, schools, as well as providing environmental and educational services to the local community (Chau 2005: 260). At CSDY, charitable practices have also generated new support from newly created local networks in the form of social capital to attract pilgrims and worshippers, which have subsequently engendered symbolic capital through enhancing the reputation of the temple, despite its status as an "illegitimate" temple in the eyes of the provincial government and the newly reorganized local government in the late 1990s. In this context, symbolic capital as an honor or prestige (Bourdieu 1986), is particularly useful in transforming the "illegitimate" status of Ms Luo's temple to a "legitimate" one in the eyes of local community. Eventually, these charitable activities granted moral authority to the temple and added to its symbolic capital, and also changed the government's perception of the temple.

Conducting charitable activities in CSDY is not unlike that at SSY in Hong Kong in the beginning of the 1950s. SSY faced the prospect of political problems with the government since they occupied a large plot of land in Kowloon and were at risk of expropriation by the government which wanted to create more space for public housing. Charitable activities greatly improved their relationship with the Hong Kong government, and the public image of the temple, by starting to fund a number of educational and charitable enterprises—kindergartens, schools, and eventually, homes for the elderly (Lang and Ragvald 1993: Ch. 4). They also allocated the gate-receipts from a box at the entrance of the temple to the Tung Wah Group of Hospitals, one of the major charitable organizations in Hong Kong. All of this charitable work was said by the SSY to be the fulfillment of their slogan, *pujiquansan*, which they translated as "To act charitably, and to advocate charity." Ms Luo and her team were very aware of the SSY's successful deployment of charitable activity to cultivate good relations with local governments. In the eyes of the government, both in Hong Kong and Zhejiang, charitable activities could help legitimize the temple's management and reassure the government that the temple's income is being used to make positive contributions to the local community, rather than merely to enrich the temple operators.

In addition, Ms Luo has also found ways to solicit support from local intellectuals and artists, by inviting selected groups from among them to the temple for activities and vegetarian meals. For example, during one of our visits, she was hosting a group of painters and calligraphers from the county, who spent a pleasant hour or two painting and performing their calligraphy in one of the halls on the grounds of the temple before lunch (Figure 6.2). Ms Luo had also recently recruited an expert young painter from Beijing to work in the temple painting murals, and he had recently completed a grand mural of the Daoist immortals on the wall of the hall in which the calligraphers and painters were engaged in their artwork. The group was clearly pleased to be hosted, entertained, and fed in this way, and Ms Luo was a skillful host for this largely secular event.

More interestingly, Ms Luo took the further step to become a Daoist nun after her ordination in Shenyang in July 2002, and such a change in her position has allowed her to assume leadership in performing elaborated rituals activities for the general public. In the previous studies of temples in China, there are very few accounts of women with a religious background managing major temples, but Goossaert (2007: 91) describes a case in Beijing in the 1940s in which a woman pursued some Daoist qualifications and then operated a temple which she had acquired.[14] But there are very few precedents in accounts of female clergy in

Figure 6.2 Ms Luo with calligraphers and painters. The wall was painted by one of the priests at CSDY.

China. Becoming a Daoist priest allowed her to be closer to the Religious Affairs Bureau under the United Front, which led her to eventually become a member of the Chinese People's Consultative Committee in Jinhua.

Ms Luo's leadership of both secular and sacred aspects of activities at the temple was also rather different from that of the most famous female religious leader, Zhengyan, the founder of the Ciji religious organization in Taiwan. Zhengyan extended her authority from religious to secular mundane matters through operating Ciji as a modern secular nonprofit organization (Huang 2009: 40). Unlike Ciji, Ms Luo first obtained success in managing the temple through attracting worshippers and gaining reputation from the community and from government officials. Only after that did she attempt to establish her religious credentials at CSDY. In our own research on all HDX temples, Ms Luo is the only secular manager who had gone the additional step of residing at the temple and even acquiring Daoist credentials.

After obtaining Daoist credentials, she began to devote more time to conducting Daoist rituals for the public and promoting Daoist longevity and health practices, such as qigong and spiritual training. Lately, some qigong and Daoist exercises have also been offered to visitors upon request. Promoting traditional Daoist religiosity through practices emphasizing health and longevity to the public is a response to the environmental pollution and hectic life brought about by market reforms and modernization in China. Elaborated Daoist rituals and chanting conducted under the leadership of Ms Luo aimed to meet the needs of the local communities. In 2008, elaborated rituals were performed to comfort the spirits of those who died in the Sichuan earthquake as well as their families. In sum, the series of activities introduced at CSDY could be seen as gestures to address civic concerns, attempts to construct new practices in the absence of a hegemonic moral order, as well as strategies to legitimize the status of the temple.[15]

Utilizing transnational ties to conduct cultural exchange at the temple

In addition, Ms Luo was able to utilize her Taiwanese origin and Hong Kong connections as social capital to facilitate contacts and exchanges that add color to the activities and programs at the temple. Through becoming a Daoist nun in 2002, Ms Luo was able to widen the scope of the translocal religious cultural exchange at the temple. This was an important and useful outcome of Ms Luo's activities from the point of view of the Chinese government. Indeed, the Chinese government has been enthusiastic in cultivating all kinds of economic, cultural, and even religious exchanges and connections with Taiwan because of the political tension between Taiwan and China, and the highly prioritized goal of fostering exchanges with Taiwan, especially during the period when the Democratic Progressive Party captured the presidency from 2004 to 2008. The classic example was to utilize the Mazu cult in Taiwan as a "Sea Goddess of Peace" and its pilgrims' visits to Meizhou in Fujian as a promotion of China's political reunification (Dean 1998; Goossaert and Palmer 2011: 261). Similarly to the Chinese government, the cultural exchanges between CSDY and various parties in Taiwan were also considered to be valuable in preparing for the future reunification of Taiwan to China. Such activities are valued by officials because they help to draw Taiwan closer to the mainland through cultural exchanges and visits by Taiwanese to important sites which are appealing to them.

In 1998, Ms Luo and her management team organized a 5-day temple tour to visit Daoist temples in the southern, central, and northern parts of Taiwan. Acting as a kind of cultural and religious ambassador through her status as a manager of a Daoist temple in China, Ms Luo shared and observed the management and religious experience at different temples in Taiwan. In 1999, Ms Luo and her team went to Taiwan again. Statues of HDX were prepared by the Jinhua prefectural-level city government as gifts and were presented by Ms Luo and her team to three senior KMT officials: Lien Chan, Wang Jin-pyng, and Chiu Chuang-huan (Figure 6.3).

On the one hand, the tour helped the local government in Jinhua to begin an informal dialogue with Taiwanese officials through religious exchange. On the other hand, it reflected that CSDY has gained the trust of the Chinese government, which indirectly enhanced the legitimacy of CSDY in Jinhua. Indeed, it is clear that Ms Luo and her temple have made positive contributions to the government. Through Ms Luo's connections in Taiwan, Taiwanese pilgrims and ritual

Figure 6.3 On behalf of the Jinhua municipal government, the management team from CSDY presented a statue of HDX to former KMT leader, Lien Chan. *Photo courtesy of Mr Chow.*

specialists were also arranged to visit CSDY and to conduct cultural exchange with Chinese religious specialists. In 1996, around two hundred religious specialists from Chinese Zhongguo Chongdaohui in Taiwan were brought to CSDY to attend the opening ceremony of the temple. The visit was labeled as a Daoist cultural exchange in which the Daoist specialists from Taiwan gave lectures to the priests at CSDY. In 1998, CSDY organized a Hong Kong and Taiwan Daoist cultural exchange tour with members from HDX Study Club and Taiwan visiting Baiyunguan, the highest Daoist authority in mainland China, and the Religious Affairs Bureau in Beijing. Indeed, these cultural exchanges have also become an important form of symbolic capital for YYY and help explain the tolerance of the Chinese government toward this "illegitimate" temple and the eventual acceptance of the temple as a legitimate one.

Besides, becoming a Daoist nun and an active member in the Daoist association also helped Ms Luo to build close connections within the Daoist religious networks in both mainland China and Taiwan. Her ordination as a Daoist priestess in China also provided legitimacy for her promotion of Daoist religious activities among Daoists within China as well as those in Taiwan. In particular, she was prompted to act due to the disappointing quality of ritual services delivered by the priests at CSDY. Religious specialists were oppressed and religious activities were shunned during the Cultural Revolution. The religious revival began in the late 1980s as a new generation began to enter priesthood. However, most of them did not receive proper training. She therefore started sending some young priests at CSDY to Chinese Daoist College for further studies.

Meanwhile, Ms Luo started looking for senior priests who entered priesthood before Communist China was established. Utilizing her personal connections in religious circles, she invited some elderly priests to Chisong to teach the younger priests. Many elderly priests were previously reluctant to teach as they were uncertain about the government's religious policy. In recent years, they became more confident about this policy, and therefore started to be willing to teach openly. It was also for a good cause, since such teaching helps to revive traditional Daoism and authentic Daoist rituals.

In addition, Ms Luo came to realize that the Daoist rituals performed by the Taiwanese priests incorporate many local folk customs and are therefore not "authentic" in her views. In the recent years, she invited Taiwanese priests to come and learn from the senior and old priests in the Mainland. Today, the Taiwanese Daoist priests from Zhongguo Chongdaohui and from temples in Taipei and Central Taiwan come to China to attend lessons given by these elderly Daoist priests in mainland China.

Indeed, the religious and cultural exchange is conducted among the religious specialists from Taiwan and those priests in CSDY, as well as among Daoists from Taiwan, Jinhua and other parts of the mainland. According to Ms Luo, Chisong plans to become a center where various Daoist priests from different parts of China and Taiwan can exchange and share ritual knowledge. CSDY's resort hotel is also a perfect site where Daoist pilgrimage tours from Taiwan and pilgrimage tours from various parts of China stopped over (see Chapter 4). The mission of going international also implies the continuous religious and cultural exchange with temples at different places. Recently, Luo and a group of Daoist priests were invited to attend the inauguration ceremony of a HDX statue at a temple in Thailand. Luo also invited the head of the Cultural Bureau in Hangzhou to write calligraphy of a commemorative plaque for the temple in Thailand.

Managing priests

A key task in managing a Daoist temple is to get some qualified Daoist priests to provide rituals and ceremonies, and to legitimize the temple as a site for the practice of an officially recognized "religion" in China. The methods of recruitment and the certification of Daoist priests, and hence the quality of their religious instruction and religious understanding, however, appear to us to be highly variable. In Zhejiang, for instance, it seems that priests and priestesses have considerable freedom to move between temples and that some of them can gain the qualifications to serve as a priest in a temple with minimal or no formal training. Since the priests and nuns are evidently free to move to other temples in other cities if they see a better opportunity elsewhere, it is not a simple matter for a secular temple manager to retain good clergy.

Ms Luo did an impressive job in managing the Daoist priests to provide professional religious services for visitors. Ms Luo stays at the temple all the time, wears clerical garb when she is at the temple, recruits, and supervises the priests directly, rather than employing a "head priest" nominated by the Daoist Association. At CSDY, there were sometimes as many as 60 priests, although the number usually fluctuated between 30 and 50 on-site priests and nuns (Figure 6.4). We interviewed some of them and discovered that they have different backgrounds and generally little religious knowledge.

During our visit in 2007, the male priests ranged in age from early 20s to late 30s or early 40s. The oldest of the priests was interested in Daoism to pursue longevity and Daoist perfection, had been a Daoist for 20 years, and had spent at least 10 years travelling among temples to find a setting which suited him. He had worked at Zugong on Jinhua Mountain for a few months, but moved to CSDY after it opened since it was not as quiet (and boring) as Zugong, and there were more opportunities under Ms Luo's guidance to learn and participate in new activities. We asked whether the management of Ms Luo's temple was different from those of the other temples in which he had stayed, and he said that it was quite different, as a result of her perspective and skills as a business woman. He seemed to us to be a more diligent and single-minded pursuer of Daoist cultivation than the other priests. He said that he preferred the slower-paced world of temple life and did not want to be part of the constant competition in the secular world. He gave lectures on Daoism periodically to the other priests at the temple.

Most of those other priests were quite young. Each had his own interests and motivations for becoming a Daoist and joining a temple. One of the young priests from Hebei told us that he had always got into fights in school, and was eventually expelled, at which point somebody advised him to go into a temple.

Figure 6.4 A priest stationed at the courtyard in front of the main altar, CSDY.

He did so, but at first he fought and quarreled even in the temple. Eventually, he learned to control his temper and become more calm through the practice of breathing exercises and *qigong*. He had worked as a priest for 3 years when we met him.

One of the priests whom we interviewed at Ms Luo's temple had grown up in a poor village and first entered a temple with only a letter of introduction from his local residence committee, stamped by the local police to indicate that he did not have a criminal record. He stayed in a number of temples for various periods, eventually settling in Ms Luo's Chisong temple in Jinhua after discovering that the conditions were much better there than at other temples in the region. Despite his lack of formal training, however, he seemed to us to be a sincere seeker of esoteric knowledge and of immortality (a classic Daoist preoccupation).

Another young priest had graduated from an art and design college, and wanted to use his skills to promote Chinese culture, but also to develop connections between science and culture, through practices such as *taiji* (also transliterated as *tai chi*) and *qigong*. He was articulate and confident in expressing these views, and felt that he could develop and promote these themes and activities at CSDY. He used his own computer for some of his work, communicating with other priests and clients by cell phone and text messaging.[16] He had once tried to develop his Daoist understandings and powers by living in a remote stone house on a mountain for a year, gathering firewood for himself and sometimes practicing Daoist meditation in the snow. But Ms Luo's temple was a more congenial (and comfortable) setting in which to pursue his interests and develop his skills.

There was also a painter among the temple priests. He had spent 4 months painting a scene of the Jade Emperor with other deities and immortals along the entire wall of one of the reception rooms in a hall next to the temple (Figure 6.2). Originally from Jiangxi, he had studied painting 10 years earlier; and several years later, he decided to pursue his art within temples, as a Daoist. He had painted in other temples in Guangxi and Guangdong, and had met Ms Luo in a temple in Jiangxi. She invited him to join her temple, and he agreed to come, and found that it was a good arrangement for his work. He had his own network of clients, and sold his paintings—mostly of Chinese deities—to customers in mainland China, Taiwan, and Singapore. Ms Luo also brought a group of secular painters to the temple, who spent some time in one of the halls doing paintings and calligraphy with themes related to the temple and the saint. Ms Luo seemed to welcome these additions to the activities and profile of the temple. However, his skills so well displayed at the temple led to other offers and opportunities, and he eventually left.

There were at least 10 female priests at CSDY in 2007. We interviewed two of them, both aged around 24 or 25. One female priest, from a town near Xian, had been a Daoist for 2 years. She learned something about Daoist deities and worship growing up in her family, since her parents were believers, and worshipped the Daoist immortal Lu Dongbin. She had learned the *erhu* and other instruments at an arts school in Xian, where she studied for 5 years. She came to this temple, after working at another temple where she led a group of temple musicians, because she had heard about it through networks of friends whom she had met at Daoist events. Her main role in Ms Luo's temple was as a leader of the six or seven musicians who played twice each day in the temple. This temple life appealed to her because she had other female friends among the group of women at the temple, and could learn many things from the lectures and mentoring of the male priests, including chanting, but she was also learning English and learning to use the computer, under the tutoring of the male priest who had graduated from an art and design college.

Another woman had also studied music at the same arts college in Xian (although they did not know each other at that time). She had also worked previously in another temple which did not have a group of musicians, and coming to this temple provided the opportunity to play and learn this type of music with other young musicians. Unlike the first woman, she was not influenced by her family (who were not religious), but by friends and peers. She had taught secular music previously to adults and children in a school, but living in a picturesque rural setting with other young people with similar skills and aims was more appealing, especially since she did not like the very competitive atmosphere in the cities. Her mother visited her at the temple, but did not really accept her choice, although her father was more accepting. She was very conscious that as an only child, she might have to help support her parents later, and felt some pressure about this obligation whenever she thought about the future. She knew she might have to take up better-paid employment eventually, but for now, she was content with the temple's social and cultural life, and with the friendships developed with other female and male priests.

Under the leadership of Ms Luo, each priest had a different role or station in the temple compound. She manages the priests according to their "specialization." There are priests who are responsible for fortune-telling and reading *qian* (divination slips) at different halls. Those who play musical instruments were arranged to perform twice each day, while also practicing to prepare for their performances in the evenings after daytime visitors had left. To Ms Luo, the temple's attractiveness and religious impact would be enhanced by regular ritual performances as well as musical performances using traditional instruments in the main hall of the temple. Elaborated rituals services were performed on the birthdays of various gods. During our visits, there were Daoist ritual performances by a group of Daoist priests and musical performances twice a day by about five musicians each time. We also observed that the visitors gathered around them at the hall during these performances (Figure 6.5).

The ambiance of the temple was good, and many were impressed by these performances. Indeed, this is the only temple of HDX in Jinhua where we found regular and well-orchestrated group performance of Daoist music and rituals. The first author was told that there were 12 musicians at the temple at one time, but some of them left to go to temples in bigger cities such as Beijing and Xian, where they could obtain higher salaries. Their musical skills were in demand in

Figure 6.5 Daoist priests performing music while worshippers are praying, CSDY.

major temples, and their networks of friends working at other temples kept them informed about salaries and opportunities. The opportunity to use their musical skills with other like-minded young people in a picturesque environment was one of the attractions of working in Ms Luo's temple for these young people, even if many of them, seeking further experiences and opportunities, would eventually move on to other temples.

Apart from assigning specific duties to priests according to their specialization, Ms Luo is also very keen to upgrade the knowledge and skills of Daoist priests at her temple. All priests and priestesses are required to attend guest lectures delivered by senior or reputable priests from Taiwan and mainland China whenever they arrive. On ordinary days, they need to practice Daoism in the evenings, try different kinds of roles within the temple's menu of services for visitors, and improve their own qualifications and experience.

Equally important, Ms Luo offered some outstanding priests the chance to have diversified exposure at other temples inside and outside China. She took some priests to Zugong and Lingyangci to help with their religious activities and rewarded them with extra pay. In 2013, she even took several of the priests on a trip to Thailand, where she had been invited to attend the official opening ceremony of a small god-statue of HDX.

Apparently, Ms Luo was the key figure in developing a range of learning and performing opportunities at the temple which attracted young people and kept them engaged and active in temple life. She vetted applicants to join the temple, counseled or sent away those who could not adapt, and kept the rest of them engaged in various services to visitors and in reading Daoist scripts, learning Daoist music and practices. She was not a strict disciplinarian, but she had Daoist credentials, and a reputation as an astute and successful business woman, both in managing secular enterprises and in running a major temple, thus doubly enhancing her influence and credibility with the male and female priests. One of Ms Luo's achievements in running the temple was to attract young people with special talents to work at the temple as priests or nuns; but at the same time, their talents made them attractive to managers of other large temples in the cities. Hence, she regularly had to meet the challenge to recruit and train new priests to replace those who eventually left.

Dynamics with local villagers in Chisong

Unlike YYY in Huang Peng village, where religious memories and practices have recently been reawakened and reinvented by villagers, Chisong villagers have all along worshipped HDX and his brother until 1958 when their temple was inundated. In fact, Chisong villagers built a new temple, which they called Chisonggong or Erxiandian ("two saints" temple), near the site of the original temple in 1993 and revived the religious practices before CSDY was built (see Chapter 3) (Figure 6.6). When Ms Luo first visited Chisonggong in the early 1990s, she donated a pair of stone lions to the villagers to place at the front of the temple. A good relationship between villagers and Ms Luo was founded.

Figure 6.6 Statues of the brothers Huang Chuping (known as Huang Daxian) and Huang
Chuqi, at Chisonggong, Jinhuashan, Zhejiang].

When CSDY was first built, villagers were very grateful to Ms Luo and were extremely supportive and cooperative to the project of building CSDY as it brought economic development for the community. One of the major improvements was in public transport. Roads were constructed and villagers could reach Jinhua city within half an hour, which led many villagers to start working outside the village. Villagers who lived next to the entrance of the temple had their houses converted into restaurants and souvenir stores. Ms Luo advised them to construct their houses with a special layout so that it would be compatible with the temple. Villagers were happy to follow, and they either got good business by running restaurants and stores themselves or in renting to others.

Ms Luo also utilized tremendous support of local elites from the village to run the temple, especially in the beginning years when CSDY was first built. Local elites, according to Chau (2005: 248–249), are important participants at village temples. These people earned their special status because of "their wealth, formal political position, informal political influence, social connections, moral authority, education, ritual knowledge, experience, leadership abilities, or a combination of these factors" (ibid.). Some of them are rich entrepreneurs or bosses of successful township enterprises, others are moral leaders who have authority and influence because of their moral strength (ibid.: 249). In the case of CSDY, the local elites solicited from the village by the temple manager are those who are cadres or those who have informal political influence, social connections, moral authority, prestige, and education. A village cadre was contracted to help run the restaurant and the resort hotel for many years after it was built in 2003. Among the few villagers, there was one outstanding one, Mr Chiang, who was employed by Ms Luo to manage the temple and in particular to cultivate good relationships with villagers. Mr Chiang was also a charismatic leader in the village. We were told a touching deed in which Mr Chiang won the hearts of the villagers. One day, a widow committed suicide by swallowing a poisonous fertilizer, a common method of suicide for women in the countryside. Her 4-year-old daughter was left behind as an orphan and was brought by the villagers to Mr Chiang for a solution. He promised to adopt her without hesitation and without consulting his wife, despite the fact that his family was not rich. This was a well-known story in the village. Through these exceptional deeds, Mr Chiang has earned moral standing in the community that helps him to exert leverage over the villagers. Mr Chiang used his moral standing to mobilize fellow villagers to comply with CSDY's development plans by vouching for them with his credibility and good intentions. With the help of Mr Chiang, Ms Luo was able to effectively solicit support and cooperation from the villagers.

At the initial stage when CSDY was built, souvenir stores and restaurants in CSDY were all contracted to local villagers for everyday management and the temple merely collected rent from the tenants. This type of "contract system" is a common practice found in many enterprises in China, which requires the shop manager to pay a lump sum on a yearly basis and be responsible for the profit or loss generated from its daily operations. As a result, villagers from Chisong were able to get new employment opportunities while Ms Luo was able to earn their cooperation and support. Indeed, these stores and restaurants were often contracted to local leaders in the village. In soliciting the support of these village leaders for the temple, the income of these leaders has also been tied to the success of the temple. Popular enthusiasm has been obtained from the villagers through engaging them in the participation of the development of CSDY. In other words, communal power from the village has been drawn upon by CSDY in reviving religious practices and developing the temple during that period. Meanwhile, Ms Luo was able to relieve herself from the burden of managing these stores as she needed to devote her energy to other buildings, which were still under construction at that time.

However, the conflict between CSDY and the villagers started to appear when more tourists started to visit both the CSDY and the peasant-managed temple, Chisonggong. One of the issues is the management of Chisonggong—the village temple which fell within the scope of CSDY. The price charged for selling incense and fortune-telling services to visitors varied from time to time. The manager of CSDY disliked this as all souvenirs stores within the temple sold things at a standard rate and the fluctuation of prices at Chisonggong affects the image of CSDY. The villagers and the temple manager obviously had different views on this issue. After several negotiations with the villagers, Chisonggong was eventually contracted to the manager of CSDY for 30 years with a payment of 160,000 RMB given to the villagers.

As CSDY has become more established, Ms Luo decided not to renew the villagers' contracts for operating the restaurants and resort hotel. Instead, she asked her cousin and brother to manage them. Meanwhile, villagers also started exploring setting up other businesses along the bank of the reservoir at the edge of CSDY, such as canoeing in the reservoir and BBQ services. Villagers began building temporary matsheds at the edge of the temple, and also ran a BBQ business there. The management team at CSDY was rather unhappy with that because the villagers did not clear the rubbish left over from the BBQ meals. The management team became disturbed about the safety and hygiene. The team reported the matter to the police, who stopped the villagers temporarily. This led to in conflict between the villagers and Ms Luo. Finally, a compromise was temporarily reached with the management team, which has since permitted the business to proceed.

Many villagers felt that they should have benefited more from the development of CSDY as it was them who contributed the land. Subsequently, the village committee planned not to renew the management contract of Chisonggong to CSDY upon its expiration. It also decided to take back half of the land rented to CSDY for the parking lots upon the completion of the contract so that the village could develop its own business there and earn more money from tourists. In addition, the rise of the local power could also be observed in the fact that the village committee initiated a road building project, which is along the reservoir to reach the town center.[17] Upon the completion of this road, tourists may choose to come to the temple using this route and thus bring new business opportunities for villagers residing along it. The changing dynamics between the temple and the local community will be interesting to observe in the coming years.

Not just an ordinary temple

Various kinds of religious services are offered in CSDY. These services generate additional reasons for people to come to the temple. In addition, individuals may also ask for ritual services from priests on various occasions, such as death rituals, openings of new shops, house-warmings, and so on. Like many other temples in Jinhua, CSDY also offers small illuminated spaces on conical towers (*guanmingdeng*) about four to six feet high, which are placed near the main altar. A counter at the main hall deals with this service. Firecrackers would be lit by a priest as a ritual to symbolize the placement of an individual's name in one of the light towers (*guanmingdeng*) and to declare the event to the deity and people. This certainly enhances the liveliness of the temple and temporarily heightened the *renao* (hot and noisy) mood; but eventually, this practice was stopped because it left clouds of smoke drifting around the front of the temple and was eventually considered by Ms Luo to be "environmentally unfriendly." Besides, small lotus boats are also purchased by worshippers or visitors and then set afloat in the reservoir, with a candle on each boat to bring blessings. For those worshippers, it was a good opportunity for them to receive blessings from their god. For ordinary visitors, it was an engaging and fun experience. Lately, however, this practice has been stopped for environmental reasons.

Over the years, Ms Luo and her team also added many features to the grounds around the temple to make it attractive to visitors even if they were not especially interested in the gods worshipped there or the Daoist services available from the priests. Although it was common in China to build temples in quiet and beautiful locations, the area around CSDY was originally not very beautiful, except for its location above a reservoir. The temple manager has greatly improved the aesthetic quality of the site through the use of park-like pathways running through trees and past ponds.[18] The area around the temple is constructed like a park to cater to different kinds of visitors, including the elderly, young people, children, tourists, and pilgrims (Chan and Lang 2011: 147). The case of CSDY supports Weller's (2006: 89) argument that nature tourism and religion run closely together in China.

Today, there is a large terrace or plaza with an ornate balustrade outside the temple where people could stroll and enjoy the scenery before or after visiting the main hall of the temple. The terrace provided stunning views of the nearby forested hills and of the large reservoir below the terrace. She also installed decorative trees, a pond, and gardens, including an enclosure where several of the mountain's iconic white goats were available for photos with visitors (recalling the sheep which Huang Chuping had once shepherded on the mountain, turned into white boulders, and then turned from boulders back into sheep with his magical powers). There were rabbits, deer, sheep, peacocks, tortoises, and swans at a particular corner of CSDY. The grounds of the temple also included a play area for children, and pavilions where visitors could sit to enjoy the views of the hills. There were outdoor speakers placed at various locations among the trees and benches on the grounds of the temple playing pleasant light music for visitors.

A number of stalls were built along the walkway from the parking lot up to the temple to sell religious paraphernalia, souvenirs, and carvings. Unlike the stalls along the road to Zugong and the stalls in front of the YYY temple, which were made of concrete and functional but unattractive, these stalls, and several of the Chisong temple's side-buildings farther up the hill, were built of finished wood which was lacquered rather than painted.

The temple has not charged admission fees since its opening, which is indeed a creative way of running a temple or park in Jinhua in the 1990s. It has therefore managed to attract a wide range of locals to visit the temple and to pray there as well. Pilgrims and spirit-mediums come as individuals and in groups (see Chapter 4). School children visit the temple on a school excursion (see Chapter 4). Tour groups were organized by companies near Jinhua for retreat purposes through Ms Luo's connections (Chan and Lang 2011: 148). Several elderly Associations in Jinhua were invited by the temple to tour there. Many families and young people visit the temple over weekends as a favorite pastime, and some domestic visitors treat it as a sightseeing spot in Jinhua because the temple is easy to access by public buses. The temple management team managed to negotiate with the bus company and have set the final destination of route outside the temple. At the beginning in 1997, the bus company only agreed to arrange for buses to come to CSDY on an hourly basis and CSDY had to cover the loss of this route if there was any. Today, not only has the bus frequency been increased, but this route has also become the most profitable for the bus company. Around ten restaurants and tea houses were found inside and around CSDY, offering vegetarian meals, elaborate meals, nostalgic country-style cuisine, and tea. Barbecue facilities were set up by villagers next to the reservoir. A resort hotel also hosted individuals, tour groups or pilgrimage tours from China and Taiwan for overnight stays (see Chapter 4).

Sometimes, wedding parties came out to the temple to take group photos. In 2003, we observed one such wedding party playing a game on the terrace where the participants form a line, with the groom at one end and the bride at the other, and the bride has to try to make her way to the groom while being blocked by the others in the line. In 2007, we discovered that many people took bridal photographs at the temple. Besides, Ms Luo sometimes organized outdoor activities in these gardens, including, during one of our visits, a tea ceremony performed by two girls from a college in the region.

Our interviews with Ms Luo in CSDY show that the number of people visiting the temple is highest during holidays (Chan and Lang 2011: 140). There were tens of thousands of visitors per day during Chinese New Year holiday, May First Labor Day holiday break, and the October First National holiday break. For the Chinese New Year, it was a customary practice to pray to the gods in the coming New Year. Visiting temples on the Labor Day and National Day breaks are new trends because these have been made into longer holiday breaks on a national level in only the past decade or so. Visitors from all around China come to temples for both recreational purposes as well as religious reasons.

Conclusions

Unlike YYY and Zugong, which are rather quiet most of the time, CSDY has a "renao" or literally "lively" atmosphere. The design and layout of the temple as a spectacular park attracts different domestic visitors seeking both sacred and secular activities during their leisure time, for example, praying, hiking, family outings, BBQ, camping, taking bridal photographs, and so on. Many worshippers burned incense and joss sticks at the temple. Occasionally, spirit mediums and together with their respective followers come as a group to pray. Priests were suitably stationed at different halls, ready for fortune-telling or answering religious queries. Well-orchestrated ritual performances and regular Daoist music performances by groups of priests were also observed at the main hall. It is clear that the religious desires of these worshippers are properly satisfied at CSDY. Indeed, religious performances are also spectacles which attract visitors to gather there. Free medical services at the temple together with the performance of local operas add to the luster of the spectacle, drawing more crowds and adding further to the lively atmosphere at the temple. Indeed, the spectacularization of activities relating to temples was a way to draw visitors for leisure and religious activities in modern society (Goossaert and Palmer 2011: 267).

In sum, the popularization of CSDY is done through its provision of religious and nonreligious services to visitors. These services reflect the multiple strategies used by Ms Luo to promote the temple and are significantly different from those adopted by YYY and Zugong. Multiple strategies adopted by CSDY include community and social services in the local region (charity and domestic tourism), or cultural exchange (visits of priests and pilgrims from different places within China as well as Taiwan), and the promotion of Daoism as a religious philosophy (lectures by Daoist priests from different places). The management team skillfully promoted the temple in the surrounding communities through having flyers distributed in markets in Jinhua, conducting charitable activities, and by bringing local groups (e.g., students, calligraphers, painters, elderlies) into the temple for various activities and events. These initiatives were sometimes curtailed later for various reasons, but show the application of marketing efforts which owes something to the business experience of her as an entrepreneur.

More importantly, Ms Luo's exceptional personal devotion to the religion differentiates her from being just another ordinary business woman. She claimed to take the temple construction and management not just as an ordinary project, but as a mission from HDX. She highlighted the experience of selecting Chisong as the site for the temple as the "message" from HDX. She justified the earlier use of the portrait of HDX and the later use of a bronze statue of HDX at the main hall as instructions received from HDX through *fuji* (spirit-writing). When the temple's legitimacy was in question, she sought help from *fuji* in YQG, where she claimed to have received the instruction of storing the religious certificate issued by the Jinhua county government in Hong Kong. Finally, she took the extraordinary initiative of gaining Daoist credentials, wearing Daoist robes, and taking on the Daoist identity. Her "religious" credentials have given her the status to manage the priests even more effectively and also work more closely with the Religious Affairs Bureau. Eventually, her religious knowledge and networks were tapped upon to upgrade the religious quality of priests, and to broaden and enhance religious services provided at the temple.

While the manager's background has allowed her to implement a series of strategies to popularize the temple and religious beliefs, it is however important to note that these strategies could only be implemented with the endorsement of the local government. For almost two decades, the temple manager has worked very hard to build good connections with different governmental offices. This is particularly significant in the case of CSDY as there was a restructuring exercise at the local government offices and the temple's legitimacy was therefore in doubt. At one point, Ms Luo confessed to the first author that dealing with the government was the most difficult task in constructing and managing the temple.

Over the years, she adopted several measures to cultivate good relationships with officials from a wide range of government offices. Since the construction of the temple, she has drawn officials into the temple's networks through inviting them to attend ceremonial activities and various secular and religious activities at the temple, as well as sitting on temple committees. Another way to construct good relationships with various government offices is to support the work of some relevant government-related welfare organizations through providing charitable activities to the underprivileged individuals identified by these organizations. CSDY also managed to give additional income to hospitals and enhanced goodwill with hospitals through inviting and paying their doctors to provide medical services for underprivileged people.

In addition, she constantly utilizes her Taiwanese identity to bring overseas pilgrims and visitors to Jinhua and the United Front Office. Her extensive secular and religious networks and interests in Taiwan and Hong Kong allow her to organize and promote group visits to her temple from outside mainland China, and to host the visitors as elaborately as she wished. These visits were important to the local government because they fostered closer ties with "overseas" Chinese, and Ms Luo's ability to bring such groups to the district was part of the reason for her influence with local officials. This is considered an important means to legitimize the status of the temple. Her appointment as a member at the Chinese People Political Consultative Committee in Jinhua county-level government further cements her status as a temple manager and eventually secures the legitimate status of CSDY.

In sum, it is the strategy of the temple manager to cultivate networks and good relationships with existing or retired officials from a wide range of government and government-related organizations, such as the United Front, Religious Affairs Bureau, county government offices, Jinhua prefectural-level government offices, Cultural Bureau, Jinhua City People's hospital, Huimin Hospital, Jinhua City Women's Association, Jinhua City Handicapped Person's Association, and so on. Tangible or intangible benefits were provided to these organizations and individuals with the expectation of receiving their support and protection. The investment in cultivating good relationships with such a wide range of offices was due to the fact that the temple's legitimacy often received inconsistent and sometimes even contradictory views from different government officials at different offices. Dean (1998: 264) noted a similar situation in Fujian:

> the Taiwan division of the United Front must compete with the Tourism Division, and the latter has to compete with the Cultural Division, and both of these with the Religious Affairs division, and all these with the party secretary and the people responsible for long-range economic planning and development. These issues frequently complicate the local coordination of policy toward a major cult center.

A recent experience provided by Ms Luo was related to the performance of Daoist rituals of "worshipping heaven" at the public square outside the Jinhua prefectural-city level government. This is an excellent example to demonstrate the inconsistent views of various government offices and the importance of cultivating wider networks with officials from different government organizations. At that time, the CSDY was invited by the Cultural Bureau to perform Daoist rituals. While Ms Luo and her team had their rehearsal in Daoist robes at the square outside the Jinhua prefectural-city level government building on the night before, they were stopped by the police (*gongan*) and were accused for conducting illegal religious activities. According to the police, religious activities should only be performed at religious sites and it was therefore deemed illegal outside the temple. Ms Luo explained to the police that they were invited by the Cultural Bureau and that this was a cultural performance, but it was not of much use. She had to call her contacts at the police office and the Cultural bureau for help. After a night's negotiations, she and other priests were eventually allowed to conduct their performance.

Finally, the support from the local society is important for ensuring the smooth operation of the temple. It is clear that CSDY would not have been built if the local villagers and local elites have not supported the project and sold their land, on which the temple now stands. Local elites from the local villagers played an important role in the management of stalls and restaurants in the initial years. In return, they received economic benefits and social status in the community. Nevertheless, the dynamics between the villagers and CSDY change from time to time, depending on the changing interests of the relevant parties and the changing developmaent path of the local area. Conflicts and grievances tend to occur in cases where the temple (CSDY) has developed very well, and in cases where temples fail to attract visitors (e.g., Zugong and YYY). It is not an easy task to maintain a balance between the interests of all parties.

Indeed, the popularization of CSDY has shown that appropriate marketing strategies and good relationships with governments as well as local communities are all equally important. A temple would struggle to become popular without the support of any of these three pillars. The way Ms Luo gets local leaders from the village and officials involved in various types of sacred and secular activities at CSDY is a strategy of legitimacy and a demonstration of the entanglement of interests between state and society.

Notes

1 A similar phenomenon also occurs in women's mosques in the Ningxia Hui Autonomous Region, where women have become notably active (see Eimer 2007).
2 Gates (1996) highlighted that many women achieved some freedom and independence as nuns in convents, but convent leadership has received almost no attention.
3 Mr Chow has been an active and key member of the management team of CSDY from 1995 to 2000.
4 Dean (2010: 247) pointed out that women from the Indonesia and Singapore branches of one of the temple networks have introduced major ritual innovations back into the local ritual arena in Putian.
5 Villagers were also keen on building the temple.
6 Goossaert and Palmer (2011: 347) have rightly pointed out that the registration of a temple is not an easy task. It often requires the temple management team to cultivate good relationships with the government, and the local religious specialists, and to attend official political meetings.
7 By 1996, there were at least seven new HDX temples in the Jinhua area.
8 See Chapter 3 for the relationships between Mr Chow and officials in Jinhua.
9 At the initial stage, three members from the Hong Kong HDX Study Club were actively involved in helping to manage the temple. They took turns to fly into Jinhua from Hong Kong to help Ms Luo to manage the temple. However, this proved difficult for them as they had jobs and other commitments in Hong Kong. A few years later, they all left and Ms Luo is the only person from that group who continues to manage the temple.
10 The opera performance attracted crowds in addition to those who came for free medical services. Donations and money rolled in as these crowds purchase incense and candles at the temples.
11 Ms Luo told us that they hope to get sponsorship for medical equipment because such equipment is expensive.

12 Huang and Weller (1998: 382–383) pointed out that Zhengyan also paid special attention to medical care.

13 Elsewhere in Suzhou and Wuxi, it was reported that a charity center or a charitable foundation that is affiliated with temples has been conducting various types of charitable activities (Laliberte, Palmer and Wu 2011: 146). They include providing scholarship to underprivileged children, offering medical subsidies to poor patients, giving poverty relief and disaster relief after the Sichuan earthquake, conducting environmental protection activities, and running a charity supermarket which sells goods below market prices to the underprivileged social groups (ibid.).

14 Goossaert (2007: 91) notes the case of Shi Zhixian, "a woman who in 1945 bought a part of a temple then managed by a Buddhist monk without a disciple. Shi then went to the Changqing guan . . . (the major temple for Daoist nuns in Peking) to become *chujia*, probably staying there for a symbolic or in any case minimal novitiate: she immediately thereafter requested that the municipal authorities confirm her as the manager of her own temple." The Changqing guan was governed by a female manager, Zeng Yiming (ibid.: 96).

15 These activities were also examined as important business strategies (Chapter 6).

16 In 2007, all but one of the priests at the temple had a cell phone; but only one had an internet connection to his computer at that time.

17 Dean (1993: 18) demonstrates that road construction reveals "the interaction of forces, creative and repressive, oppressive and evasive, cooperative and co-optive."

18 Tea-planting and reforestation efforts are found to aestheticize the environment around the black Dragon King Temple (Chau 2006: 225–29).

7 A popular temple in Guangzhou built and managed by a secular entrepreneur

Introduction

The most successful of the HDX temples in China, in a suburb of Guangzhou, was run by an overseas Chinese entrepreneur who learned and applied his construction, marketing, and investment skills in the capitalist metropolis as well as in development projects in Guangdong, and applied some of the same methods and calculations to the problem of building, managing, and marketing a successful temple. In this chapter, we review the strategies and initiatives of this entrepreneur—Dr William S.L. Yip (hereafter, following the pinyin, Dr Ye). In the conclusions, we summarize and also compare the management and strategies of Dr Ye at the Guangzhou HDX temple with those of Ms Luo and her colleagues at the Chisong Daoyuan temple in Jinhua, described in Chapter 6.

What unites the two cases is that both temples were launched by entrepreneurs who committed themselves to building and managing a Daoist temple, and who developed a variety of creative initiatives to make their temples impressive while also cultivating and achieving good relationships with the local government. For an entrepreneur to launch a major temple project and obtain the right to manage it at least for several decades illustrates the diversity of possibilities despite the apparent restrictions in the regulations about temples. To make such a project successful with the local population and also with the local government is even more impressive. Our information about the two temples in these two chapters is not entirely symmetrical, partly because the interviews and temple visits with Dr Ye and his staff, and with Ms Luo and her staff, followed to a considerable extent the topics and themes which were most interesting for them, and on which they were keen and willing to share information with us.

For example, as a builder, Dr Ye was keen to talk about the unique and striking architectural features of the temple, the costs of building it and dealing with the debts incurred before he took on the project, and the careful management of temple finances. As an entrepreneur skilled in business practices such as marketing, promotion, and good relations with local governments for projects in the area, he was also ready to discuss these topics with us.[1] However, he was not much involved with the priests, who operated in their own microcosm within the temple.

However, at Ms Luo's temple, she was not particularly interested in discussing accounting or architecture, and was much more willing and interested to talk about the various charitable projects and donations which she had initiated in the area from the temple. As a credentialed Daoist nun who vetted and supervised the priests, she was also very interested in the arrangements to enhance the religious credibility of the temple experience through selecting competent priests and ensuring that they received further education and training in Daoism and in the various kinds of temple services. She brought some of the priests to meet us, and facilitated our interviews with a number of those priests, as described in Chapter 6.

Although the focus of the research at each temple was somewhat different as a result of the differences between the two contexts and the different emphases of Dr Ye and Ms Luo, we are able to describe the initiatives and strategies used by these entrepreneurs and their staff to promote and legitimize each temple in the local community and with the local government, and to add features and activities to make the temple experience impressive and interesting for both tourists and worshippers.

In the concluding section of this chapter, we summarize the themes and findings in these two case studies of arguably "successful" temples, and make some comparisons with the research and analysis of other scholars who have studied the differences in strategies, management, and popularity among temples in other cities (e.g., Ashiwa and Wank 2006; Chau 2006; Goossaert and Fang 2009; Dott 2010; Sutton and Kang 2010; Svensson 2010).

The Guangzhou Huang Daxian temple

By far the best located of any of the temples in our study is the Guangzhou Huang Daxian temple. It stands near the site of the first major temple to this deity in the Guangzhou area, built in 1899 just across the river from urban Guangzhou in a then-rural district known as Huadi ("flower district"). The temple was converted to an orphanage in the 1920s, and finally destroyed in the 1930s (Lang and Ragvald 1993: Ch. 2). After Lars Ragvald rediscovered the site in 1985 with the help of local cadres and elderly local residents, the local government began to take an interest in compiling information about the original temple, and finally decided to build a new HDX temple on the site in order to enhance the fame and prestige of the district, Fangcun, and to attract visitors and investors from Hong Kong.

The Fangcun government apparently raised at least 10 million RMB for the project through a bank loan, and spent the money acquiring the land and starting the construction, including some site preparation and a gateway at the entrance. However, they ran out of money in 1995, and were faced with a problem: a site ear-marked for a major temple, millions of RMB spent, and no temple. Searching for other sources of funds, they identified a Hong Kong-based Canadian-Chinese developer, Dr Ye, whose company had built apartment complexes in Fangcun, and approached him for help.

Dr Ye had a good reputation and high status in the area as a builder of high-quality apartment complexes since the early 1990s, and as a well-connected business man in the region.[2] He had served as President of the Canadian Chamber of

Commerce in Hong Kong, and had previously accompanied the Canadian Prime Minister and a group of businessmen to Beijing to meet the then-Prime Minister Zhu Rongji in Beijing. This was well-known in Guangzhou. Dr Ye was a very good choice, if he was willing.

The Fangcun officials asked him to take on the project, pay off the bank loan, and complete the work, in return for control over the project and management of the temple for 40 years.[3] (This, at least, was the final result of the negotiations). Initially reluctant, he finally agreed, starting the serious planning in late 1997. Construction was completed about 14 months later, with work in the final stages going on day and night to meet the deadline for opening the temple at the Spring Festival in February 1999. The new statue of the deity, which was cast in bronze in Guangzhou, was modeled on the image of HDX at the Seseyuan temple in Hong Kong. The total cost of the project was more than 30 million RMB, with further costs expected for later phases in the development of the temple.

Some of the funds were used to pay the owners of houses next to the temple, who would have to be relocated. This costs the developer an average of about 600,000 RMB per household for the six households just behind the temple. (Some were re-housed in apartments in the buildings across from the temple.) He also paid off the debts accumulated in the course of the earlier partial construction of the gate of the temple compound.

As part of the agreement, the local government committed to substantially widening the road in front of the temple to accommodate arrivals of the expected busloads of tourists from Guangdong and Hong Kong. Dr Ye wanted them to add signs on the street along with directions to the temple to be placed inside the nearest subway station, but the officials were reluctant to do so. Nevertheless, they widened the road in front of the temple so that tour buses could easily stop and disgorge large numbers of tourists in front of the gate.

Dr Ye told us during one of our visits that he hoped to recover the cost within the first 25 years or so of the 40 years in which he has the right to operate the temple, and to get profit from it, if profits are available, in the remaining 15 years of the lease. This is an exceptionally long-term perspective, and suggests that profit is not a key reason for his involvement.

Some of the cost was incurred in building a large plaza to accommodate worshipers in front of the main hall, as in the Seseyuan temple in Hong Kong. After agreeing to build and manage the temple, Dr Ye had spent several months visiting other cities in mainland China to observe the architectural features of those temples while thinking about how to build a temple which would be both impressive, and durable over the longer term. While many large new temples are built on hillsides to increase their visibility and showcase their striking temple-architecture, this temple was located in an area of flat delta-land with no nearby hills. So, Dr Ye decided to raise the profile and visibility of the temple by putting it on a raised plaza or platform, with a broad stairway from the gateway entrance going up to the platform. This required that they sink the pillars supporting the platform and temple going 18–25 meters into the ground to carry the weight of the temple and raised platform and the expected crowds on the platform, and to avoid any future

Figure 7.1 The Guangzhou HDX temple (main building), 2001.

problems of subsidence of the ground under the temple. The orientation of the temple also had to be correctly determined by *fengshui* considerations: it faced south, but slightly west of due south, because (so they were advised), only the emperor's palace can face exactly due south. Even the toilets at the temple were carefully engineered with natural lighting and ventilation and high ceilings, to be the best such facilities at any temple in China.[4] If the temple was to be his cultural contribution and legacy in the district, and also an example of his professional expertise as a builder, he wanted it to be exemplary. Indeed, he said that he had spent more time on it, including the design, planning, construction, and liaisons with local government, than for any other construction project in his career as a builder (Figure 7.1).

The Fangcun temple opened in February of 1999. The new temple was controlled under a joint-venture agreement in which the Hong Kong-based builder's company owned 90 percent of the project and the Fangcun government owned 10 percent. The builder's intention was to ensure that the Fangcun government retained a stake in the temple, and in its success. Later, the local government privatized the company which held the Fangcun government's 10 percent share of the temple, and the builder then bought that remaining 10 percent.[5]

In effect, the temple is now controlled by a private Hong Kong-based company, which hires and pays all of the staff except the Daoist priests, who are appointed by the Daoist Association. At the time, this was unprecedented for any major urban temple in China, and there were some political risks. However, Dr Ye helped to ensure good relations with the local government, which would be crucial for the temple's longer-term legitimacy and security, partly by appointing a secular temple-manager who had previously worked as an official in the Fangcun government and had many contacts with and good knowledge of the local political apparatus, and knew how to ensure good working relationships with the government.[6]

Dr Ye also invited a committee of government officials and members of the Guangzhou Daoist Association to meet regularly to go over the accounts of the temple, and recommend any useful expenditures in the local community. One of these expenditures in 2004 was a donation of about $200,000 RMB to the hospital located not far from the temple. The following year, on the basis of a suggestion from the Religious Affairs Bureau, the temple planned to donate $300,000 to assist one of the local ethnic minorities living in a suburb of Guangzhou to build tourist facilities in their village.

The priests

As of 2003, there were nine Daoist priests at the temple—nearly half of the temple-based Daoists active in Guangzhou at that time and the largest group of Daoist priests at any of the Guangzhou temples.[7] There were three senior priests, one of whom specialized in ritual, one who managed the other priests, and one who represented the Guangzhou Daoist Association.

Dr Ye did not play an active role in selecting or managing the priests, all of whom were sent by the Daoist Association. However, he found that with a variety of backgrounds speaking different dialects, and with little formal training in rituals, they were unable to sing in tune and unison during the temple ceremonies which required some group chanting and singing. So, he hired a singing instructor to train them to a higher level of performance (and noted to us the irony that a secular manager had to arrange to train Daoists how to sing). The senior priests were each provided with a room with a bathroom, which was unusual in local temples at that time, and reportedly led to some envy among priests in other temples in the city. But despite these enviable working conditions in the best-constructed and most modern of the Guangzhou temples, he was unable to be more selective in choosing them.

Dr Ye transferred about 800,000 RMB each year to the priests via the head priest, who had arrived at the temple about 6 months after it was built. The head priest decided how the funds were allocated. Priests can also receive income from ritual performances, and there was a service counter at the temple where visitors could arrange these performances. (There was apparently no standard price list for various ceremonies, and prices were negotiated between the priests and their clients.)

In the first few years, there were some difficulties in the work and behavior of the priests, and Dr Ye found it necessary to develop some rules for their behavior. For example, they had to return by 11:00 p.m. if they went into the city; and if they returned later than 11:00 p.m., they had to sign in at the gate. No outsiders are allowed into the temple after temple hours; and in particular, the priests cannot bring guests or family members into the temple for overnight stays. Eventually, the temple managers set up a "management negotiation committee" (*kuan li xie tiu wei yuan hui*) to deal with difficulties between the secular managers and the priests, comprised of a high official from the Guangzhou Religious Affairs Bureau, a district director from the Fangcun municipality, and a retired chief of the Religious Affairs Bureau who were experienced in handling discussions and negotiations with clergy.

Fortune-tellers attract visitors to many rural and suburban temples; but in discussions with the local government it was agreed that it was too sensitive to bring fortune-tellers into a major new temple in the provincial capital and as of 2003, the Bureau of Religious Affairs was not willing to allow fortune-tellers at the temple. Dr Ye was very careful to avoid what might appear to the local authorities to be "superstitious" activity, especially because the temple had a high profile in the city, and was also very visible to authorities in Beijing. However, during the Spring Festival, some fortune-tellers operated openly from booths along the street leading into the temple. (On the comparable ban on fortune-telling in major urban temples in Shanghai, see Yang 2003: 217–218.) Thus, the tradition of seeking the deity's advice through fortune sticks (in the practice called *qiu qian*) was available to visitors during the New Year period, without apparent interference by the local authorities, as long as it did not occur within the temple compound. There were also a number of tables along the street at which hawkers sold incense as well as religious and secular souvenir items such as statues, pendants, small decorated swords, and so on.

Location and transportation

The temple is well-located because there is a very large local population who are potential worshippers, and who can visit the temple without difficulty. In its "catchment area"—Guangzhou and suburbs—citizens are aware of the popularity of HDX in Hong Kong from their Hong Kong relatives and from Hong Kong television programs, which are watched by most residents in Guangzhou (Zhu and Ke 2001). The Guangzhou temple thus has the potential to attract visitors and worshippers from among the eight million urban residents of the city. Conveniently, there is a new subway line in the city which includes a station about 300 meters from the temple. While not as close to a subway station as Hong Kong's HDX temple, the Guangzhou temple benefits from this transportation link, which brings visitors from other parts of Guangzhou quickly and in comfort. The Liwan district of Guangzhou, which includes the former district of Fangcun, included nearly 900,000 residents, as of 2010, with another 2.7 million residents just across the river in the urban-core area of Guangzhou City.[8]

One of the routes from the subway to the temple is through an underground shopping mall, and there are signs within the subway station and in the shopping mall indicating the proper exit to take to get to the temple. Clearly, it has become an attraction which benefits other businesses in the area, and draws visitors from other parts of the city to an otherwise obscure and unimpressive suburb of Guangzhou.

Visitors, worshippers, and revenues

During our visit on the first day of the Spring Festival in January 2001, we observed a steady stream of worshippers, and calculated that around 60,000 people visited the temple on that day, many of whom arrived by subway (estimating the number of visitors to the temple on that day by periodically counting the number of persons ascending the steps onto the main plaza during a 2-minute period throughout the day). While not quite as packed and busy as the Seseyuan's HDX temple in Hong Kong during the same New Year period, the Fangcun temple was thronged with worshippers bowing, carrying incense, putting paper money into collection boxes, and trying to navigate through the crowds. The temple staff who were responsible for regularly removing incense sticks from the giant metal urns and putting them into large baskets for disposal wore goggles, gloves, and rubber aprons to protect themselves against the swirling smoke and drifting ash from the incense (Figure 7.2). They had to empty these large baskets of incense sticks as many as two hundred times, on very busy days.

We conducted a small-scale survey on the day before the beginning of the Spring Festival, to learn more about these visitors and worshippers. Lang used student interviewers who approached arriving visitors before they entered the temple with a few questions about where they resided and whether they had visited the temple previously. The survey indicated that about 77 percent of the visitors were from Guangzhou, with about 34 percent living nearby in Fangcun or regularly passing by the temple, while about 6 percent of the visitors lived in other parts of the Pearl River Delta (Lang, Chan, and Ragvald 2005). Dr Ye's staff had also done a survey with similar results: about 85 percent of worshippers and visitors were from Guangzhou, 10 percent from other towns in the Pearl River delta, and 5 percent from "other places." These "other" visitors included individuals and tour groups from Malaysia, Singapore, and other Southeast Asian countries, as well as from Hong Kong. The managers of the temple noted these tour-group arrivals, and told us that they recorded 67 tour groups in July, 68 in August, and 52 in September, with an average of 30–40 people in each group, usually arriving by chartered bus. Other tour groups arrived by bus from the Pearl River Delta. The managers provided a free guided tour for any group larger than five persons.

The fact that most of the visitors were from Guangzhou, and very few were from Hong Kong, was evidently a surprise to local officials. There has been no local tradition of worship of this deity in the city since the 1940s, although Guangzhou residents know about his fame in Hong Kong. This is not, therefore, merely a "tourist-temple," and it has gained a significant share of local religious activity among nearby urban-dwellers. Only a third of the respondents in our survey were first-time visitors to the temple; another third had visited two or three times, while the final third of our respondents were frequent visitors. We concluded from these data that about two thirds of the visitors were local people whom we may call periodic or regular worshippers of the deity.

The temple managers estimated that during the year, about 600,000 visitors purchased an admission ticket at the gate, while about 180,000 people entered without payment—VIPs, elderly, children, and coupon holders. The normal

Figure 7.2 Guangzhou HDX temple staff, with goggles (to protect against incense smoke).

admission fee was 5 RMB; but for 50 RMB, visitors could buy coupons for 18 visits, thus saving 40 RMB.

The temple's success in attracting large numbers of residents of Guangzhou produces a steady flow of funds into temple accounts from the 5 RMB admission fee and from donations. Shops at ground level and in the temple's basement store offered a wide range of goods, including decorative items with religious themes, DVDs about Daoism, books on fortune-telling and palm-reading, toys in the basement shop, and a higher class of merchandise in the ground-floor shop such as gold-covered icons and statues of deities produced in Foshan. The shop was at that time the only part of the temple facilities which had air conditioning and partly for that reason, was especially popular with local and overseas visitors during the summer.

The temple also offered a hall for ancestral tablets, in which the ancestors and deceased worshippers received regular offerings of incense, fruit, and tea, with classical paintings on the wall and Daoist music playing softly through small speakers. Visitors could get their own or an elderly relative's tablet installed on the wall, covered by a red square of paper with the name, indicating that the person is still living, but would have that space after death. Meanwhile, both before and after death, the person received the benefit of the deity's benevolence and the care of a Daoist who looked after the hall and prepared the offerings. This could be arranged through the temple's service counter next to the main hall. The service counter also advertised the various kinds of donations available, such as funds for a stone lion in front of the temple, for a brass bell, or for decorative calligraphy carved into stone plaques, or for a gold covering for the deity's statue. Visitors could also rent a niche in one of the small conical "light towers" in the main hall, which would bring "blessings" for a year from promixity to the deity.

Handling the cash from the donation boxes required some special attention because the boxes regularly filled up with often crumpled paper money, much of it in small bills. During a tour through the basement rooms under the temple, we observed a group of staff sitting around a low table piled high with a mound of paper money from the donation boxes, and methodically pulling out, unfolding, sorting, and counting the bills. (Unfortunately, we were not able to watch this process at length, unlike Adam Chau's experience when he lived in the Heilongdawong temple complex and was able to hang around—delighted to be able to observe them counting the money—at the temple; Chau 2006: 112.)

Dr Ye was very concerned to make sure that all of the funds were properly deposited, so that he could retain the trust of the local government. So he established a regular practice that after the counting of donations and gate receipts was completed, all of the funds were transported the next morning over to the bank for deposit in the temple's bank account. This was essential in order to provide proper records in the event of questions or audits from the local government. It was also a good way to ensure that funds which accumulated in the temple did not get diverted or redirected to other destinations. He employed three professional accountants, one based in Hong Kong, to keep the records of revenue and expenditures.

The Hong Kong builder and his local manager had worked out an arrangement to send a portion of these funds each month to the local government. Eventually, the Religious Affairs Bureau suggested that it was not appropriate for temple revenues to go directly into government accounts. Consequently, a foundation was set up, with representatives from the builder's company, the Daoist Association, the Religious Affairs Bureau, and the Fangcun and Guangzhou governments. The foundation determined the allocation of these funds directly into local educational and charitable programs in Guangzhou (beginning in 2004). This arrangement is similar to the way in which the Seseyuan in Hong Kong directs some temple revenues into local charitable and educational activities, with advice from officials appointed by the government to sit on the Seseyuan's Board of Directors. Of course, such revenues depend on the popularity of each temple. The daily expenses of Dr Ye's temple were, with more than 80 staff, quite high, and for a time, were larger than the gate receipts and donations during much of the year.

The temple also passed money to the Fangcun government to cover additional public services during the Spring Festival, particularly, the fire department (which provided a fire truck on stand-by near the temple) and additional police to ensure public order (compare Chau 2006: 217). The relationship with the local police seemed to be amicable; and on the first day of the New Year, we observed three senior police officers in full regalia arriving to visit the temple. Dr Ye was waiting for them, and hosted them in the temple's VIP hall for a chat over tea. The VIP hall, furnished in the usual heavy and expensive traditional chairs and meeting table, featured photos of Dr Ye with various dignitaries, politicians, and scholars who had visited the temple.

During the first Lunar New Year in which the Fangcun temple was open (1999), it attracted about 550,000 visitors during the Spring Festival month (Figure 7.3). In the following year (2000), however, the temple only attracted about 350,000 visitors during the same period, according to the temple builder, who told us that some other temples in Guangzhou had also noticed a substantial decline (as much as 30–40 percent) in the flow of worshippers. It is possible, and some of the temple managers believed, that the repression of Falun Gong and the intensified scrutiny of some kinds of religious activity had affected the willingness of some Guangzhou residents to visit temples.

Promotion and marketing

In any case, the temple managers decided to use advertising to try to attract more visitors. Before the Lunar New Year in 2000, they placed 30-second ads on Hong

Figure 7.3 Crowds in Guangzhou HDX temple courtyard.

Kong television stations, and print-ads in two Guangzhou newspapers. They also conducted a survey of worshippers at the temple to find out how they had learned about the temple. On the basis of the results, the managers changed their advertising campaign for the 2001 Lunar New Year period, placing newspaper ads only in the Guangzhou Daily. From their surveys, they had discovered that most visitors to the temple had seen the ads in this newspaper, and hence that this was the most cost-effective way to reach potential worshippers.

As an example of how a newspaper-ad is used to promote visits to a temple, we quote the advertisement in Guangzhou Daily published on January 24, 2001:

> During the Spring Festival, the temple is a good place to visit, with many things to see and many things to do; lion dancers welcome the New Year, and the God of Wealth welcomes guests. There are many good things here to bring you wealth. New scenery has been added, such as millions-of-years-old oddly-shaped stones, a pool where you can liberate fish and turtles [to accumulate merit], a God of Wealth Hall, a Confucius Holy Hall, a Guangong Hall and a Guanyin Hall . . . all in a special park-like design. . . . There is free incense available with purchase of a ticket for entry to the temple [for those who don't want to buy incense], and visitors purchasing the entry-ticket can get a coupon for a second free entry later.

The ad concluded with information on opening hours and detailed instructions on how to get to the temple by bus or by subway. At the temple, visitors could also get multiple-entry tickets: 10 tickets for 30 RMB, or 18 tickets for 50 RMB, saving a couple of RMB on each visit if they became regular visitors. Children shorter than 1.2 meters and elderly above the age of 60 entered free. For some months, there was actually a temple website which also provided this kind of information on the temple's features, services, transportation, and promotions (the website was later closed).

The temple managers had to be careful about this kind of marketing, and checked with the authorities before launching the newspaper ads (otherwise, the newspaper would not have agreed to run such an ad). At that time, this was the only temple which had been allowed to advertise in a local newspaper, and very likely this was because of the commitment of the local government to making the temple a success after the very large investments in its construction. But the local "climate" for such temple promotions can vary over time, and the temple benefitted from a possibly temporary local relaxation in media policy in regard to religions. Several years later, such an advertisement would have been turned down (so we were told by temple management), and hence the temple had to tone down public promotions and give up the use of newspaper ads.

But the extraordinary local advertisement quoted above shows how the managers were able to take advantage of opportunities and official tolerance at that time in order to publicize the various features of the temple, marketing it with a combination of religious and secular attractions. They stressed utility (getting wealthy), the variety of "goods" available (the chance to worship a number of well-known deities, in addition to the principal deity, Huang Daxian), aesthetic enjoyment, and convenience (easy to get there by public transportation).

They used other methods of promotion also with a lower visibility, including temporary tables set up in public spaces around the district (sometimes but not always seeking approval from a local neighborhood affairs office), with some free gifts for inquirers, such as a small fan with a picture of the temple. They also sent or carried brochures about the temple to local travel agents.

To plan these kinds of activities, they contracted a marketing firm to design a questionnaire and collect data on visitors both inside and outside the temple and to handle liaisons with local media. They supplemented this kind of data with a record containing the names and addresses of more than a thousand visitors to the temple, which they obtained from donations, purchase of tablets in the memorial hall, and names of people who came to the temple and wanted to be notified when a free distribution of rice would be arranged. They used this list to contact these visitors again to publicize special events and new features at the temple, and try to build a growing database of devotees and interested persons. Several of the other temples we studied tried to compile such lists using records of people who donated or who paid fees for Daoist ceremonies. But the Fangcun temple managers have developed by far the most extensive database of visitors and interested persons and have used it for further promotions and publicity.

In the early 2000s, the manager said that the temple received as many as 3,500 visitors on some days; but on most days, about 800 to 1,200 people get a ticket and go through the gate into the temple. The first and fifteenth day of the lunar calendar of each month are particularly busy days in most temples, and the temple had to hire additional temporary staff helpers on those days. On the day of the deity's "birthday" in 2004, about 30,000 people visited the temple. To further publicize the god's birthday, the temple gave away 20,000 one-catty bags of rice to local elderly, which considerably increased the crowds at the temple on that day. (For some of the elderly, this was not just free food: it was rice blessed by the god.) With a regular flow of visitors even on "quiet" days, and huge crowds on special days such as the god's birthday and during the Spring Festival, this is an extraordinarily successful temple.

As a new and grandly built temple with a very impressive flow of visitors, dedicated to a deity closely associated with Hong Kong and alleged (by many Hong Kong worshippers) to be very perspicacious and able to advise and help devoted followers in the quest for success, prosperity, and family advancement, the temple was also interesting to local elites. Indeed, on the eve of the Spring Festival in 2001, the temple provided special access to a highly select group. It is considered to be valuable to go into a major temple immediately after midnight on "New Year's Eve" when the Spring Festival begins, and to be one of the first to offer incense to the deity. Such devotion supposedly attracts the deity's special attention and favor; and as a result, large crowds typically queue outside the gates of major temples to be among the first to offer incense and benefit from the deity's grateful benevolence. The Guangzhou HDX temple offered this benefit on that evening to about 300 selected VIP guests, including high officials from the

Religious Affairs Bureau and from the city government, along with some family and close friends of the guests, and some major donors to the temple. They arrived late in the evening for the event and were received by Dr Ye and his staff as VIPs (see also Chau [2006: 219] on local officials who go to a temple "under cover of darkness," and have relatives or subordinates deliver donations).

For the regular visitors to the temple, the managers arranged a different kind of reception: they had three of the priests dress up as the "god of wealth," and working in shifts, they stood in front of the temple and greeted visitors during New Year with a hearty *gong xi fa cai* (the typical New Year greeting), and were ready to shake hands and pose for photos, free of charge. While this is a bit like the use of Santa Claus figures in shopping malls during the Christmas season, it has a more religious cast, even though both the "god of wealth" and Santa Claus are jovial figures deployed to entertain and take photos with visitors during festivals. The first time they were deployed at the New Year, the "god of wealth" greeters gave out free "red-packet" envelopes to all visitors. Although the amount was small (10 cents, or 1/10th of an RMB), it caused chaos as people pushed and shoved to get the envelopes. The police asked the managers not to do this for the following year; so, in subsequent years, the "god of wealth" only greeted visitors, shook their hands, and posed for photos but did not give out "lucky money" envelopes.

The temple management had also compiled a list of names and addresses of visitors who had bought niches in the memorial hall or made donations or had made inquiries about future activities at the temple, and used this list for some of their promotions.

Other temple managers had certainly noticed the success of this temple. One of the other big Daoist temples in Guangzhou is the Sanyuan Gong, which is much older and has a long history in the city. It attracts local worshippers and some tourists, but evidently far fewer than the number of visitors to the HDX temple. They had also noticed the drop in temple-visitors after the crackdown on the Falun Gong, and were considering ways to increase the flow of visitors in the future. Representatives from the Sanyuan Gong came over to the HDX temple to see how they had managed to make the temple so successful, telling Dr Ye that they wanted to "learn from you" (how to increase the appeal of a temple for visitors). They were impressed by some of his architectural innovations, including a stone staircase up to the main podium of the temple, and they eventually installed a similar feature in their own temple, commissioning the same company used by Dr Ye for the project.

Enhancing the temple's features

Dr Ye continued to add new features to the temple in order to make it increasingly attractive and interesting. One of his innovations was to install the few remains of the original temple, built in 1899 and destroyed in the 1920s and 1930s, in a new garden next to the main hall of the temple. As described in Chapter 2, the temple built by Liang Renan and his patrons on the site in 1899 was confiscated by the local Nationalist government around 1919 or 1920, and turned into an orphanage in the 1920s. Later, the building was progressively destroyed by the Japanese, to create more space for river-defence against guerrillas in the 1930s, and by local people who looted the remains for building material. But a few pieces of the temple remained, lying on the ground in what was mainly a rural area up to the 1950s. Eventually, a coffin factory was built on the site.

When Lars Ragvald finally found the site with the assistance of local cultural affairs cadres, in 1985, those pieces were used by the factory workers as places to sit while eating lunch (Lang and Ragvald 1993: 22), but none of them were aware that these were the remaining pieces of a HDX temple which had once existed on the site. That visit alerted the local cultural affairs cadres about the cultural and potential economic significance of the site, and led by various processes to an eventual decision to rebuild the temple on the site (see also Lang and Ragvald 2005). When Dr Ye later took over the project, on the invitation of the local government, he also inherited those relics from the original temple (Figure 7.4). During our first visits to the new temple, they were still stored in the basement. Later, they were moved up into a space on the grounds of the temple. Finally, Dr Ye commissioned the construction of a garden with a small pond and a memorial wall into which were placed those remaining pieces of the original temple. He also added some other unique items to the decorations, including a 4-meter-long piece of wood excavated from a 2,200-year-old shipyard in Guangzhou, which was given to him by the local government for his assistance with that project, and which he placed above the entrance to one of the halls.[9]

Figure 7.4 Relics from the original temple built in 1899, which was destroyed in the 1930s, reinstalled in a commemorative wall in the garden, Guangzhou HDX temple.

A second type of innovation was the addition of a number of unusual features to the grounds of the temple complex. One of these was the planting of lychee trees in the temple's garden near the stairway up to the main plaza. These were actually tended not by temple staff, but by workers sent each month by the Provincial Agriculture Department to look after them. Lychees are a highly prized seasonal fruit in southern China, but these lychees, growing on the grounds of a temple to a famous deity, would be especially valuable to believers, and some were auctioned to people who wanted such auspiciously nurtured fruit, while others were given away to honored visitors and guests. The grounds of the temple also featured large, unusually shaped white stones in the garden. For devotees of the deity, these would symbolize the saint's miracle of turning white boulders into sheep. Dr Ye had met the famous architect I.M. Pei, and asked him about the carved stones in front of the Bank of China building in Hong Kong, for which Pei had been the architect. He wanted something similar for his temple. Eventually, it was suggested that he pursue the search in Guangxi province, and he finally found a number of striking natural white boulders and had them imported into Guangdong and installed in the garden of the temple. (These are the stones mentioned in the temple's advertisement in the Guangzhou Daily quoted above.) During that visit to Guangxi, he had also heard a performance of singers and had endeavored to recruit ten of the girls to come to Guangzhou to sing in the temple.

A third major enhancement to the temple complex was the installation of 5,000 characters from the text of the Daoist canon, the *Daodejing*, in ceramic tiles on a wall about 12 meters long and 4 meters high behind the main hall of the temple. The characters were selected by Daoists from one of the Daoist temples in Hong Kong, the Fengying Xian Guan, with further work on the text, to add punctuation in order to make it more easily readable, provided by scholars at The Chinese University of Hong Kong. Each of the ceramic tiles contained a relief-style character from the text. Dr Ye had to spend considerable time in Foshan finding a company with the expertise and craftsmen to produce durable tiles with the characters from the Daodejing, and to cement them into the wall. Ultimately, it required about a year of testing the technology for the tiles before they were ready to be installed. He hoped to sell each of the tiles to a donor for about 1,000 RMB per character, with profits going to the local government. We saw the result on one of our visits. It must have pleased the Guangzhou Daoist Association, and added further orthodox religious credentials to the temple.

According to the account in Ge Hong's writings about Daoist immortals, Huang Chuping had not apparently read or used the *daodejing* in his own pursuit of immortality. But the wall led directly into classical Daoism, bypassing the particular emphases on the life and quests of Huang Chuping. Thus, the wall helped to "mainstream" the temple's religious legitimacy for official visitors from the government and the national Daoist Association. Dr Ye's intention was to introduce something new and striking in the temple to enhance its religious legitimacy, and he even kept the plans a secret for some time so that other temples would not take his idea and produce such a wall before the preparatory work for his own wall had been completed.

A fourth enhancement of the temple was the addition of smaller halls for other deities in the temple complex, including a hall containing a white-jade statue of the Buddhist deity Guanyin. Like Lao Wang's addition to the Heilongdawang temple of a hall for Heilongdawang's mother, to attract worshippers concerned more with family problems (Chau 2006: 120), Dr Ye added icons and worship sites for other popular non-Daoist deities to increase the range of attractions at the temple for visitors and believers. This apparently did not cause any significant trouble with the Daoist Association, since it helped to draw more visitors to what was, after all, a temple to a Daoist saint which provided a major source of employment and income for local Daoist priests and for the Association. During this period, the bronze statue of HDX was also enhanced with a paint containing real gold, using funds donated for the purpose by a wealthy Guangzhou resident.

A fifth project was a community-meeting space behind the temple in which local community groups could hold outdoor events, and in which Cantonese opera and folk songs were performed for visitors and local elderly during the god's birthday. Dr Ye had noticed that in the years after the opening of the temple, more parents were bringing children to the temple (whereas this was rare during the first year or so after it opened), and so he wanted to introduce more features which appealed to children (and hence, to their parents in planning local trips for their kids), including children's performances on the open-air stage, and demonstrations of various arts and crafts such as papercutting.

A sixth project was to install a car park for 200 cars, making the temple accessible not only by bus and subway, but also, for wealthier urbanites willing to drive to the temple in their own cars. Of course, this is only a partial list of the plans, projects, and strategies of Dr Ye and his staff, and the planning and funding of these projects and events was constantly evolving, with new experiments almost every year.

The local political environment for a major temple can also change, becoming more liberal or more restrictive as political changes are promoted at the national or provincial levels and as new leaders take office. When the temple was first opened to the public, local officials were very cautious, but became much happier about it later, so we were told, as it succeeded in drawing large numbers of visitors, produced revenues for the government and the Daoist Association, and was clearly well-managed in terms of oversight of temple operations. But city officials also have to take their cues from shifts in national policy. When the shift is toward a more restrictive regulatory regime for religious activity sites, this can create new challenges for managers at major temples.

For example, despite Dr Ye's many political connections and extensive experience with government officials in Guangzhou, and his caution in trying to keep temple activities well within the limits of official tolerance, the local government began to take a more restrictive approach to some of the practices in temples in 2012, including one of the key sources of revenue, the sale of niches in the memorial hall for deceased persons, with the spirit tablets placed on the wall and priests regularly providing offerings and performing memorial

Table 7.1 Revenue at Guangzhou Huang Daxian temple*

	2012 HK$000s	2011 HK$000s
Source of revenue:		
Service income from memorial halls	5,436	16,303
Entrance fee income	2,344	2,346
Donation income	633	581
Sale of souvenir and consumable goods	5,164	5,241
Total	13,577	24,471

* Source: *Canada Land Limited Annual Report* 2011/2012[10]

services. This is a lucrative source of income in many temples. According to Canada Land's Annual Report for 2011/2012 (filed in Australia), the revenue from the niches in these memorial halls was about HK$16.3 million in 2011, but declined to about HK$5.4 million RMB in 2012 (*Canada Land Limited Annual Report* 2011/2012, p. 48). Dr Ye, in the Chairman's message in the Annual Report, noted that "For the past twelve months, none of the niches were trans-acted due to regulation of the authorities, and we are still under negotiation with the local authorities."

Other revenue at the temple, from the entrance fee at the gate, donations, and sales of "souvenir and consumable items," were comparable to 2011 (see Table 7.1), but the big decline in memorial hall income had a major impact on temple revenue and led to a net loss for the company of about HK$6.6 million for 2012, and prompted some cost-cutting measures to deal with the reduced income (*Canada Land Limited Annual Report* 2011/2012: 4). The boundaries between what is "acceptable" at a temple and what is "unacceptable" for local authorities can depend on the size and visibility of the temple (small rural tem-ples can get away with much more than major urban temples), and the views of new national or local leaders about the practices at such temples. Complaints from the Religious Affairs Bureau can probably also induce local officials to crack down on some practices at some times. Thus, the shifting political envi-ronment can present continuing challenges to the political skills of the managers of a major temple.

However, the evident success of Dr Ye and his team in providing an impres-sive Daoist temple and attractive tourist destination in a major city might lead some observers to wonder whether he would try to replicate this project in some other major city. Indeed, he acknowledged that he had been considering the possibility of a similar large temple in Singapore. He thought the land there was very expensive, but the Singapore government had apparently assured him that it would be cheaper for a religious site, and that they would inform him if a suitable plot of land became available. He found the prospect interesting, because there were some 20 million overseas Chinese in Southeast Asia, with no major Daoist temple in the region, and a major HDX temple in Singapore might attract many of them, especially in view of the deity's fame in Hong Kong. As far as we know, such a project was never launched in Singapore, but the fact that he was considering it in the early 2000s after completing and launching the major temple to HDX in Guangzhou suggested that his entrepreneurial vision, emboldened by the evident success of his first major temple project in China, was being extended to other possible opportunities for temple-projects in other good locations.

But he still prioritized location as a key factor in a decision about whether to launch a temple project. He declined to consider a similar project in Macau for example, on the grounds that the population in Macau was simply not large enough to provide ample business for a HDX temple; and in any case, temple-goers in Macau were already accustomed to visiting the major Mazu temple in that city. He also discarded the idea of building a major temple in either Jinhua in Zhejiang, or Xiaqiao Mountain in Guangdong, for the same reason: transportation to those sites for tourists and worshippers, at that time, was not well-developed enough to attract the tens of thousands of visitors and worshippers each month which would justify and pay for the kind of grand project which he had completed in Guangzhou.

Conclusions

In this chapter, we provided a case study of a temple to HDX in Guangzhou launched and managed by a nonlocal secular entrepreneur. In Chapter 6, we described another case study of a temple in Jinhua also launched and eventually managed by another nonlocal entrepreneur. Both temples are ornate, colorful, and well maintained, with a variety of religious services provided by busy groups of priests. Both temples have been strikingly successful in attracting visitors, and the abilities and enterprise of these two managers seem to us to have been crucial for the success of each temple.

There are several other cases in the literature on temples in China, which show the importance of skilled and politically astute temple managers. For example, Chau (2006) describes the activities of Lao Wang, the local entrepreneur and also temple boss of the Heilongdawang temple in Shaanbei, who deployed his temple-ambitions and political skills to develop that temple from the 1980s, Ashiwa and Wank (2006) note the success of the abbot Shenghui, appointed by the China Buddhist Academy in Beijing to run the Nanputuo temple in Xian, who used those kinds of skills to reorganize temple management in the late 1990s, Svensson (2010) relates the activities and success of the abbot of the Ciyun Temple in Wuzhen during the same period, and Sutton and Kang (2010) note the importance of the two local men who developed a City God temple project at Songpan even in the face of the resistance of local government officials.

However, apart from a few references to entrepreneurs operating temples (e.g., Goossaert and Fang, 2009: 41), there has been very little attention devoted to the phenomenon of secular entrepreneurs successfully launching and managing major temples. These two chapters have provided a detailed account of two such cases, including the strategies and initiatives which were adopted by the two entrepreneurs in the drive to make their temples successful.

We begin with a summary of the similarities, and then note the differences, in the two cases. There are a number of similarities between the development and management of the Guangzhou Huang Daxian temple, by Dr Ye, and of the Chisong temple in Jinhua, by Ms Luo and her colleagues.

First, both projects were actually initiated and supported by officials in the local government, mainly because they wanted to promote economic development in their districts (as chronicled in many other studies, e.g., Goossaert and Fang, 2009 and elaborated in Chapter 3), using the cultural capital and historic significance of the original HDX temples near each site to put up new temples in order to attract tourists and investors. Dr Ye and Ms Luo were asked by officials whether they were willing to take on these projects, despite the fact that both were, at the time, secular entrepreneurs operating businesses in the district. Both Dr Ye and Ms Luo evidently had misgivings or reservations, but they were persuaded to take on a temple project, and subsequently invested a considerable amount of their time and resources in these projects.

Second, both Dr Ye and Ms Luo and her colleagues devoted a large amount of planning effort and funds to ensuring that each temple was built to a high standard, with many enhancements of the buildings, gardens, and other features on the site to make the setting as attractive as possible. We have described a number of these enhancements in the two temples.

Third, both entrepreneurs skillfully promoted the temple in the surrounding communities through advertising (e.g., in Guangzhou) and flyers distributed in markets (in Jinhua) and by bringing local groups (e.g., students, calligraphers, painters and elderlies) into the temple for various activities and events. These initiatives were sometimes curtailed later for various reasons, but show the application of marketing efforts in both cases which owe something to the business experience of both entrepreneurs.

Fourth, both entrepreneurs diligently and successfully cultivated good relationships with the local government departments, partly through funneling some of the temple's income into the local government or into various local charitable projects, and partly through shrewd appointments to the temple-management team. In the Guangzhou HDX temple, Dr Ye recruited a former official with the Fangcun government to serve as the on-site temple manager and to liaise with local government offices. In the Chisong temple, Ms Luo succeeded in appointing a representative from the Jinhua government to a temple management committee, and also recruited a cadre from the nearby village, who could help with relationships with the villagers and with the district government.

The Fangcun temple had such a high profile in that urban district that a local manager who had worked in the district government would help greatly with relationships with the various branches of that government. He would also still be working in the district with a fairly high-profile position in a major and well-connected enterprise, no doubt with a higher salary. Ms Luo's temple was in a quiet rural area, and it would have been more difficult—and less useful—to try to recruit a cadre from the city government to engage in on-site management. But the rural cadre who assisted Ms Luo in managing the temple and temple–village relationships served a similar function in her temple.

There were also important differences between the two temple projects. First, the Guangzhou temple benefited from an excellent location, with several million potential visitors living nearby, most of whom are familiar with the deity and with Huang Daxian's great popularity in nearby Hong Kong from Hong Kong relatives and Hong Kong media which they can access in Guangdong. They could go to the temple easily by taking the Guangzhou subway to Fangcun, followed by a 10-minute walk from the Fangcun subway station to the temple. But the Chisong temple in Jinhua was in a rural district, above a reservoir, at least 30 minutes by bus from the nearest city, Jinhua, which has only a fraction of the population of Guangzhou. Most residents in Jinhua had no exposure to the stories and legends about HDX, or to worship of the saint, until the various temples to HDX began to be built in the area from the early 1990s.

Is location important in the success of a temple? It has been proposed that location was one of the key conditions for the success of the HDX temple in Hong Kong (Lang and Ragvald 1993), and other analysts have also noted the importance of the location of a temple (e.g., Chau 2006: 86). Location can be important; other things being equal, because a temple conveniently located close to a large population of potential worshippers, and easily reachable by other potential visitors such as tourists and curious locals, has better prospects of attracting visitors than a remote and hard-to-reach temple far from any substantial number of worshippers or tourists. Of course, there may be other temples that are equally convenient; so, after location, the features of the temple then become a key factor in determining which of the conveniently located temples attracts the most visitors. However, other things being equal, location and convenience are very important.

Of course, some famous rural temples and monasteries in remote locations have sufficient religious or historical significance to attract pilgrims and tourists, especially if those temples are very ancient or very grand or sit in spectacular settings perched on mountainsides overlooking scenic valleys, or are located near major tourist attractions. However, the temples discussed in this chapter, and most new temples in mainland China, cannot rely on fame or historic significance or proximity to major tourist destinations to attract visitors. So, Dr Ye's temple had major advantages over Ms Luo's temple in terms of this "location" factor (which of course includes transportation to the site of the temple), and indeed, the very good location was one of the factors in Dr Ye's decision to take on the project. This makes it all the more impressive that Ms Luo has managed to make her rural temple successful, partly by reducing the "location disadvantage" by inducing the local bus company to run more buses to the temple, and installing a large parking lot next to the temple, thus making it easier and more convenient for Jinhua urbanites to travel to the temple by bus.

This is a good example of the point that a locational disadvantage can be overcome with transportation innovations. The reader may recall that for the Zugong temple discussed in Chapter 5, the local government considered trying to reduce the locational disadvantage by building a cable-car up to the temple, but abandoned the plan because it was prohibitively expensive at that time. For the Guangzhou temple project, Dr Ye undoubtedly assessed the locational advantages of the Fangcun site for his temple before committing his time and resources to the project, but he also did not neglect to publicize the transportation routes to the temple in advertising its features to Guangzhou residents through the newspaper ads. We can say that both Dr Ye and Ms Luo were acutely aware of the location–transportation issue, and crafted their strategies according to the circumstances of each temple.

Second, Dr Ye was entirely secular in his management of the temple, leaving the priests to conduct their activities according to their training (although he did try to improve their singing and chanting performances by hiring a trainer to teach them to sing in unison), whereas Ms Luo became deeply immersed in the theory and practices of Daoism (an interest which preceded her involvement with the Chisong temple), eventually achieving ordination as a Daoist cleric, and devoted herself much more intensively to selecting priests, arranging and supervising their religious activities, and upgrading their Daoist expertise through lectures, evening studies, and visits by Daoist experts from other cities. Both Dr Ye and Ms Luo appear to have successfully navigated the potentially difficult interactions between priests and secular managers. Ms Luo's particular path to this outcome, through ordination as a Daoist clergy, may be one of the most striking and unusual features of the success of her temple management.

A third difference between the two cases is that Dr Ye has apparently never had a significant problem with the local government's recognition of his temple, whereas Ms Luo had to deal with the consequences of changes in the local government's structure and the transfer out of officials who had originally supported the project, which eventually led to a potential threat to the temple's legitimacy as a registered and approved temple. She met these difficulties successfully, but had to work hard to bolster the temple's local support and its community-related activities. The quiet struggle over the possession of the temple registration document recounted in Chapter 6 is the most extraordinary incident we have encountered among all of these temples in regard to temple legitimacy. But both temples are now well-established in their local communities and apparently accepted by the local government agencies.

Fourth, Ms Luo in the early years engaged in intensive local charitable activity with periodic free medical services for elderly and scholarships for local students as part of her strategies to gain support, legitimacy, and approval in the district. By contrast, Dr Ye funneled revenue from the temple into branches of the local government, particularly for services such as police and fire department assistance on days when the temple was particularly crowded. There was little attempt to initiate local charitable services in the district, although he did provide a major donation to a local hospital near the temple. This is partly because the local district governments in Guangzhou already have extensive public services for education, health, welfare, and so on, and there would be little space (or tolerance) for an organization attempting to augment or replace those services. By contrast, in Jinhua in the late 1990s and early 2000s, the rural population in districts around the temple was still underserved in terms of health and education, and so Ms Luo's outreach activities made some contributions while not alienating the local government.

But as Jinhua developed and became wealthier, and public services more extensive, Ms Luo eventually stopped some of the earlier charitable activities such as free medical and optical care for rural elderly, choosing instead to develop Daoist longevity activities, which would not compete directly with secular public services. Clearly, some of the early strategies adopted by Ms Luo were suitable and useful for some period of time, but were not necessarily supportable over the longer term. She used her resources and ideas to experiment with creative additions to local welfare, continuing those which were sustainable, and abandoning those which were not.

We should note that in both of these cases, the initiatives, innovations, and temple enhancements adopted by these entrepreneurs were experimental, and designed to test what worked and was useful. It is a dynamic process, and certainly continues. The nature of religious entrepreneurialism is that it does not cease as long as creative entrepreneurs remain committed to and engaged with the success and growth of their temple projects. It is actually with some regret that we have to conclude our accounts of these developments up to the time of writing, because we are certain that this process will continue and will produce further interesting and creative enhancements to each of these successful and popular temples.

Finally, we should note that we have assessed the relative success of each temple partly on the basis of their ability to attract visitors, whom we have referred to as "worshippers" and "tourists." Both "tourists" and "worshippers" can contribute to temple revenues, through purchase of entry tickets and of various religious and secular items in temple shops and restaurants. The promotion of the temple in a district or region can attract both kinds of visitors. Priests who offer services at a temple for fees no doubt prefer "worshippers," and local government agencies responsible for economic development probably prefer "tourists." But temple managers such as Ms Luo and Dr Ye seem to be promoting and enhancing their temples to make them attractive to both kinds of "visitors."

But in fact, there is no clear line between "tourists" and "worshippers," as a number of scholars have pointed out from their own research (e.g., Goossaert and Fang 2009; Dott 2010; Sutton and Kang 2010; Svensson 2010). Many tourists are attracted by the spectacles at a large temple, and the historical significance of the site, but are also willing to try the "religious" activities as part of the experience (e.g., Sutton and Kang 2010: 122), while "pilgrims" and "worshippers" at these temples also visit them partly for the same gratifications that the temples provide for tourists—rich experiences of colors, music, and incense, spectacular locations, impressive halls and statues, and so on (Dott 2010: 27). In fact, all religions provide a mix of "religious" and "sensual" experience, and successful religious entrepreneurs usually understand this as they design their religious sites.

Notes

1 Interviews with Dr Ye were conducted in Guangzhou in 2003 and 2004 (by Graeme Lang and Selina Chan), and with the head priest (by Selina Chan) and in Guangzhou and Hong Kong in 2000 and 2001 (by Graeme Lang and Lars Ragvald).

2 Dr Ye founded the company Canada Land in 1972, to develop properties for sale to Asian interests, and eventually returned to Hong Kong and China in 1991 to develop real estate and tourists attractions in Guangzhou. In 1997, he was appointed as a member of the People's Consultative Committee of Guangzhou, elected President of the Canadian Chamber of Commerce in 1998, and eventually elected as Guangzhou Municipal Honorable Citizen. He received the Honorary Doctor of Laws degree from his alma mater, Concordia University in Montreal, in 1998 (*GEG Annual Report*, 2012: http:// www.galaxyentertainment.com/uploads/investor/59239f66d0f92dc7aca359a22144894c fc8bb768.pdf, accessed May 9, 2014; *Canada Land Limited Annual Report* 2011/2012).

3 We were told that the final agreement included a lease on the land for 70 years, while control over the management and finances of the temple was for 40 years. Presumably, Dr Ye's company could continue to receive income from the temple, in principle, after 40 years, even if the Daoist Association took over the management, thus assuring the builder that major investments in an impressive and durable temple would not be lost by conversion of the land to other uses.

4 Toilets are not a small matter in a temple which would receive thousands of visitors each day during peak periods. The reason for carefully engineering the toilets was to ensure that there were no unpleasant smells in any part of the temple compound despite the presence of toilets for visitors on the grounds of the temple.

5 Jean Oi has noted that in Guangdong, there have been other cases where non-mainland owners who originally had only partial ownership of a local firm were recently allowed to buy up the local state's share and take full ownership. Thus, the eventual full "privatization" of control over the Fangcun temple, through Dr Ye's purchase of the government's 10 percent share of the enterprise must be seen within the context of evolving policies toward "privatization" in Guangdong. See Jean Oi, "After state socialism: political constraints on privatization in China," presented at the 40th Anniversary Conference of the University Service Centre, on 'The State of Contemporary China', at The Chinese University of Hong Kong, January 5–7, 2004, p.12. However, part of the reason for Dr Ye's acquisition of the remaining 10 percent of the shares was that he did not want to deal with the privatized local company to which the local government had allocated the local government's 10 percent share of the temple. His offer to the local government was, "either you buy my 90 percent of the temple, or I'll buy that local company's 10 percent share." Of course, they chose the latter.

6 The Annual Report for Canada Land Limited 2012 (p. 12), provides a glimpse of the way the company deals with local government relations: "The Company does not establish any policies on risk oversight and management of material business risks. A significant portion of the Group's operations is conducted in the People's Republic of China (the "PRC") where growth is rapid and the legal framework is occasionally uncertain when compared to the more developed economic nations in the world. In the opinion of the Board, through constant contact with appropriate officials inside and outside government and discussions with external advisers the Group reduces unnecessary risk to the minimum."

7 The Sanyuan Gong, the main historic Daoist temple in Guangzhou, had four Daoist priests at that time, in 2003.

8 Statistics Bureau of Guangzhou. September 2012. ("统计年鉴 2012" [in Chinese]).
9 When the ancient shipyard was being excavated in Guangzhou and prepared for exhibition in the city as part of Guangzhou's archaeological heritage, Dr Ye noticed that the site would be susceptible to flooding. He invited some high officials to his office to outline a solution which involved drains and a covering over the site, which he would donate to the city. They agreed, and when the work was completed, they gave him a large piece of the wooden structure from the original shipyard as a gesture of appreciation. Eventually, he had it cleaned and preserved and added it to the temple's decorations,
10 *Canada Land Limited Annual Report* 2011/2012, accessed May 8, 2014, at: http://member.afraccess.com/media?id=CMN://3A375062&filename=20120625/CDL_01308336.pdf. The Report refers to the temple (without naming it) as a "tourist attraction" operated by the company in Guangzhou.

8 Conclusion

Introduction

This book interrogates the complex process of reviving, building, and managing a series of temples in China with the purposes ranging from the revival of religious life to economic and tourism development over a period of more than 20 years. We have provided a general analysis of the construction and management of a series of temples as well as in-depth studies of selected temples. Temples are not examined separately as independent case studies, but as part of a common network formed by local and transnational communities. Three themes have been addressed. First, this book has given a detailed account of the process of how different local governments played an active role in initiating a series of temple-building activities without having the intention of reviving religious practices. Second, our book analyzes the different marketing strategies used in managing temples and attracting visitors, as well as the complex dynamics involving the transnational, national, and local forces behind the scenes. Third, it examines how the symbol of HDX has been appropriated and relocalized in Jinhua for place-making and identity construction.

In this concluding chapter, we will discuss these three themes in an attempt to demonstrate that the series of temple-building activities and management is relevant for a general understanding of economic, cultural, and social development in China. We start with the issue raised at the beginning of the book: Why have so many temples dedicated to HDX been constructed? How do the local governments trigger the reawakening of legends and memories relating to HDX in local communities to legitimize a series of temple-building activities? What functions did these temples serve in the economic and political goals of state officials? How did local authorities and local intellectuals attempt to enhance the authenticity of each project in terms of local heritage and history? What are the effective strategies which popularize temples? What is the impact on local religious life and local identities?

Temple construction and the politics of memories

Our book has demonstrated that the overseas Chinese did not play an active role in reviving local memories although it was they who triggered the revival of the legends of HDX in Jinhua during their initial visits there. Neither have they played an active role in most of the temple-building projects. Exceptions were found in cases of Dr Ye and Ms Luo. Overseas Chinese who went to Jinhua are from different social and cultural backgrounds and have different motivations. Some have distinctive religious affiliations in Hong Kong and went with the curiosity of searching for the roots of HDX. Others were interested in exploring business opportunities (see Chapters 3 and 4). Unlike the overseas Chinese in Fujian (Dean 1998; Kuah-Pearce 2000), the majority of these overseas Chinese do not pay regular visits to Jinhua. The passion that motivated most of the pilgrims over the search for the hometown of HDX in Jinhua quickly cooled down as they were unable or unwilling to be closely connected to the local communities and authorities.

Local governments in Jinhua were the ones who have taken up the leadership of reawakening, compiling, and promoting histories and legends relating to HDX, although the overseas Chinese were the first to introduce knowledge and information on HDX to Jinhua through transnational networks. This is different from existing research on the revival of temples and religious practices in China, which noted that a bottom-up approach has been taken, with local villagers playing the lead role in driving the revival rather than the government. Various local governments compete with each other through mobilizing intellectuals and locals to revive, invent, and select memories and legends that highlight different connections to HDX.

Historical texts and oral narratives of HDX legends have been recalled, remembered, as well as selectively and creatively promoted by different local governments together with intellectuals, temple managers, and local villagers. Such a process is also different from existing research on social memories and religion, in which the people themselves took the lead in remembering the communities' difficult past (e.g., Jing 1996; Mueggler 2001). Instead, the oral narratives recovered by the local government, intellectuals, as well as locals in Huang Peng village and Chisong county reflect the everyday life of peasants and universal moral virtues. A wide range of stories relating to HDX has been revived to account for different stages of his life. HDX has been portrayed as an authentic person who lived there and had overcome natural disasters and problems encountered by the peasants in the farming communities, healed and helped the poor, as well as resisted unreasonable requests of emperors with his magical powers after becoming an immortal.

The retrieving of oral narratives of the past is closely related to the conditions of the present and aspirations for the future. Jing (1996) investigates how thirst for revenge and communal recovery in the present has conjured up memories of suffering, and the new Confucius temple serves as a means to reconcile with the traumatic past. Mueggler (2001) demonstrates how social memories of wounded community are constantly recalled in the struggle for "ethical justice and reconciliation" in the present and future. Historical memories recalled in the process of temple revival reveal the desire to work with the state in the present to attain aspirations for economic development and modernity in the future (Flower 2004: 681). Our examination of legends revived at different places in Jinhua shows that the past has been retrieved, remembered, or invented primarily to justify temple-building activities in different local communities. Based on legends and historical texts found and endorsed by the local governments in Jinhua, the official authorities have identified Jinhua as the overall hometown of HDX in a broader sense. Huang Peng village at Lanxi is now recognized as the official birthplace of HDX, while Jinhua Mountain and Chisong county are considered places where HDX practiced Daoism. Subsequently, a number of temples dedicated to him were built in these places.

Nevertheless, legends are narratives of multiple memories as well as conflicting accounts of the past in the present. They brought understanding to the competition between governments, as well as between people and governments. We have shown that it is the authority of the prefectural-level government which settles the hometown controversy and not historical evidence. These narratives of HDX endorsed by the local government have been contested by entrepreneurs and local villagers based on their different interests. Villagers from Xianqiao and entrepreneurs from Yiwu are currently trying to develop temple-related tourism by claiming that their villages are also important places linked to HDX through legends and interpretations of historical texts. Memories of HDX in legends are clearly an ongoing process of struggle between different parties in the present.[1] Indeed, memories are dynamic processes of construction and reconstruction in response to the changing socioeconomic interests of various parties in the changing present.

Temples as spectacles and sites for enriching experience

To be a popular temple which draws lots of visitors, it is usually either a community center which is related closely to the life of the people, or is an interesting site which attracts different kinds of visitors, including both tourists and petitioners. Anthropologists who studied China have paid adequate attention to temples as community centers that draw in people from village communities. Community temples play a significant role in conducting public events and charitable activities, thereby attracting villagers and creating bonds among them (e.g., Tsai 2002; Chau 2006; Goossaert and Palmer 2011: 256). Efficacy of the deity is another obvious reason which draws worshippers. Recently, some researchers began to pay attention to temples at tourist spots in which the majority of the visitors are tourists, but the strategies to attract visitors have not been discussed. Some of these temples were renovated or promoted by local governments because they fall within the geographical scope of heritage sites (see McCarthy 2010; Sutton and Kang 2010). Other grand temples in tourist spots were renovated by businessmen, or contracted to them, for developing local economy or ethno-religious tourism (e.g., Sutton and Kang 2010: 105; Svensson 2010). These studies are confined to examining temples as tourist sites, without any detailed account of how the governments initiate the revival and construction of temples, and whether with support from locals or capital from overseas worshippers or investors. Indeed, there are very few studies on the management of temples, the development of temples as enterprises, or the commoditization of religion.[2] Yang (2005) mentioned that nontemple Daoists in Shanghai and elsewhere are entrepreneurs who provide religious services outside of "religious activity places." Chau (2006: 122) also suggested that "we can view Longwanggou as a petty capitalist enterprise based on the provisioning of Heilongdawang's efficacious responses, and increasingly in a manner resembling convenience stories and one-stop shopping malls."

In our studies of temples, we attempted to find out strategies to increase the attraction of temples to various kinds of visitors. This approach does *not* treat the temple as merely a profit-making entity in which managers are not really concerned about "religion," because a temple's appeal to worshippers or potential worshippers is also clearly important for the success of a temple that aims at attracting such people and induce return visits. But it does deploy many of the same categories of assessment as are used in the study of other kinds of enterprises. We have profiled the strategies and initiatives of several of these temple managers in some detail, including those of Ms Luo and Ms Hu in Jinhua, and of Dr Ye in Guangdong. These accounts do not provide the same level of detail as in the small number of other publications which also profile the strategies of a shrewd and successful temple manager (e.g., Chau, 2006, on temple boss Lao Wang), but they cover a picture of development of temples for more than a decade and nevertheless add to our knowledge of the variety of ways in which creative temple managers have attempted to make their temples popular, successful, and authentic.

We noted that temple managers work hard to promote their temples, for some of them at least, because they are competing with other temples for visitors. Other scholars have also commented on this "competition" between temples. For example, in *Miraculous Response: Doing Popular Religion in Contemporary China*, Adam Chau writes,

> Different temples quite consciously compete with one another in promoting their own deity's magical power, and in the process different ways of provisioning *ling* [efficacy] are invented, modified, or expanded. The case of Longwanggou presents several examples of these kinds of conscious manipulation of what is called 'business models' in the world of business (i.e., ways of generating revenue). Of course, any innovation should still be framed in culturally acceptable idioms or one risks provoking cycnicism and losing support of worshippers.
>
> (Chau 2006: 120)

> In an effort to further expand the temple's service repertoire, temple boss Lao Wang decided a few years ago to build an elegant, new temple hall for Heilongdawang's mother, Longmu niangniang, so that people with problems and anxieties relating to reproduction and child rearing and who normally go to goddess temples would also come to the Heilongdawang Temple for help. Images of one-stop shopping easily come to mind.
>
> (Chau, 2006: 120–121)

Apparently, each temple is unique and the "formula" for getting popular is not always the same. Different strategies could be divided into two categories: improvement in hardware or software. The hardware includes the physical features of the temple, including both the main hall and statues, and the other buildings and grounds of the temple. They include an impressive statue of the temple's principal deity and a variety of other god-statues, chosen on the basis of the deities which are popular or interesting to potential visitors and each with his or her own worship-space (e.g., a separate hall or side-hall within the temple compound); ornate and colorful exterior and interior walls, ceilings, arches, paintings, and furniture; a large and clean plaza in front of the temple with urns for placing incense sticks; plants, shrubs, and trees around and within the temple compound; if possible, a pond or fountain; good views from within or near the temple of surrounding landscapes; an impressive view from within the temple compound of the main hall of the temple.

However, the software provided by the temple is equally important. The software includes the provision of a rich experience to visitors in both sacred and secular aspects. The temple managers have to be as creative as possible in offering a complete suite of different services to visitors. These services include credible-looking clergy performing religious activities such as chanting or singing or other forms of musical performance, as well as being available for consultations with visitors (i.e., fortune-telling and palm-reading); longevity exercises, clean and family-friendly hiking tracks, nice restaurants, lodges, shops in which good-quality religious, quasireligious, and secular (e.g., cultural) souvenirs are available for sale at reasonable prices; and attentive, easily accessible staff to answer questions, accept and record donations, and answer enquiries and provide directions at the temple.

Strategies adopted at Fangcun HDX temple and CSDY in Jinhua show that both the hardware and the software of the temples are of excellent quality. The physical setting is decent and the temple is well-maintained and new structures and new services are constantly added to increase attraction and add new experiences for visitors. In both temples, quality and diversity of religious services are important for attracting visitors. Indeed, it is an advantage if temples have qualified religious specialists and trustworthy ritual services.[3] Both temple managers tried to ensure that the on-site clergy provided a good quality and variety of religious services. Regular, well-orchestrated Daoist music and professional ritual performances are impressive features of temples, which are however always absent in many Chinese temples in China today because of the disruption brought about by the Cultural Revolution. Charitable activities performed by temples is an important means of upholding moral values in contemporary society and building their reputation, besides being an attraction to visitors and serving as a reminder of the traditional practices of temples. They all granted an "authentic" religious experience to the worshippers.

Moreover, religion also provides "spectacle," with a range of sensory experiences—sights, sounds, colours, smells, music, singing, paintings, statues, uses of lights and shadows, striking architecture, and so on. This is part of the reason that many tourists visit religious sites but also part of the reason that it is interesting and satisfying for many people with religious motivations to visit the same sites repeatedly. As noted in Chapter 4, there is very often no sharp distinction between "the tourist" and "the pilgrims" at many of these temples (see also Oakes and Sutton 2010; Dott 2010). Many "tourists" are influenced and impressed by the religious atmosphere at temples and may even try some of the religious activities for the sake of the experience, or if they were initially non-believers, may eventually become "worshippers" or "pilgrims," as many also savour or enjoy the spectacles at a temple and go there partly for those reasons.[4] At temple festivals, and on special days such as the Spring Festival or the birthdays of the gods, it seems to be the case that a "hot and noisy" (*renao*) experience is important: crowds of people, lots of different kinds of activities, a lively atmosphere—the crowds themselves become part of the appeal of going to these festivals (Chau 2006). Today, various groups of visitors came to CSDY for different activities. Some came because of the reputation of the temple as a *renao*, fun place, while others did so for the efficacy of the deity in answering prayers.[5] We found tourists coming as a group on weekends to enjoy barbeque or camping, families arriving for leisure, groups of retirees coming for qigong exercises, while couples were taking bridal photographs there. Many also bowed or prayed at temples. Visitors are also invited by the temple manager to come to CSDY from time to time. Some of these are from the local district (students, elderly, officials, calligraphers), and some are from the manager's networks outside the district, while others are from other cities or from overseas (Taiwan). The coming and going of these groups, while only occasionally visible to the other visitors coming to the temple or through temple publicity, also add to the atmosphere of a busy and lively temple. Managers at CSDY and Fangcun temples are generally aware of these kinds of effects, and do their best to improve the "temple experience" for that reason.

For YYY and Zugong, the management teams are competent in building the hardware, including the construction of grand temples. Nevertheless, the maintenance of the physical building is not always conducted properly, as was found in the case of YYY. Most importantly, the management teams at Zugong and YYY seem to be less competent in providing the visitors with a memorable experience. Both temples appeared to be rather quiet and empty most of the time, and also did not have a reputation for the efficacy of the deity in answering prayers. The major promotional strategy of these temples is to authenticate HDX as a cultural heritage in Jinhua and to assert Jinhua as the hometown of HDX while connecting with HDX's translocal ties. We have recounted the details of the promotional strategies adopted by the municipal government, the Jinhua office of the United Front, the cadres in the Double Dragon Cave Management Committee, and the government-sponsored HDX Cultural Research Association. HDX has been represented and promoted as a religion and a cultural heritage in Jinhua through media power and creative branding strategies, cultural tourism festivals, and conferences.[6] Although strategies of HDX adopted by local governments in authenticating legends have successfully constructed and spread the portrayal of Jinhua as HDX's hometown, those strategies merely enhanced the reputation of HDX in

Jinhua, and they are not effective in drawing visitors to specific temples operated by the local governments.

Temple managers at Zugong and YYY are rather cautious not to promote the associated religious beliefs because religious activities could easily be viewed as superstition by the authorities (see Chapter 4). In both temples, the management teams experienced difficulty in managing the priests and in improving religious services. They were reluctant to be involved in religious matters although the manager at YYY had to turn to religious activities eventually because no tourists had come to visit. In both temples, the management teams promote HDX as cultural heritage and their temples as tourist sites. Nevertheless, both temples neither offer particularly exotic temple buildings or objects for tourists to gaze at nor provide a special, enriching experience to tourists, and thus both temples do not attract crowds during ordinary days. Jinhua as the "authentic" hometown alone is also not appealing enough to attract many overseas pilgrims to visit the temples and the visits to Zugong and YYY are not a particularly fruitful experience which could sustain regular visits. This is rather different from the experience of pilgrims from Taiwan/Southeast Asia to Fujian because their visits were enriched by secular (visiting kinsmen at hometown) as well as sacred activities (Dean 1998).

To the locals and visitors, they are also not concerned with the historical "authenticity" of HDX as that was portrayed by the government. To them, a temple becomes an "authentic religious place" when it is crowded with worshippers and visitors, filled with incense and smoke and exudes a religious aura. To the locals, "authenticity" is determined by whether HDX has become a significant part of their religious or economic life. They are more concerned with whether the temples have satisfied their religious desires (e.g., efficacy of the deity), and whether these temples have brought new economic opportunities and improved their livelihood as was promised by the temple builders.[7] In both YYY and Zugong, new temples neither played a significant role in enriching the religious life of locals nor directly increased villagers' income greatly. In contrast, the CSDY and Fangcun HDX temples have enriched the religious life of the locals, while the local communities have also benefited economically from the development of CSDY.

In addition to providing an enriching experience to the visitors, the management teams are also required to have good relationships with the local governments and support from the locals. We have shown that good relationships with the locals could be built through meeting their needs in both the religious and economic aspects, such as conducting charitable activities in the local communities. In addition, we have highlighted the importance of governmental endorsement and support to the temples. This is particularly important in China because different temple-development strategies have also led to a wide range of religious and cultural activities at temples, which may be questionable in the eyes of the governments. These activities include entertaining pilgrimage tours organized around spirit mediums, fortune-telling, palm-reading, and divination services, which could easily be considered as superstition by the state. Indeed, the popularization of the worship of HDX and the appearance of spirit mediumship focusing on HDX in different communities are consequences that are also not necessarily anticipated nor welcomed by the state. These religious activities at temples would be suppressed by the state if they are considered as negative superstition. How do various actors (temple managers, priests, locals) escape from the state's tight control of these religious practices?

A dichotomous view of state domination and local resistance does not explain the practice of religious activities in post-reform China. Palmer, Shive, and Wickeri (2011: 208) have pointed out that religious practices do not necessarily follow what was set in the laws and regulations by the central government because the local authorities implement them in different ways and with various interpretations. Similarly, the case of Longwanggou temple in Shaanxi shows that religious activities were neither completely compliant with the party–state ideology nor were entirely autonomous (Chau 2005: 260). Negotiations between the people and local state took place all the time (ibid., see also Yang 2004, 2008). Ashiwa and Wank (2006) show that actual practices are results of implementation of state policy through the interaction of three parties: religious association, Religious Affairs Bureau, and the temple administration team. This is complicated in China by the greater interest of state agencies in promoting the cultural, heritage, and tourism features of temples that bolster the economy, which lies in contrast to the religious motivations of some priests, temple managers, festival organizers, and worshippers in promoting the more specifically religious features of a temple's activities and services (Ashiwa and Wank 2006). Indeed, religious activities are considered legitimate, and hence would be encouraged only if they are positive cultural and touristic activities (e.g., Jing 1996; Dean 1998, 2003; Flower and Leonard 1998; Feuchtwang 2000; Eng and Lin 2002).

To gain continuous support from the local governments, temple managers came up with several strategies. First, as in previous research, they use "folk culture" and cultural heritage as justifications for activities conducted at the temples. Touristic and economic development is an effective coverage which leads to religious rejuvenation in the context of market economy. Second, the moral authority of the temple that was established through charitable activities to a wide range of underprivileged groups, offers legitimacy to activities performed by the temple. Indeed, these charitable activities did not only provide satisfaction to those who receive the medical services or educational subsidies directly, but also pleased the local government as it relieved part of the burden of relevant government departments. Third, economic benefits to the local governments are not only limited to the provision of charitable services to the local communities under their jurisdiction, but also in the form of direct donation as well as supplementary pay to the local police who maintain law and order in the district where the temple is located. Fourth, the temple manager was also clever enough to utilize HDX in Jinhua as a symbol for promoting China's political reunification. This is more sophisticated than that as portrayed by Dean (1998), in that it was primarily the government that promoted this ideology in legitimizing the revival of Mazu in Fujian. In our studies, not only has the Chinese government played the reunification card, but Ms Luo has also utilized her role skillfully as a

Taiwanese to blend in with the ideology of reunification. In addition to arranging regular visits of the Taiwanese religious specialists and tours to Jinhua and Beijing, which were presented as cultural exchange between China and Taiwan, the temple management team also acted as the messenger on behalf of the Jinhua prefectural-level city government to send statues of HDX to three senior KMT officials.

Relocalizing HDX in Jinhua

It is clear that overseas Chinese, local governments, temple managers, intellectuals, and locals are all involved in reviving and relocalizing HDX through temple-building projects and reawakened memories. Temple-building projects have revived, reinvented, and enriched the religious life of villagers, especially in Chisong and Huang Peng, Lutian, Rengang, as well as many other worshippers of HDX who live inside and outside of Jinhua and Guangdong. Some of them were drawn to HDX because he is a local religious icon from the past. For instance, villagers in Chisong built and renovated old temples dedicated to the deity in reviving their religious practices. Others learned about HDX from the media and overseas Chinese. They were also drawn by his reputation overseas and sometimes because of the deity's efficacy in healing and in answering petitions. For instance, worship of HDX in Huang Peng village was popularized although neither villagers recalled any earlier temples for HDX in their village nor any form of worship of HDX took place in the past.[8]

Nevertheless, it is important to note that the revival or invention primarily focuses on HDX and not his brother, who was also worshipped by the peasants in Jinhua in the past. Apparently, this is due to the influence of overseas Chinese who worship HDX exclusively.[9] Today, the majority of temples constructed in Jinhua are dedicated to the worship of HDX only and he is well-known in Jinhua, but not his brother, although both statues of HDX and his brothers are still in the newly rebuilt Chisonggong as well as the renovated old temples, Erhuangjunci. Similarly, most legends and memories revived also focus on HDX, and there was very little mention of his brother who is also an immortal. To the locals, "forgetting" the brother is as important as remembering HDX himself because of the latter's connection to overseas pilgrims. Indeed, the revival or invention of religious beliefs is an active local response to the transnational connections.

Moreover, the revival of memories and temple-building projects has led to the making of local places. Places or localities are "here in relation to a there" by imagination (Casey 1993; Feuchtwang 2004: 24), and are often known as a process of making in the context of globalization (see e.g., Appadurai 1996; Lu 2002).[10] Feuchtwang (2004: 4) argues that place-making is "a process of centering" by various forces and in different forms. Places are constructed through the territorialization of state, capitalism, and local history (ibid.: 177). In Jinhua, we have demonstrated that the building of temples by capital from different sources, the performance of religious, social, touristic-economic activities, and the reawakening of memories relating to HDX, form a complex process of making places. Local villagers in Chisong, Lutian, and Huang Peng were proud that their villages have been associated with HDX, who is famous abroad and hence attract tourists and pilgrims.[11] Today, one could also find locally grown vegetables named after the immortal in Lanxi, which are recent inventions that seek attention and consumption from domestic and international tourists. Restaurants or teahouses or BBQ stores next to CSDY or Zugong were named after HDX by the locals, who were looking to attract tourists. Places are made by "the actions and constructions of people tracing salient parts of their daily lives" (Feuchtwang 2004: 10) through religious and tourism-related economic activities. New identities of local places are formed through the forces of socioeconomic development and cultural interaction around local and transnational ties. While Jinhua is acknowledged as the hometown of HDX in tourist brochures, Huang Peng in Lanxi is known as the home village of HDX where he was born. Villagers from Huang Peng in Lanxi were proud to share the same native village with HDX. Xianqiao town in Chisong is remembered by the villagers as the place where HDX and his brother died and became immortals while fighting a natural disaster. Chisong, Lanxi, Yiwu, and Jinhua Mountain are places where HDX conducted different activities according to legends recalled by various groups. Landmarks relating to HDX were highlighted at different places in Jinhua, in the form of temples or relics, as a result of state power, investment projects, and narratives of local histories.

While these local places are made with new identities through the reawakening of memories, temple-building projects, and tourism-related activities, a transnational Chinese identity has also been promoted by the local governments through utilizing the symbol of HDX.[12] Indeed, the local governments have utilized HDX and its legends as intangible cultural heritage, so as to inculcate Chinese cultural nationalism and solicit investments and visits from overseas Chinese. Nevertheless, different visitors granted different meanings to their visits to Jinhua: as an exotic tour to China, an experience of Chinese culture in mainland China, an opportunity to explore business opportunities, as well as roots-searching and pilgrimage experiences. Apparently, the politics of surrounding the deity's native roots have been well-played by different actors for their own interests. A complex, multifaceted process of identities is formulated and negotiated by overseas pilgrims according to their respective experiences with the symbol of HDX in Jinhua. New imaginaries of HDX as a symbol of multifaceted Chinese identities, or local place identities, have emerged. Indeed, the symbol of HDX has now been re-established and relocalized with multiple and diverse meanings through the process of blending religious beliefs and cultural heritage, local religion and economic development, as well as the local and transnational Chinese identities. This process of "relocalizing" HDX in Jinhua is grounded in the everyday experience of the religious, economic, and cultural life of villagers, the exotic and enriching tours of tourists or visitors, the religious repertoire of petitioners and pilgrims, the marketing strategies of temple managers, the various economic and political agendas of local governments, the practices and negotiation of cultural nationalism, as well as the transnational flows of capital, people, ideas, and goods.

Notes

1 The remembering of the temple in Dachuan was a creative act which serves the interests in the present (Jing 1996), while the remembering and revival of the temple in Ya'an makes the present responsibility of the state in building the road explicit (Flower 2004).

2 In Taiwan, Huang (2009) accounted the structure and bureaucracy of the managerial staff and the charismatic leadership of Chen Yen while explaining the global development of Tzu Chi.

3 In principle, each province and most cities have a Daoist Association which can provide some trained clergy for local Daoist temples, in return for some share of the temple revenues for the priests and the Association, and some participation in decisions on how the temple is operated. In practice, there are many problems which arise in these relationships (Goossaert and Fang 2009).

4 We should also reiterate that "worshippers" is a very broad category with a wide range of possible approaches and attitudes toward "worship" (see also Lang and Ragvald 1993, Ch. 5, on "Believers", and Chau 2006, Ch. 5, on "Beliefs and Practices"). Some religiously inclined visitors to a temple are interested in the doctrines and beliefs about immortality, the afterlife, the prescriptions for a virtuous life, and so on; but many others are primarily interested in getting some supernatural assistance or advice about some particular problem. Hence, "petitioners" is often a more accurate account of the visitor's motivations than "worshipper." It is also the case that many "petitioners" are not fully convinced that the deference and the offerings will be noticed or have any effect, and take a pragmatic approach to the act of petitioning or showing respect to the deity ("If it works, I will return to give thanks and make more offerings, but if not, maybe the deity was distracted, or there was nothing there after all, or, maybe we should try another deity next time since this deity didn't do much.") So, even the "worshipper" category of visitors is a far too simple concept to capture the range of secular and "religious" motivations of visitors to a temple.

5 Chau (2006: 243) also mentioned that visitors visited the temples because of the efficacy of the deity.

6 Similar strategies are found in promoting other temples (Dean 1998).

7 Weller (2000: 477–478) argues that religion practices in Taiwan vary. Religion satisfies individuals as "embedded members of social networks" and "caters to asocial individuals."

8 The popularization of religious beliefs however does not necessarily imply the popularization of the temple. While Huang Peng villagers worship HDX, they do not necessarily support YYY. Instead, the worship has often been conducted at the Gunglu temple (see also Chan and Lang 2007).

9 Nevertheless, the influence from overseas communities on memories of local ritual practices in Jinhua is limited although religious exchanges between the Taiwanese and Chinese priests have been conducted at one temple. This is also different from the situation in Putian, Fujian where overseas Chinese are well-known for reintroducing and shaping the local ritual practices through religious exchange between ritual specialists (Dean 2010: 249–250).

10 Places are sometimes made as a result of nostalgia and nation-building (Lu 2002).

11 Although overseas pilgrims do not pay regular visits to these temples, villagers were enthusiastic in recalling their visits as ways to affirm the special status of the temples.

12 The "revival" of Buddhism is noted as a process of how the state has circulated the symbol of Buddhism as culture and affected the Buddhist discourse and performance (Zhe 2011: 45–46). The turning of religion into culture is an innovative revitalization (ibid.: 45).

Appendix

The lives of a saint—compiling stories about Huang Chuping in Jinhua, Zhejiang

Deities and saints have identities that are comprised of their personalities and their specializations. A river god might be temperamental, capricious, and only interested in the affairs of river-travellers and fisherpeople (and incompetent to deal with droughts and plagues). A "high god" might be authoritarian, stern, and jealous, demanding total loyalty, but guarding his people from enemies as long as they remain faithful, and laying down the law about what "faithful" means in daily life (but uninterested in minor family troubles and illnesses). A mother-goddess might be kind and nurturing, sympathetically listening to the troubles and ills of women, children, and devotees and willing to help if she can (but unlikely by personality, character, and abilities to help kings win battles against rivals). Most deities have such identities.

But identities of deities can drift and diversify when their worshippers inhabit or migrate into different social and political environments. Some specialized deities become generalized as the social character and occupations of their worshippers, and hence the nature and variety of their needs expand as they migrate into cities. The attributed personality and interests of a deity might also vary between farmers and businesspeople, between the educated and the illiterate, or between men and women. These differences and divergences can be illustrated with many examples from the histories of religions and from the sociological study of religious beliefs.

In our case study, we have focused on a deity whose origins are in fourth century CE Daoist literature about Daoist saints and whose worship seems to have been confined to people in villages and small towns in a rural region around Jinhua for more than a thousand years. It was only in the late nineteenth century, as far as we know, that public or semi-public worship of this figure emerged far to the south, in Guangdong, among mostly educated urbanites in the region around Guangzhou, and was subsequently carried to Hong Kong and popularized among urban residents from the 1920s to the 1970s.

The worship of the deity has been revived in Jinhua, and various parties in Jinhua are rebuilding the deity's identity using icons, images, and stories which they have uncovered or constructed from the bits and pieces which remained. Some of the new Jinhua images have also appropriated features of his identity carried to Jinhua by visiting Hong Kong worshippers. The traditions about the deity overlap and contain some similar features in the two main settings in which he is worshipped—in Guangdong/Hong Kong, and in Jinhua—but there are also striking differences.

In Guangdong, as noted above, there was little evidence for worship of Huang Chuping before the 1890s, when it appeared among a small group of people in the Guangzhou area during a time of plagues and political turmoil. The deity's strong interest in those troubles and crises was amply illustrated in his *fuji* messages to his followers and to the world in the late 1890s and the first few years of the twentieth century (Lang and Ragvald 1998). Subsequently, a much-simplified version of the deity's capacities and interests was carried down to Hong Kong in 1915, and it was only there that the deity survived the devastations and suppressions of folk religion in China between the 1920s and 1970s.

In Hong Kong, the deity came eventually to be perceived as a generalist with a keen interest and a perceptive understanding of the troubles of urbanites in a free-wheeling capitalist metropolis and to be able to help them in their struggles for business success and upward mobility for their families. The deity is not much interested in wars, plagues, farming, rainfall, relations with governments, or international affairs, but he has a reputation for advice about capitalist investments and business decisions, and about paths to success in the educational system of Hong Kong, as well as his older reputation for providing healing services and advice (Lang and Ragvald 1993). In an era where modern medicine is the first choice for almost all Hong Kong residents, the deity is still thought to be capable of providing recommendations for herbal medicines and semi-magical cures for obstinate illnesses, a specialty which was part of his "charisma" in Guangzhou, and in Jinhua. Indeed, the Seseyuan's HDX temple in Hong Kong still provides herbal medicines for worshippers in a building next to the temple plaza. But HDX is firmly a generalist for Hong Kong's anxious and upwardly mobile urbanites and few of the worshippers now seek medical prescriptions.

Most people in Hong Kong know the deity's personality and interests in this way. If they have any knowledge of his fourth century CE origins as a Daoist hermit, it is only the story, purveyed by the two temples devoted to his worship in Hong Kong, that he went up into the mountains to seek Daoist perfection, and when his brother went to search for him he demonstrated his powers by turning white rocks into sheep at his call. Later he devoted himself to helping others, particularly with medicines and healing but without details of particular acts, miracles, or demonstrations of power and virtue.

In Jinhua, by contrast, the stories, legends, and reconstructions of his acts, powers, and interests are much more detailed and diverse. Indeed, most Hong Kong worshippers know none of this and would be surprised by all of the various miracles and interventions attributed to this figure during his life in Jinhua. These stories can be placed into several different "categories" according to their subjects and outcomes. Indeed, some cultural affair intellectuals in Jinhua, after compiling many of these stories, have tried to set up such categories to make sense of the diversity. These collections of stories, compiled in Jinhua by local cultural affairs scholars and intellectuals in the early 1990s, deserve a fuller treatment by specialists, who could compare them to partly similar collections of stories about other Daoist saints and also search for antecedents in local gazetteers.

There are several issues in dealing with these stories. One is the provenance of the stories and the methods used in collecting them. We have little information about provenance, except claims from officials and compilers in Jinhua that these are oral legends collected through interviews with local elderly people. In a few cases, the booklets they produced record the name of the person who told the story and the names of the interviewers (e.g., in Shi 1995: 163–164, the "nine-hill tea" story, where two informants are mentioned, along with the two people who recorded the story from the informants). But this kind of information is not provided for most of the stories.

We do not know where and how the researchers found these informants. We have talked to the compiler of one of these collections, who worked as a fortune-teller at the YYY temple in Lanxi, and he claimed that the stories were collected from about 10 elderly villagers in Huang Peng village near the temple. But he also admitted that he had exercised some creative licence in putting these stories into the book about his village. We were not able to determine how much of a particular story was "original," and how much of the story was a result of the fortune-teller's own embellishments. We also cannot say whether these stories were edited after they had been compiled or whether there were some elaborations added by the compilers or editors. We cannot compare original transcripts or notes from any of these interviews with the final published versions of each story.

We also do not know whether any of these stories were borrowed from the traditions about other Daoist saints or whether they might be the result of merging the histories of some local Daoist saints into a single figure, through the collapsing of stories about other saints into a sequence of legends about the most popular or durable of those saints. We have observed this phenomenon already in regard to stories about "Huang Daxian" in Mt. Luofu in Guangdong (Lang and Ragvald, 1993: 142–145). It would not be surprising if some similar "merging" of saints' biographies have occurred in Jinhua.

One of the processes which occurs in the development of some religions is the compilation and editing of stories about the founder of a religion, or about a saint, usually long after that founder or saint has died and the subsequent production of a canonical or quasicanonical literature about the founder or saint. It seems that this proceeds from the transmission of oral stories within particular communities, to transcriptions of those stories by persons wishing to preserve the stories outside of individual memories, to later editing and sometimes borrowing from other similar texts coming from other communities, after the exchanges of some of these texts among groups of followers.

If a formal organization develops with a mission to rationalize and endorse an authoritative version of the stories and traditions, a "canonical" text may be developed through some collaborative process and is then taught to subsequent generations of believers (and may be enforced if the organization is authoritarian and concerned to suppress rival authorities).[1]

A kind of "semiofficial" biography of Huang Chuping did indeed develop in the form of the southern Guangdong/Hong Kong version of the saint's life, which was transcribed in Guangdong in the late 1890s and eventually adopted and promulgated at their temple in Kowloon by the Seseyuan.

As related earlier in the chapter, the first version of the saint's life was the fourth century capsule-biography by Ge Hong (perhaps based on some earlier oral traditions or some earlier lost written accounts), which was consulted by Daoists in Guangdong in the late nineteenth century, and then transmitted, through spirit-writing, purportedly as the deity's own "autobiography," recorded during the spirit-writing session, and then republished as if it was a direct revelation to these believers from the deity himself. This "autobiography" is endorsed and made available to believers by the Seseyuan, and although there are no rival "autobiographies" which need to be suppressed or refuted, the account is a kind of weak form of a canonical gospel.

Of course, the Seseyuan also has the much more extensive record of the deity's instructions and guidance in the volumes of spirit-writings produced by Liang Renan in the late 1890s, but these are unknown outside the Seseyuan and have not been used by the Seseyuan to try to produce a more complex authoritative version of the saint's life, teaching, and miracles. Thus, the saint's life story, for worshippers who take the trouble to inquire, consists of that very simple version focusing on the saint's journey into the hills as a young shepherd to pursue Daoist cultivation, and his brother's search for him, and then the rocks-into-sheep story, with some reference to further healing acts and help for those in need.

But in the case of the far more diverse Jinhua stories about Huang Chuping, there is (as yet) no religious organization which has the mission and motive to provide a canonical view of the saint's life and to compile stories of the saint's virtue and powers into a coherent biography.[2] The reasons why no such organization developed to preserve and enforce an orthodox version of the saint's life could be explicated but that would require an analysis of the development of authoritarian religious organizations committed to preserving and enforcing orthodoxy in preaching and belief, and the analysis would have to take account of the differences between monotheistic and polytheistic religious cultures. Such an analysis is far beyond the scope of this book. We merely wish to note that these stories have been collected and published in Jinhua without much apparent attempt to shape them into a systematic account of the life, teachings, virtues, and miracles of the saint.

However, the local government has sponsored the collection and publication of stories and legends about HDX (Chuping), not for religious reasons but to mainly bolster the legitimacy of Jinhua's claim to be the homeland of the saint and (as argued in Chapters 3 and 4) to promote the virtues and morality of helping others and service to the people which was supposedly exemplified in the life of the saint.

Here, we will briefly outline some of these stories, to illustrate their much greater diversity compared to the simpler Hong Kong/Guangdong version of the saint's life. The stories are paraphrased in italics under each theme. In the stories, the figure known in Hong Kong as "Huang Daxian" is identified as Huang Chuping, the name of the saint given by Ge Hong in his account of the saint's life before he became an immortal.

First, we note that while the Hong Kong/Guangdong biography of the saint highlights the miracle of turning rocks into sheep, the Jinhua stories also include an explanation of the saint's ability to make this kind of magical transformation. It turns out that he had already turned some sheep into rocks first:

> The saint was looking after the sheep on the mountain, while also trying to learn Daoism from an old Daoist. He heard someone crying for help, and ran down the hill to the river, where he saw a boy struggling and nearly drowning. He jumped into the river and saved the boy, and escorted him back to his home. But when he returned to the mountain, four of the sheep were missing. He found only one, which had hurt its leg and thus couldn't go far. The other three were gone, possibly eaten by a tiger. Since he found it hard to help people and also look after sheep, he asked the Daoist to teach him the magic needed to turn the sheep into rocks [so they couldn't run away while he was busy helping people, and so the tigers couldn't eat the sheep while he was busy with pursuing Daoist arts]. He had to pass three tests to gain this power: sit in the sun for ten days, sit among snakes and insects without disturbing them, and walk on fire. Finally, the Daoist was satisfied, and gave him a golden whip with which to strike the sheep and turn them into stones. The account continues with the story of Chuping's brother searching for him, at the request of their elderly father, observing Chuping's powers using the whip, and joining Chuping and the Daoist to learn Daoism together.
>
> (Ma 1993: 36–42)

The Jinhua stories also include further accounts of the saint turning sheep into rocks. In the first story, he turns sheep into rocks to cover a box, thus hiding it and the gold inside the box from a rich man:

> When Huang Chuping was reading under a tree, he observed a box carried up the hill, which he opened [presumably after those who carried it had left], which contained gold obtained by a greedy rich man through blackmailing (or cheating) local people. Huang Chuping got his sheep to lie on top of the box, and then turned the sheep into stones which covered it. When the greedy rich man came with his servants to retrieve the box, he couldn't find it. After they left, Huang Chuping gave all of the money to local poor people.
>
> (Shi 1995: 147–148)

In the second story, *the saint saves a girl*, he uses the same sheep-transforming power:

> A local girl caught some fish in a river, which she exchanged for rice in the local market, but it turned out that the fish were grandsons of the god of the sea, who punished the girl by covering her with scales. She then jumped into the water and disappeared, leaving her mother crying sadly by the riverside. The saint came upon the scene, and guessed what had occurred. To recover the girl from the water, he turned a number of sheep into large stones, and threw them into the water, which lowered the water level and made it easier

to retrieve the girl from the river. Then he procured some herbs in the nearby hillside, made medicine, and cured her of the scales after several months of treatment. According to the story, she became very beautiful. Thereafter, she and her mother set aside a day each year to venerate the saint.

(Shi 1995: 159–160)

Tigers appear in several of the stories, in which Huang Chuping outwits one or more tigers and protects the local villagers. In the first story, *Distracting the tiger*, the saint confronts and also outwits the tiger:

Huang Chuping was a ten-year-old shepherd, reading on the hillside while his sheep grazed, with some other children nearby. Suddenly the children cried out that a tiger was approaching and was going after one of them. Chuping told the children to climb into a tree, and then used his whip to strike the sheep, causing them to cry out, which then attracted the tiger. Chuping then used the whip on the tiger, striking it in the eye. The tiger ran off, but soon returned. But Chuping carried a bleating sheep in the opposite direction from the children, thus attracting the tiger away from them and saving their lives. He then climbed into a tree, from which the tiger could not dislodge him. The tiger bit the tree, but the sap from the tree was bitter, and the tiger went to drink some water, and then returned to the tree. Chuping had left his clothes in the tree, and mistaking the clothes for the boy, the tiger finally knocked down the tree, but found only clothing. By that time, Chuping had escaped with the sheep and the children. The story spread, and he was praised by villagers for his bravery.

(Wang 2007: 20)

This story was taken to be an example of his virtuous concern for helping others. In another story, the saint used a different method to intimidate tigers:

Two quarrelsome tigers on the mountain had been terrifying villagers with their fierce tiger-fights, but the saint frightened them into silence by arranging a more fierce and thunderous fight between two bulls. The battle between the bulls scared the tigers so much that they gave up their own fights. *[The account relates the saint's intervention to the well-known local tradition of Jinhua bullfights, which had continued up to the present]*.

(Ma 1993: 11–14)

It is not clear how old Chuping was supposed to be at the time of this second incident. If he had already achieved the powers of Daoist perfection, as illustrated by the stories of turning sheep into stones, an inquirer might wonder why a Daoist saint who can turn sheep into stones cannot do the same to tigers. Perhaps, within local conceptions about animals, tigers are too powerful to be easily transformed into stones. Or perhaps, as implied in the first story about transforming sheep into rocks, a power granted to the saint by the old Daoist, this magical power only worked on sheep (and would not work on tigers). If the original miracle stories about white boulders and sheep derive from the similarity, at a distance, between an irregular white boulder and a sheep resting in the grass, then the transformation of a striped tiger into a white boulder, or of a white boulder into a tiger, is less likely to arise in the imaginations of observers. It is also far less likely that both white boulders and tigers would ever be observed at the same time on a hillside. In any case, the stories about Chuping's encounters with tigers probably reflect the fears about wild tigers which evidently afflicted local villagers living near some mountains and forests in China where tigers roamed until at least the late nineteenth century (Elvin 2004).[3]

There are further stories about Huang Chuping's responses to misbehavior and oppressions by the rich and powerful, in which he contrives to cheat or punish greedy rich men who have been cheating or oppressing others.

> A local magistrate and a rich man had forced villagers to go into the mountains to dig for treasure *[presumably, either buried treasure or valuable metals such as gold]*. When Huang Chuping returned to the area and heard about this, he used some tricks to induce the rich man and the magistrate to become suspicious of each other and to fight, which caused them to lose money and reputation, while relieving the pressure on the villagers.
>
> (Wang 2007: 21)

This kind of story might be interpreted by some analysts as a reflection of contemporary tensions in Chinese society and as a veiled critique of everyday oppressions of the "common people" by political and economic elites. But in compiling these stories, local intellectuals would have to be careful not to appear to be promoting anti-regime messages, especially since it was the local government which was paying for the publication of these stories. If there are contemporary messages in the stories, they have to be carefully crafted to appear to refer to those long-ago times. There are certainly precedents in Chinese literature for the use of ancient stories to introduce oblique critiques of modern conditions. But we have no way to confirm that this is the case in these stories.

Some stories seem to reveal tensions between local people and the imperial regime, such as stories about deceiving an emperor for the benefit of local villagers:

> An emperor, visiting the area on a hunting expedition, became hungry and stopped near the mountain to eat. His party encountered an old lady who gave him some porridge, which he liked very much. After he returned to the capital, he asked the Jinhua villagers to send corn for his porridge from the area. There was a drought at that time, however, so it was impossible for them to grow corn for the emperor. The villagers asked the saint for help, and so he converted an area in which he grew herbal medicines to growing corn, and used the water with which he irrigated the herbal crops to irrigate the corn. This corn was used by the villagers, however, and was not sent on to the capital.
>
> (Wang 2007: 20)

There is what appears to be another version of the same story, in an earlier collection of stories:

The emperor liked hunting, but while in the area he encountered a black tiger, and tried to leave, but had lost his way. He was hungry, and eventually fainted. When his servants found him, they took him to a village, where an old man [not an old lady as in the story above] cooked some corn into a porridge, which the emperor liked very much. Back in his palace, his cook was unable to duplicate this porridge using local corn, and so he ordered the Jinhua villagers to send him their corn, threatening to kill them if they did not comply. The villagers were sad and afraid, and asked the two saints (Chuping and Chuqi) to use his (or their) power to produce good corn. The saint [or the two saints] used blessed or 'spiritual' water to help them and to make medicine, and eventually went up to heaven.

(Ma 1993: 69–76)

Some of the stories are about small-scale and personal family assistance by the saint. In one of these stories, the saint also resists marriage in order to devote himself to further Daoist cultivation:

The saint, at age 15, came to a village and heard someone crying. A house had burnt down, and all the pigs and sheep were dead. A man and his mother who lived there had also died in the fire. Only the man's wife and daughter were left alive, and were crying. (The man had been a local "doctor" adept in curing snake bites). The saint was carrying some money given to him by an old Daoist to help him pursue his Daoist cultivation. He used the money instead for the funeral, and to build the man's wife and daughter another home. The saint stayed with them for three years, until he was 18 (and the girl was 17). She loved him, and he also loved her, and her mother hoped they would marry. Instead, he finally departed, without telling them he was leaving, but wrote them a brief letter about it before he left. When they discovered he had left, they tried to run after him, but they couldn't find him.

(Ma 1993, p. 24–30)

In what appears to be a related story, the saint feels some regret for leaving a woman whom he loved in order to pursue Daoist perfection:

The girl whom he loved missed him very much, and eventually became sick. Meanwhile, Chuping, while herding the sheep and pursuing perfection, noticed two sheep who were touching their necks together in affection. He cried, thinking about the girl. His Daoist master noticed and suggested that she might be sick now, and he should visit her. But Chuping knew he could not go back, so he sent a deer to see her, carrying some herbal medicine to cure her illness. She took the medicine and recovered, but wanted to send a message back to Chuping with the deer. But the deer refused to leave. Finally, she realized that he had sent the deer to be with her. Her mother wanted her to forget Chuping and marry somebody else, but she refused. Local people who learned about the story were amazed, especially as the deer helped the girl with farm work, performing some of the tasks of a cow.

(Huang 1998: 12–13)

Other stories also feature the saint's resistance to the appeal of a beautiful woman:

> At the age of 40, Chuping was living in a temple and using herbs to cure local poor people. Everyone praised his good will. One night, during a rainstorm, a beautiful girl knocked on his door, seeking shelter. Her parents had died, and she was traveling to her uncle's home, and needed to stay for only one night. He allowed her to stay the night, but slept in the kitchen while she occupied his room. During the night, she rushed to him claiming she feared monsters, and hugged him tightly, and asked him to stay with her for the night. He pushed her away angrily, and warned her that if she tempted him again, he would kick her out. The next day, she refused his offer of breakfast, and left. But she had left a golden ring in the washbasin, and so he ran after her to give it back. It turns out that she was a goddess, who had come to test his virtue. Since he had passed the test, he was allowed to become an immortal.
>
> (Ma 1993: 43–45)

Some stories show the saint helping local farmers with rain:

> During a drought, there was so little water that the farmers could not even grow turnips. So, they prayed to the saint, and it rained. In a second story, they feared they did not have enough fertilizer so he created a formula for them which used material from the walls of huts. The saint also provided various crop-protecting services for farmers: for example, crafting an apparently magical jar which preserved grain against insects and the usual forms of decay.
>
> (Wang 2007: 19–20)

There are other stories in which he helped impoverished villagers during a famine:

> Long ago, there were no crops, and the villagers needed to eat grass roots and tree bark. Chuping asked his sheep to help to find food. One of the sheep found a rock which it could not break apart (which contained seeds for crops) and returned and tried to get the saint's attention (presumably by bleating). The saint, misunderstanding the sheep's cries, gave it grass to eat, but it continued to pester the saint for several days. Finally, Chuping followed the sheep to the rock, and used an iron axe to split the rock. Inside, there were seeds for growing crops. The sheep by that time was very tired, and lay down on the hillside and never moved again. But the villagers now had seeds for crops. They named the hill the "lying down sheep" hill to memorialize the incident.
>
> (Shi 1995: 160–162)

Some stories are about healing diseases or physical ailments. Several of the stories also include interactions with other deities or saints, who come down to earth to test Chuping's virtue before granting him further powers or recognition as Daoist saint and eventually as an immortal.

Finally, we discovered that among the stories collected by an elderly temple-based fortune-teller in Huang Pan village from about 10 local elderly, several stories included incidents from the life of Huang Chuping and his brother Chuqi when they lived in the village (according to the local claims). One of these stories, which a local business man claimed he had also heard as a child growing up in that village, explains how and why the two brothers eventually left the village:

> Huang Chuping and Huang Chuqi, who lived in the village at that time, had constructed a kind of "dragon bed" for treating illnesses. The bed had a "head" at one end of the bed which opened and produced a vapour when a person lay on the bed and held the "dragon head." The two brothers stood on either side of the bed, and held the sick person during this procedure. The bed [*according to the story*] healed sick people after this "treatment." However, the emperor heard about this "dragon bed," and was angry because the "dragon" is a symbol for the emperor, and only the emperor can use the "dragon" symbol for any purpose. The villagers told the brothers about the emperor's dangerous anger, and so the brothers put the dragon-bed into the river, and fled down the well (which they had dug earlier, in the village) and disappeared, to reappear later on Jinhua Mountain. They never returned to the village.
>
> (*Huangpeng Cunzhi* 1997: 244–245).

It is not clear from this story how the "dragon-bed" event fits into the lives and careers of the two local boys who eventually became Daoist saints on the mountain. Presumably, they were already adults at the time (especially since according to another local story they had industriously dug a well in the village which produced disease-healing water), but there are no other accounts, among the stories compiled by local scholars, that the brothers had returned to the village from the mountain and practiced Daoist healings in their home village. Of course it is impossible to know when such a story was first related in the village, but if it was told to the business man long before the revival of interest in HDX in the late 1980s, as appears to be the case, by an elderly person who grew up in the village in the early twentieth century, it is possible that the story is much older and comes from a local stream of stories about Chuping and Chuqi which connected them to the village and which were possibly told and re-told only in that village. (It would be necessary to search for possible literary antecedents of such a story in earlier compilations of Daoist folklore before proceeding to the hypothesis that it might have a local origin.)

It is also notable that the Hong Kong version of the cult, with a focus on Huang Chuping, has affected not only the temple iconography in a number of the Jinhua temples but has also seeped into the explanations and rationalizations of local "experts."

For example, the "two saints" version of the cult presents some puzzles. If both Huang Chuping and Huang Chuqi were active in the area and both achieved the powers of an immortal, we asked the elderly fortune-teller in Huang Pun village, why does the YYY temple next to the village only enshrine Huang (Chuping) Daxian and not also his brother Huang Chuqi? One obvious answer was the involvement of the Hong Kong Seseyuan in supporting the construction of that temple with a major donation, and hence, that the "one-saint" version of the cult was imported back to Lanxi and to the village as a result of Hong Kong influence. But the village fortune-teller did not give this reply, even though he was based in the same large temple financed and influenced by the Seseyuan.

Instead, he said that Huang Chuping is worshipped as the "Daxian" of the two brothers because he never married, whereas the older brother, Chuqi, married and had children (before leaving them in his old age to join Chuping on the mountain). We treat this as probably an "ad hoc" explanation in response to a question from us and not as a real local explanation which antedates the building of the YYY temple.

But the interaction and mixing of local and nonlocal stories and traditions makes all such accounts provisional, and it is only our best guess. It is possible that the preferential focus on Chuping is much older than the influence of the Hong Kong version of the cult since the late 1980s and we also note that most of the stories compiled by the fortune-teller and the local intellectuals and published in the 1990s are mostly about Chuping's life and activities.

Notes

1 For example, in the formation of the canonical Christian texts, oral traditions from the first century CE were evidently preserved within particular early-Christian communities and eventually committed to writing as "gospels" relating the life, preaching, and miracles attributed to Jesus. There is considerable debate about how these stories were transmitted, when, and how they were eventually transcribed in written documents, how the compilers used other available texts, and how the texts were revised in subsequent edited collections. But it is clear from comparisons of the four "canonical" gospels (Matthew, Mark, Luke, and John) that several versions of the venerated person's life with somewhat different details remained within the canon despite some irreconcilable differences in the texts. There were also other stories, texts, and "gospels" which were not included in the final officially endorsed canonical bible and eventually disappeared because they were not recopied by church scribes (see, e.g., Ehrman 2005, 2014). Several of these texts were recovered by archaeologists in the twentieth century CE (e.g., the "gospel of Judas").
2 It seems that there was no single organization in Jinhua which attempted to control the worship of this saint and to prevent rival versions of the saint's biography and teachings from being propounded by some other organization. Folk religion in China generally does not operate this way. Worshippers are often illiterate and rely on oral traditions and personal stories for their conceptions of the deity and his powers. Also, there is no "priesthood" with a vested interest in establishing themselves as the only legitimate professional exponents of a particular saint's life and teaching.
3 Dr Patrick Hase, who was a district officer in Hong Kong's New Territories in the late 1970s and 1980s, collected a number of stories from elderly villagers about encounters with tigers in the area prior to World War II. The skin of one of those tigers was displayed for many years in one of the local temples.

References

Aijmer, G. and Ho, K.Y.V. 2000. *Cantonese Society in a Time of Change*. Hong Kong: Chinese University of Hong Kong.

Anagnost, A. 1997. *National Past-times: Narrative, Representation, and Power in Modern China*. Durham: Duke University Press.

Apolito, P. 2005. *The Internet and the Madonna: Religious Visionary Experience on the Web*. Chicago and London: The University of Chicago Press.

Appadurai, A. 1996. *Modernity at Large*. Minneapolis: University of Minnesota Press.

Ashiwa, Y. and Wank, L.D. 2006. The Politics of A Reviving Buddhist Temple: State, Association, and Religion in Southeast China. *The Journal of Asian Studies*, 65(2):337–359.

Ashiwa, Y. and Wank, L.D. 2009. Making the State in Modern China: An Introduction Essay, pp.1–21, in A. Yoshiko and D.L. Wank (eds) *Making Religion, Making the State*. Stanford: Stanford University Press.

Bourdieu, P. 1986. The forms of capital, pp. 46–58, in R.G. John (ed) *Handbook of Theory and Research for the Sociology of Education*. New York: Greenwood Press.

Brickell, K. and Datta, A. (eds). 2011. *Translocal Geographies: Spaces, Places, Connections*. Burlington: Ashgate Publishing Ltd.

Brown, D. 1996. Genuine Fakes, pp. 33–47, in T. Selwyn (ed) *The Tourist Image: Myths and Myth Making in Tourism*. Chichester: Wiley.

Burawoy, M. 2000. *Global Ethnography: Forcers, Connections and Imaginations in a Postmodern World*. Berkeley: University of California Press.

Casey, S.E. 1993. *Getting Back into Place: Toward a Renewed Understanding of the Place-World*. Bloomington: Indiana University Press.

Chan, S.C. 2005. Temple-Building and Heritage in China. *Ethnology*, 44(1):65–79.

Chan, S.C. and Lang, G. 2007. Temple Construction and the Revival of Popular Religion in Jinhua. *China Information*, 21(1):43–69.

Chan, S.C. and Lang, G. 2011. Temples as Enterprises, pp. 133–153, in C.A. Yuet (ed) *Religion in Contemporary China: Revitalization and Innovation*. London: Routledge.

Chau, A.Y. 2005. The Politics of Legitimation and the Revival of Popular Religion in Shaanbei, North-Central China. *Modern China*, 31(2):236–278.

Chau, A.Y. 2006. *Miraculous Response: Doing Popular Religion in Contemporary China*. Califronia: Stanford University Press.

Chau, A.Y. 2009. Expanding the Space of Popular Religion: Local Temple Activism and the Politics and Legitimation in Contemporary Rural China, pp. 211–240, in A. Yoshiko and D.L. Wank (eds) *Making Religion, Making the State*. Stanford: Stanford University Press.

Chen, S.X. 2006. Dui Ruhe Tisheng Huangdaxian Wenhua Luyou Cengci De Qianjian [A preliminary investigation on how to improve Huangdaxian cultural tourism]. *Huangdaxian Wen Hua*, 2(3):30.

Chhabra, D., Healy, R., and Sills, E. 2003. Staged Authenticity and Heritage Tourism. *Annals of Tourism Research*, 30(3):702–713.

Dean, K. 1993. *Taoist Ritual and Popular Cults of Southeast China*. Princeton: University Press.

Dean, K. 1998. *Lord of the Three in One: The Spread of a Cult in Southeast China*. Princeton: Princeton University Press.

Dean, K. 2003. Local Communal Religion in Contemporary South-east China. *The China Quarterly*, 174:338–358.

Dean, K. 2010. The Return Visits of Overseas Chinese to Ancestral Villages in Putian, Fujian, pp. 235–264, in O. Tim and D.S. Sutton (eds) *Faiths on Display*. Lanham: Rowan and Littlefield.

Dean, K. and Zheng, Z. 2010. *Ritual Alliances of the Putian Plain*. Leiden and Boston: Brill.

Dott, R.B. 2010. Spirit Money: Tourism and Pilgrimage on the Sacred Slopes of Mount Tai, pp. 27–50, in O. Tim and D.S. Sutton (eds) *Faiths on Display*. Lanham: Rowan and Littlefield.

DuBois, T.D. 2005. *The Sacred Village: Social Change and Religious Life in Rural North China*. Honolulu: University of Hawaii Press.

Ehrman, D.B. 2005. *Lost Christianities: The Battles for Scripture and the Faiths We Never Knew*. New York: Oxford University Press.

Ehrman, D.B. 2014. *How Jesus Became God: The Exaltation of a Jewish Preacher from Galilee*. New York: HarperOne.

Eimer, D. 2007. Beyond belief. *Post Magazine* [*South China Morning Post*], November 11:17–20.

Elvin, M. 2004. *The Retreat of the Elephants: An Environmental History of China*. New Haven: Yale University Press.

Eng, I. and Yi-Min, L. 2002. Religious Festivities, Communal Rivalry, and Restructuring of Authority Relations in Rural Chaozhou, Southeast China. *The Journal of Asian Studies*, 61(4):1259–1285.

Fan, L. 2003. The Cult of the Silkworm Mother as a Core of the Local Community Religion in a North China Village: Fieldstudy in Zhiwuying, Baoding, Hebei. *The China Quarterly*, 174:359–372.

Fang, L.M. 1995. Chisong Gong [The palace of Chisong], pp. 155–156, in F. Shi (ed) *Chisong Huangdaxian*. Hai Kou: NanHai Chu Ban Gong si.

Fentress, J. and Wickham, C. 1992. *Social Memory*. Oxford: Blackwell.

Feuchtwang, S. 2000. Religion as Resistance, pp. 161–177, in *Chinese Society: Change, Conflict and Resistance*. London: Routledge.

Feuchtwang, S. 2004. Theorising Place, pp. 3–32, in F. Stephan (ed) *Making Place: State Projects, Globalisation and Local Responses in China*. London: UCL, Portland: Cavendish.

Feuchtwang, S. and Wang, M. 2001. *Grassroots Charisma: Four local leaders in China*. London: Routledge.

Fisher, G. 2012. Religion as Repertoire: Resourcing the Past in a Beijing Buddhist Temple. *Modern China*, 38(3):346–376.

Flower, M.J. 2004. A Road Is Made: Roads, Temples, and Historical Memory in Ya'an Country, Sichuan. *The Journal of Asian Studies*, 63(3):649–685.

Flower, M.J. and Leonard, P. 1998. Defining Cultural Life in the Chinese Countryside: The Case of the Chuan Zhu Temple, pp. 273–290, in V.B. Eduard, F.N. Pieke, and W.L. Chong (eds) *Cooperative and Collective in China's Rural Development: Between State and Private Interests.* Armonk: M.E. Sharpe.

Gates, H. 1996. *China's Motor: A Thousand Years of Petty Capitalism.* Ithaca: Cornell University Press.

Goossaert, V. 2007. *The Taoists of Peking, 1800–1949: A Social History of Urban Clerics.* Cambridge: Harvard University Press.

Goossaert, V and Fang, L. 2009. Temples and Daoists in urban China since 1980. *China Perspectives*, 4:32–41.

Goossaert, V and Palmer, A.D. 2011. *The Religious Question in Modern China.* Chicago: The University of Chicago Press.

Graburn, H.H.N. 1989. Tourism: The Sacred Journey, pp. 21–36, V.L. Smith (ed) *Hosts and Guests: The Anthropology of Tourism.* Philadelphia: University of Pennsylvania Press.

Halbwachs, M. 1992. *On Collective Memory*, C.A. Lewis (trans and eds). Chicago: University of Chicago Press.

Hall, S. (ed). 1997. *Representation: Cultural Representations and Signifying Practices.* London: Sage/The Open University.

Harvey, D. 1990. Between Space and Time: Reflection on the Geographical Imagination. *Annals of the Association of the American Geographers*, 80(3):418–434.

Herrou, A. 2011. Networks and the 'Cloudlike Wandering' of Daoist Monks in China Today, pp. 108–132, in C.A. Yuet (ed) *Religion in Contemporary China: Revitalization and Innovation.* London: Routledge.

Huang, C.J. 2009. *Charisma and Compassion: Cheng Yen and the Buddhist Tzu Chi Movement.* Cambridge: Harvard University Press.

Huang, C.J., Valussi, E., and Palmer, D.A. 2011. Gender and sexuality in Chinese Religious Life, pp. 107–123, in P.A. David, G. Shive, and P.L. Wickeri (eds) *Chinese Religious Life.* New York: Oxford University Press.

Huang, C.J. and Weller, P.R. 1998. Merit and Mothering: Women and Social Welfare in Taiwanese Buddhism. *The Journal of Asian Studies*, 57(2):379–396.

Huang, Z.Q. 1998. Zhongtou Chisong. *Wu Xing Huangdaxian Gushi Zhuankan (Special Edition on Huangdaxian Stories)*, 3(102):24–25.

Huangdaxian Chuanshuo Yu Huangdaxian Dao Jiao Yinyue Bei Lie Ru Jinhua shi Shou Pi Sheng Feiwuzhi Wenhua Yichan Daibiaozuo Minglu [The Legends of Huangdaxian and His Daoist Music are Added to the First Jinhua City's First List of Intangible Cultural Heritage]. 2006. *Huangdaxian Wen Hua*, 2(3):49.

Huangdaxian Wenhua Secretariat 2007. "Huangdaxian Chuanshuo Shen Bao Zhejiang Sheng Feiwuzhi Wenhua Yichan Xiangmu" [The Legends of Huangdaxian Applying as Zhejiang Province's List of Intangible Cultural Heritage]. *Huangdaxian Wen Hua*, 1(4):47–48.

Huangpeng Cunzhi Bianzuan Xiaozu [Huangpeng Cunzhi Editorial Committee]. 1997. *Huangpeng Cunzhi* [Huangpeng Village Gazette]. Beijing: Zhongguo Shuji Publishing Co.

James, L.W. 1985. Standardizing the Gods: The promotion of T'ien Hou (Empress of Heaven) Along the South China Coast, 960–1960, pp. 292–324, in D. Johnson, A. Nathan, and E. Rawski (eds) *Popular Culture in Late Imperial China.* Berkeley: University of California Press.

Jing, J. 1996. *The Temple of Memories, History, Power, and Morality in a Chinese Village.* Stanford: Stanford University Press.

Jinhua Huangdaxian Wenhua Yanjiu Hui [Jinhua Huangdaxian Cultural Research Association]. 2007. Guanyu Da Xiang Huangdaxian Wenhua Pinpai Ban Hao Huangdaxian Wenhua Luyou Jie De Jianyi [The Recommendations to Enhance the Brand Name of Huangdaxian and Huangdaxian Cultural Tourism Festival]. *Huangdaxian Wen Hua*, 1(4):4.

Jinhua Huangdaxian Yanjiuhui Bangongshi [Office of Jinhua Huangdaxian Research Association]. 2006. Jinhua Huangdaxian Yanjiuhui Wenhua Chengli Yi Zhou Nian [The First Anniversary of Jinhua Huangdaxian Cultural Research Association]. *Huangdaxian Wen Hua*, 2(3):44.

Jordan, D. 1972. *Gods, Ghosts, and Ancestors: The Folk Religion of a Taiwanese Village.* Berkeley: University of California Press.

Jordan, K.D and Overmyer, D. 1986. *The Flying Phoenix: Aspects of Chinese Sectarianism in Taiwan.* Princeton: Princeton University Press.

Kang, X. 2009a. Old Age, and Temple Work: A Case From Northwestern Sichuan. *China Perspectives*, 4:42–52.

Kang, X. 2009b. Three Religions, and a Tourist Attraction: Contesting Sacred Space on China's Ethnic Frontier. *Modern China*, 35(3):227–255.

Kuah-Pearce, K.E. 2000. *Rebuilding the Ancestral Village: Singaporeans in China.* Aldershot: Ashgate Press.

Laliberte, A. 2004. *The Politics of Buddhist Organizations in Taiwan: 1989–2003.* London: RoutledgeCurzon.

Laliberte, A, Palmer, D., and Wu, K. 2011. Religious Philanthropy and Chinese Civil Society, in A.D. Palmer, G. Shive, and P.L. Wickeri (eds) *Chinese Religious Life.* New York: Oxford University Press.

Lang, G. 1989. Oppression and Revolt in Ancient Palestine: The Evidence in Jewish Literature from the Prophets to Josephus. *Sociological Analysis*, 49:325–343.

Lang, G., Chan, S.C. and Ragvald, L. 2005. Temples and the Religious Economy, pp. 149–180, in Y. Fenggang and J.B. Tamney (eds) *State, Market, and Religions in Chinese Societies.* The Netherlands: Brill Publisher.

Lang, G., Chan, S.C, and Ragvald, L. 2005. Temples and the Chinese Religious Economy. *Interdisciplinary Journal of Research on Religion*, 4(1):1–27.

Lang, G. and Ragvald, L. 1993. *The Rise of a Refugee God: Hong Kong's Wong Tai Sin.* Hong Kong: Oxford University Press.

Lang, G. and Ragvald, L. 1998. Spirit-Writing and the Development of Chinese Cults. *Sociology of Religion*, 59(4):309–328.

Lang, G. and Ragvald, L. 2005. Grasping the Revolution: Fieldwork on Religion in China. *Fieldwork in Religion* 1(3):213–228.

Lanxi Huangdaxian Research Association. 1995. *Huangdaxian Zhiliao Xuanbian* [Huangdaxian Research Material]. Lanxi: Lanxi Publishing House.

Lewis, I.M. 1989. *Ecstatic Religion: A Study of Shamanism and Spirit Possession* (second edition). New York: Routledge.

Lu, H.Y. 2002. *The Politics of Locality: Making a Nation of Communities in Taiwan.* New York and London: Routledge.

Ma, J. 1993. *Huangdaxian Chuan Qi* [The Legends of Huangdaxian]. Hong Kong: Hong Kong Kim Ling Publishing Co.

MacCannell, D. 1976. *The Tourist: A New Theory of the Leisure Class.* New York: Schocken Books.

Massey, B.D. 1999. Power-Geometries and the Politics of Space and Time, Hettner Lecture 1998, Department of Geography, University of Heidelberg.

McCarthy, K.S. 2010. Economic Development and the Buddhist-Industrial Complex of Xishuangbanna, pp. 157–182, in O. Tim and D.S. Sutton (eds) *Faiths on Display*. Lanham: Rowan and Littlefield.

Miaoxie Huangdaxian De Dianshiju 'Chisong Hun' Kaishi Chou Pai [The TV Drama "Chisong Hun" depicting Huangdaxian is preparing for filming]. 2006. *Huangdaxian Wen Hua*, 1(2):27.

Misztal, B. 2003. *Theories of Social Remembering*. Maidenhead and Philadelphia: Open University Press.

Mueggler, E. 2001. *The Age of Wild Ghosts: Memory, Violence, and Place in Southwest China*. Berkeley: University of California Press.

Mueggler, E. 2007. Spectral Chains: Remembering the Great Leap Forward Famine in a Yi Community, pp. 50–68, in C.K. Lee and G. Yang (eds) *Re-Envisioning the Chinese Revolution: The Politics and Poetics of Collective Memories in Reform China*. Washington: Woodrow Wilson Center Press; Stanford: Stanford University Press.

Oakes, T. and Sutton, S.D. 2010. Introduction, pp. 1–26, in O. Tim and D.S. Sutton (eds) *Faiths on Display*. Lanham: Rowan and Littlefield.

Palmer, A.D. 2009. China's Religious Danwei, Institutional Religion in the People's Republic. *China Perspectives*, 4:17–30.

Palmer, A.D., Shive, G.L, and Wickeri, L.P. (eds). 2011. *Chinese Religious Life*. New York: Oxford University Press.

Peng, Z.Q. 2006. Ying Nuli Tuxian Huangdaxian Wenhua Dui Goujian Hexie Shehui De Zuoyong: Jianji Fan Mixin De Wenti [Should Highlight the Contribution of Huangdaxian Culture in Building a Harmonious Society]. *Huangdaxian Wen Hua*, 2(3):2–3.

Putterman, L. 1995. The Role of Ownership and Property Rights in China's Economic Transition, *The China Quarterly*, 144(144):1047–1064.

Qian, X.X. 1998. Erxianqiao De Chuanshuo [The Legend of Two Saints Bridge]. *Wu Xing Huangdaxian Gu Shi Zhuan Kan*, 3(102):22–23.

Ryan, C. and Gu, H. 2010. Constructionism and Culture in Research: Understandings of the Fourth Buddhist Festival, Wutaishan, China. *Tourism Management*, 31(2):167–178.

Schwartz, B. 1991. Social Change and Collective Memory: The Democratization of George Washington. *American Sociological Review*, 56:221–236.

Shi, F. (ed). 1995. *Chisong Huangdaxian*. Hai Kou: NanHai Chu Ban Gong si.

Shi, K. 2007. Chuyi Dui 'Huangdaxian Chuanshuo' De Baohu [On Protecting the Legends of Huangdaxian]. *Huangdaxian Wen Hua*, 1(4):23–24.

Siu, F.H. 1990. Recycling Tradition: Culture, History, and Political Economy in the Chrysanthemum Festivals of South China. *Comparative Studies in Society and History*, 32(4):765–794.

Sullins, D.P. 2006. Gender and Religion: Deconstructing Universality, Constructing Complexity. *American Journal of Sociology*, 112 (2):838–880.

Sutton, D.S. and Kang, X. 2010. Making Tourists and Remaking Locals: Religion, Ethnicity, and Patriotism on Display in Northern Sichuan, pp. 103–126, in O. Tim and D.S. Sutton (eds) *Faiths on Display*. Lanham: Rowan and Littlefield.

Svensson, M. 2010. Tourist Itineraries, Spatial Management, and Hidden Temples: The Revival of Religious Sites in a Water Town, pp. 211–234, in O. Tim and D.S. Sutton (eds) *Faiths on Display*. Lanham: Rowan and Littlefield.

Tsai, L.L. 2002. Cadres, Temple and Lineage Institutions, and Governance in Rural China. *The China Journal*, 48:1–27.

Urry, J. 1995. *Consuming Places*. New York: Routledge.

Wang, N. 2000. *Tourism and Modernity: A Sociological Analysis.* Oxford: Elsevier Science Ltd.

Wang, Y. 2007. Huangdaxian Chuanshuo De Daode Yu DangDai Sixiang Daode Jianshe [Moral Virtues of Huangdaxian and Cultivation of Contemporary Moral Values]. *Huangdaxian Wen Hua*, 1(4):19–21.

Watsons, S.R. 1994. Memory, History, and Opposition under State Socialism: An introduction, pp.1–20, in W.S. Rubie (ed) *Memory, History, and Opposition under State Socialism.* New Mexico: School of American Research Press.

Welch, H. 1965. *Taoism: The Parting of the Way.* Boston: Beacon Press.

Weller, P.R. 2000. Living at the Edge: Religion, Capitalism, and the End of the Nation-State in Taiwan. *Public Culture*, 12(2):477–498.

Weller, P.R. 2006. *Discovering Nature: Globalization and Environmental Culture in China and Taiwan.* Cambridge: Cambridge University Press.

Williams, C.A.S. 1960. *Encyclopedia of Chinese Symbolism and Arts Motifs.* New York: Julian Press.

Wong, S.H. 1985. A study of Huang Daxian [in Chinese], *The Journal of the Institute of Chinese Studies of the Chinese University of Hong Kong*, XVI:223–239.

Woon, Y.F. 1984. *Social organization in South China, 1911–1949: the Case of the Kuan Lineage of K'ai-p'ing County.* Ann Arbor: Center for Chinese Studies, University of Michigan.

Yan, Y. 2011. The Changing Moral Landscape, pp. 36–77, in A. Kleinman, Y. Yan, J. Jing, S. Lee, E. Zhang, T. Pan, F. Wu, and J. Guo (eds) *Deep China: The Moral Life of the Person.* Berkeley; Los Angeles; London: University of California Press.

Yan, H. and Bramwell, B. 2008. Cultural Tourism, Ceremony and the State in China. *Annals of Tourism Research*, 35(4):969–989.

Yang, D-R. 2003. The Education of Taoist Priests in Contemporary Shanghai, China. D. Phil. Dissertation, London School of Economics and Political Science.

Yang, D-R. 2005. The Changing Economy of Temple Daoism in Shanghai, pp. 113–148, in F. Yang and J.B Tamney (eds) *State, Market, and Religions in Chinese Societies.* The Netherlands: Brill Publisher.

Yang, D-R. 2011. From Ritual Skills to Discursive Knowledge: Changing Styles of Daoists Transmission in Shanghai, pp. 81–107, in A.Y. Chau (ed) *Religion in Contemporary China.* Oxon: Routledge.

Yang, M.M.-H. 2004. Spatial Struggles: Postcolonial Complex, State Disenchantment, and Popular Re-appropriation of Space in Rural Southeast China. *Journal of Asian Studies*, 63(3):719–755.

Yang, M.M.-H. 2008. Introduction, pp. 1–42, in M.M.-H. Yang (ed) *Chinese Religiosities: Afflictions of Moderntiy and State Formation.* California: University Press.

Zelizer, B. 1995. Reading the Past Against the Grain: The Shape of Memory Studies. *Critical Studies in Mass Communication*, 12 (2):214–239.

Zhao, W.Q. and Zhao, X.F. 1995. Huangdaxian Weihe Qu Xianggang: Xiqiaoshan Kaocha Ji [Why did Huangdaxian go to Hong Kong? An investigation at Xiqiaoshan], pp. 76–78, in Lanxi Huangdaxian Research Association, *Huangdaxian Zhiliao Xuanbian* (Huangdaxian Research Material). Lanxi: Lanxi Huangdaxian Research Association.

Zhe, J. 2011. Buddhism in the reform era: a secularized revival? pp. 32–52, in C.A. Yuet (eds) *Religion in contemporary China: Revitalization and Innovation.* London: Routledge.

Zhu, J.J.H. and Ke, H. 2001. Political Culture as Social Construction of Reality: A Case Study of Hong Kong's Images in Mainland China, pp. 188–217, in H. Shiping (ed) *Chinese Political Culture, 1989–2000.* Armonk: M.E. Sharpe.

Glossary

Baiyunguan	白雲觀
Baojiguan	寶積觀
Cai Sheng	財神
Chishanxiaozu	慈善小組
Chishi Yan	叱石巖
Chisong Daoyuan	赤松道院
Chisong HDX Association	赤松黃大仙會
Chisong HDX Research Association	赤松黃大仙研究會
Chisong Zi	赤松子
Ciji	慈濟
Daling village	大嶺村
Daodejing	道德經
Daoist	道教
Dimu	地母
Dongyang	東陽
Erhu	二胡
Erhuangcunci	二皇君祠
Erxiandian / Chisong Gong	二仙殿 / 赤松宮
Erxianqiao	二仙橋
Fangcun	芳村
Fengshui	風水
Fengying Xian Guan	蓬瀛仙館
Fuji	扶乩
Furoujiping	扶弱濟貧
Fuweijikun	扶危濟困
Ge Hong	葛洪
Ge Hong's Shen Xian Zhuan	葛洪神仙傳
Gongan	公安
Guangmingdeng	光明燈
Guangxia	廣廈
Guanyin	觀音
Guerxianci	古二仙祠
Gunglu temple	公魯廟

Huadi	花地
Huang Chuping	黃初平
Huang Chuqi	黃初起
Huang Daxian Ci	黃大仙祠
Huang Gongfu	黃公符
Huang Peng village	黃溢村
Huang Yeren	黃野人
Huangdaxian (HDX)	黃大仙
Huangpeng Cunzhi	黃溢村誌
Huitu Liexian Quanzhuan	繪圖列仙全傳
Ichendalou	義診大樓
Jianfeng	尖峰
Jieyang	揭陽
Jin dynasty	晉朝
Jindong	金東
Jing Mimeng	驚迷夢
Jinhua Guan	金華觀
Jinhua	金華
Jinhuashan	金華山
Lanjiang	蘭江
Lanxi	蘭溪
Liang Junzhuan	梁鈞傳
Liang Renan	梁仁菴
Lingyangci	靈羊祠
Lingyangdao	靈羊島
Longcandong	龍藏洞
Longwanggou	龍王溝
Lu Ban	魯班
Lu Dongbin	呂洞賓
Luofu	羅浮
Luotangqing	落湯清
Lutian	鹿田
Mao Gengzhi	毛根之
Mazu temples	媽祖廟
Mou	畝
Muchenyuan	穆澄源
Peishan Pujitan	菩山普濟堂
Pujiquansan	普濟勸善
Qian	籤
Qigong	氣功
Qiu qian	求籤
Renao	熱鬧
Rengang	稔崗
Sanju daoshi	山居道士
Seseyuan	嗇色園

Shankoupeng village	三口馮村
Shengbei	聖杯
Shengjingyuan	勝景園
Shenxian Zhuan	神仙傳
Taiji / Tai chi	太極
Tudi	土地
Wang Huai	王淮
Wanshenge	萬聖閣
Wuhaixianjing	物外仙境
Wupo	巫婆
Wutaishan	五台山
Xianghuo	香火
Xianjing	仙井
Xianqiao	仙橋
Xianyiguan	仙奕館
Xiaqiao Mountain	西樵山
Xing Shi Yaoyan	醒世要言
Xingshanzhie	行善嫉惡
Xinhui	新會
Xiqiaoshan	西樵山
Xiufu	修復
Yangshikeng	羊石坑
Yangyingcun	羊印村
Yanshanchene	揚善懲惡
Yiwu	義烏
Yuan Yuan Yuan	緣源園
Yuanqingge	元清閣
Zhang Liang	張良
Zhao Gong	趙公
Zhibingjiuren	治病救人
Zhongguochongdaohui	中國崇道會
Zhongtou village	鐘頭村
Zugong	祖宮

Index

admission fee (temples) 28, 61, 78, 82, 90, 101, 115, 128
admission ticket (temples) 61, 84, 127
authenticity 4–5, 41, 49–51, 54, 56–57, 68, 91, 145, 151

Biographies of Immortals see also *Shenxian Zhuan*
Buddhism, Buddhist 22, 26, 63, 70, 82–83, 93, 95, 120, 136, 138, 155

charity (charitable activities) 62, 64, 70, 72, 74, 81–84, 99, 101–102, 116–117, 120, 129, 141–142, 147, 149, 151–152
Chisong Daoyuan (CSDY) 33, 44, 47, 51, 57, 60–64, 66–67, 69–70, 90, 94–119, 149–151, 154; charitable activity 101–102, 142
Chisong Huang Daxian (HDX) Association 31–33, 39, 45, 54, 57, 97–98, 100
Chisonggong 30, 33, 40, 42–44, 47, 51, 57, 60–62, 96, 111–114, 153
Christian, Christians 19, 166
cinnabar 12, 16
cultural heritage 4–5, 8–9, 28, 39, 44, 47, 49–58, 60, 65–66, 68–71, 95, 144–145, 147, 150–152, 154
Cultural Revolution, and religion 3, 24–25, 43, 46, 49, 53, 67, 77, 93, 106, 149

Daoism 12–13, 34, 49, 58, 65, 90, 94, 98, 106–107, 111, 117, 122, 128, 135, 141, 147, 160
Daoists 12–13, 22–23, 76–77, 90, 106, 125, 135, 148, 159
Daoist Association 28, 54, 56, 76, 89, 106–107, 124–125, 129, 135–136, 155

Daoist herbal medicine *see also* medicine: Daoist herbal medicine, remedies, prescriptions
Double Dragon Cave (Double Dragon Scenic Park) 30, 32, 42, 52, 54–57, 60, 67, 70–71, 85, 87–88, 91, 93, 150

economic development and temples 4, 28, 35, 42, 44–46, 49, 51–52, 68, 72, 78, 86, 112, 139, 142, 152, 154
entrepreneurs and temples 61, 100, 112, 121–22, 138–139, 142–143, 147–148
environment and religion 28, 104, 114, 120
Erhuangcunci 41, 173
Erxiandian 111

Fangcun 25, 122–126, 139–140
fortune-tellers, qiu qian 18, 20–21, 26, 74, 78, 110, 113, 116, 126, 128, 149, 151, 158, 165, 166
fuji (spirit-writing) 14, 20, 22–23, 62, 65, 96, 99, 117, 157
Fujian: temples, worship 5, 65–66, 70, 93, 97, 104, 118, 151–152, 155

Ge Hong 11–12, 16–17, 23, 50, 135, 159
gender, and religion 81, 94–95; *see also* women
guangmingdeng 80
government (local government) 1–10, 12–13, 18–22, 24, 28, 30–36, 38–40, 42–74, 76, 78–79, 82, 84, 86, 88, 91–94, 96–100, 102, 104–106, 117–119, 121–126, 129–131, 133–143, 145–147, 150–154, 157, 159, 162
Guangzhou: historical HDX temples 9–10, 13, 17–20, 26, 157; Guangzhou HDX Temple 25, 282–9, 121–144

Hong Kong: worship of HDX ix, 8, 10, 12–13, 16, 18–22, 29–30, 32–33, 45–46, 48, 54–55, 93, 96, 102, 140, 157; Hong Kong tourists and pilgrims: 9, 23–26, 31–34, 39, 42–43, 51, 58, 62, 65–70, 73–74, 80, 83, 85, 97, 99–100, 106, 117, 126–127, 146

Huang Daxian (HDX): biography in *Shenxian Zhuan* 10–11; 'autobiography' in *Jing Mimeng* 16; worship in Hong Kong ix, 10, 16, 18–23; *see also* Hong Kong, worship of HDX; veneration in Guangdong 14–18, 23–28; stories compiled in Jinhua 36, 57, 157–166; HDX heritage in Jinhua 4–5, 39, 44, 47, 49–50, 51–68, 150–152

Huang Daxian temples *see also* Chisong Daoyuan, Chisonggong, Erxiandian, Guangzhou Huang Daxian Temple, Lingyanci, Rengang, Seseyuan, Yuanyuanyuan, Xinhui HDX temple, Zugong temple

Huang Chuping 10–14, 16–19, 23–25, 37, 112, 115, 135, 156–161, 164–166

Huang Chuqi 10–13, 16, 18, 24–25, 29, 112, 163, 165–166

Huang Gongfu 17, 24

Huang Peng (village) 33, 36–39, 41, 47, 70, 72, 74, 77–78, 81–83, 111, 146–147, 153–154, 158

Huang Yeren 23

Huitu Liexian Quanzhuan (Illustrated Complete Biographies of Ranked Immortals) 13

identity, identities: of deities 156; of persons 3, 22, 37, 47, 50, 54, 64–69, 117–118, 145, 154; of places 154

intangible cultural heritage 5, 9, 50, 53, 55–57, 68, 70, 154

Illustrated Complete Biographies of Ranked Immortals see *Huitu Liexian Quanzhuan*

Japan: Japanese occupation of south China 19–20, 22, 25, 43, 134

Jing Mimeng 14–16

Jinhua: fieldwork ix, 7; government, officials 32, 35, 42–43, 49–50, 52–56, 58, 62–63, 66–70, 78, 82, 84–85, 88, 93, 97–100, 118, 139, 146–147, 150, 153; HDX temples 3, 5, 9, 13, 25, 30, 32, 42–44, 51, 61, 66, 70–91, 139, 140

Jinhua Guan 30, 32, 35, 42–43, 47, 51, 57, 60–62, 70, 88, 174

Lanxi 9, 30, 33–36, 38–43, 45, 47, 51, 58, 70, 71–74, 76–77, 81–85, 91, 93, 147, 154, 158, 166

legend (legends) 3, 5, 8, 10, 11, 13, 29, 31, 33–41, 43–47, 50–58, 62–64, 68–71, 73, 85, 88, 140, 145–147, 150, 153–154, 157–159

legitimacy of temples 4, 23, 33, 38, 47, 82–83, 88, 99–100, 102, 106, 118, 152, 166

Liang Renan 14–20, 24–26, 46, 133, 159

Lingyanci 39

longevity 12, 19, 55, 90, 99, 104, 107, 142, 149

Luofu, Luofushan: Huang Daxian worship 12, 23–24, 58, 158

moral virtues 50, 52–56, 62, 64, 69, 146

medicine: Daoist herbal medicine, remedies, prescriptions 12, 14, 16–20, 26, 38, 52, 81–82, 157, 161–163

plague (1890s) 14–15, 45, 157

priests (Daoist) 151–152, 155; CSDY 94–96, 98, 103–104, 106–111, 114–118, 120, 122; Guangzhou HDX temple 121–122, 124–126, 133, 136, 138, 141; Jinhua 13, 52; Lingyanci 39; YYY 74–81, 83–84, 87, 92–93; Zugong 88–90, 92

qiu qian: see fortune-tellers

Religious Affairs Bureau 34, 66, 83–84, 98–100, 104,106, 117–118, 125–126, 129, 133, 137, 152

Rengang (village) 24, 26, 153

revival (of temple) 1–2, 5, 7–8, 14–15, 23, 28–29, 31, 34, 44–45, 53, 73, 92, 106, 145–147, 152–153, 155, 165

Rhapsodies on [one hundred] subjects see *Shilei fu*

Seseyuan (SSY) 19, 21–26, 30–34, 43–46, 51, 58, 60, 62, 65–66, 73–78, 84, 102, 123, 127, 129

Shenxian Zhuan (Biographies of Immortals) 11–13

Shilei fu (Rhapsodies on [one hundred] subjects) 12–13

spirit mediums 38, 62–63, 70, 72, 79, 81–83, 92, 96, 115–116, 151 state (in China) and religion: 3–4, 6–7, 46, 49–50, 53–4, 56, 69, 71–73, 78, 82, 89, 98, 118–119, 145, 151–152, 154

Taiwan, Taiwanese and religion 3, 5, 9, 14, 31–32, 39, 51, 56–57, 62, 64, 66–68, 74, 94–100, 104–106, 111, 116–118, 150–151, 153
temple management 1, 4, 6–7, 49, 62, 68, 70–72, 78, 86, 88–89, 91–92, 94, 100, 115, 119, 131, 133, 138–139, 141, 153
tourism, tourists 1–9, 23–24, 28, 30, 32, 34–35, 39, 42, 45–52, 54–55, 57–62, 67–74, 80, 82, 85–93, 113–118, 122–123, 125, 127, 137–143, 145, 147, 150–154
transnational 1–5, 30–33, 37, 45, 48–50, 52, 56–59, 61–62, 68–69, 71, 94, 96, 104, 145–146, 153–154
transportation, importance for temples 39, 44, 77, 85–86, 91, 112, 126, 131–132, 138, 140–141

United Front 7, 34, 52, 65, 70, 84, 99, 104, 118, 150

women, and religion 14, 63, 70, 79, 81–83, 86, 94–96, 100–101, 103, 109, 119, 156; *see also* gender

Xianyiguan 30, 38, 47, 51, 70, 84, 175
Xiqiaoshan: HDX statue 26–27
Xinhui: Huang Gongfu commemorations 17; HDX temple 24

Yuanqingge (YQG) 22, 31–32, 39, 42–45, 51, 54, 58, 62, 65–66, 70, 85, 93, 96–97, 117, 199
Yuan Yuan Yuan (YYY) 34, 43, 47, 51, 57, 66, 70–93, 99, 106, 111, 115, 116, 119, 150–151, 158, 165

Zugong temple 30, 42–43, 47, 51, 57, 60–62, 66–67, 71, 76, 84–93, 96, 99, 107, 111, 116, 141, 150–151, 154